MCSE CAREER MICROSOFT®!

MCSE Career Microsoft®!

by William C. Jeansonne

IDG Books Worldwide, Inc.
An International Data Group Company
Foster City, CA • Chicago, IL • Indianapolis, IN • Dallas, TX

MCSE Career Microsoft®!

Published by
IDG Books Worldwide, Inc.
An International Data Group Company
919 E. Hillsdale Blvd., Suite 400
Foster City, CA 94404

www.idgbooks.com (IDG Books Worldwide Web site)

Library of Congress Catalog Card No.: 97-73913

ISBN: 0-7645-3141-7

Printed in the United States of America

10 9 8 7 6 5 4 3

1E/RZ/RS/ZX/IN

Distributed in the United States by IDG Books Worldwide, Inc.

Distributed by Macmillan Canada for Canada; by Transworld Publishers Limited in the United Kingdom; by IDG Norge Books for Norway; by IDG Sweden Books for Sweden; by Woodslane Pty. Ltd. for Australia; by Woodslane Enterprises Ltd. for New Zealand; by Longman Singapore Publishers Ltd. for Singapore, Malaysia, Thailand, and Indonesia; by Simron Pty. Ltd. for South Africa; by Toppan Company Ltd. for Japan; by Distribuidora Cuspide for Argentina; by Livraria Cultura for Brazil; by Ediciencia S.A. for Ecuador; by Addison-Wesley Publishing Company for Korea; by Ediciones ZETA S.C.R. Ltda. for Peru; by WS Computer Publishing Corporation, Inc., for the Philippines; by Unalis Corporation for Taiwan; by Contemporanea de Ediciones for Venezuela; by Computer Book & Magazine Store for Puerto Rico; by Express Computer Distributors for the Caribbean and West Indies. Authorized Sales Agent: Anthony Rudkin Associates for the Middle East and North Africa.

For general information on IDG Books Worldwide's books in the U.S., please call our Consumer Customer Service department at 800-762-2974. For reseller information, including discounts and premium sales, please call our Reseller Customer Service department at 800-434-3422.

For information on where to purchase IDG Books Worldwide's books outside the U.S., please contact our International Sales department at 415-655-3200 or fax 415-655-3295.

For information on foreign language translations, please contact our Foreign & Subsidiary Rights department at 415-655-3021 or fax 415-655-3281.

For sales inquiries and special prices for bulk quantities, please contact our Sales department at 415-655-3200 or write to the address above.

For information on using IDG Books Worldwide's books in the classroom or for ordering examination copies, please contact our Educational Sales department at 800-434-2086 or fax 817-251-8174.

For press review copies, author interviews, or other publicity information, please contact our Public Relations department at 415-655-3000 or fax 415-655-3299.

For authorization to photocopy items for corporate, personal, or educational use, please contact Copyright Clearance Center, 222 Rosewood Drive, Danvers, MA 01923, or fax 508-750-4470.

ABOUT IDG BOOKS WORLDWIDE

Welcome to the world of IDG Books Worldwide.

IDG Books Worldwide, Inc., is a subsidiary of International Data Group, the world's largest publisher of computer-related information and the leading global provider of information services on information technology. IDG was founded more than 25 years ago and now employs more than 8,500 people worldwide. IDG publishes more than 275 computer publications in over 75 countries (see listing below). More than 60 million people read one or more IDG publications each month.

Launched in 1990, IDG Books Worldwide is today the #1 publisher of best-selling computer books in the United States. We are proud to have received eight awards from the Computer Press Association in recognition of editorial excellence and three from *Computer Currents*' First Annual Readers' Choice Awards. Our best-selling ...*For Dummies*® series has more than 30 million copies in print with translations in 30 languages. IDG Books Worldwide, through a joint venture with IDG's Hi-Tech Beijing, became the first U.S. publisher to publish a computer book in the People's Republic of China. In record time, IDG Books Worldwide has become the first choice for millions of readers around the world who want to learn how to better manage their businesses.

Our mission is simple: Every one of our books is designed to bring extra value and skill-building instructions to the reader. Our books are written by experts who understand and care about our readers. The knowledge base of our editorial staff comes from years of experience in publishing, education, and journalism — experience we use to produce books for the '90s. In short, we care about books, so we attract the best people. We devote special attention to details such as audience, interior design, use of icons, and illustrations. And because we use an efficient process of authoring, editing, and desktop publishing our books electronically, we can spend more time ensuring superior content and spend less time on the technicalities of making books.

You can count on our commitment to deliver high-quality books at competitive prices on topics you want to read about. At IDG Books Worldwide, we continue in the IDG tradition of delivering quality for more than 25 years. You'll find no better book on a subject than one from IDG Books Worldwide.

John Kilcullen
CEO
IDG Books Worldwide, Inc.

Steven Berkowitz
President and Publisher
IDG Books Worldwide, Inc.

Eighth Annual Computer Press Awards ≥ 1992

Ninth Annual Computer Press Awards ≥ 1993

Tenth Annual Computer Press Awards ≥ 1994

Eleventh Annual Computer Press Awards ≥ 1995

IDG Books Worldwide, Inc., is a subsidiary of International Data Group, the world's largest publisher of computer-related information and the leading global provider of information services on information technology. International Data Group publishes over 275 computer publications in over 75 countries. Sixty million people read one or more International Data Group publications each month. International Data Group's publications include: **ARGENTINA:** Buyer's Guide, Computerworld Argentina, PC World Argentina; **AUSTRALIA:** Australian Macworld, Australian PC World, Australian Reseller News, Computerworld, IT Casebook, Network World, Publish, Webmaster; **AUSTRIA:** Computerwelt Osterreich, Networks Austria, PC Tip Austria; **BANGLADESH:** PC World Bangladesh; **BELARUS:** PC World Belarus; **BELGIUM:** Data News; **BRAZIL:** Annuário de Informática, Computerworld, Connections, Macworld, PC Player, PC World, Publish, Reseller News, Supergamepower; **BULGARIA:** Computerworld Bulgaria, Network World Bulgaria, PC & MacWorld Bulgaria; **CANADA:** CIO Canada, Client/Server World, ComputerWorld Canada, InfoWorld Canada, NetworkWorld Canada, WebWorld; **CHILE:** Computerworld Chile, PC World Chile; **COLOMBIA:** Computerworld Colombia, PC World Colombia; **COSTA RICA:** PC World Centro America; **THE CZECH AND SLOVAK REPUBLICS:** Computerworld Czechoslovakia, Macworld Czech Republic, PC World Czechoslovakia; **DENMARK:** Communications World Danmark, Computerworld Danmark, Macworld Danmark, PC World Danmark, Techworld Denmark; **DOMINICAN REPUBLIC:** PC World Republica Dominicana; **ECUADOR:** PC World Ecuador; **EGYPT:** Computerworld Middle East, PC World Middle East; **EL SALVADOR:** PC World Centro America; **FINLAND:** MikroPC, Tietoverkko, Tietoviikko; **FRANCE:** Distributique, Hebdo, Info PC, Le Monde Informatique, Macworld, Reseaux & Telecoms, WebMaster France; **GERMANY:** Computer Partner, Computerwoche, Computerwoche Extra, Computerwoche FOCUS, Global Online, Macwelt, PC Welt; **GREECE:** Amiga Computing, GamePro Greece, Multimedia World; **GUATEMALA:** PC World Centro America; **HONDURAS:** PC World Centro America; **HONG KONG:** Computerworld Hong Kong, PC World Hong Kong, Publish in Asia; **HUNGARY:** ABCD CD-ROM, Computerworld Szamitastechnika, Internetto online Magazine, PC World Hungary, PC-X Magazin Hungary; **ICELAND:** Tolvuheimur PC World Island; **INDIA:** Information Communications World, Information Systems Computerworld, PC World India, Publish in Asia; **INDONESIA:** InfoKomputer PC World, Komputek Computerworld, Publish in Asia; **IRELAND:** ComputerScope, PC Live!; **ISRAEL:** Macworld Israel, People & Computers/Computerworld; **ITALY:** Computerworld Italia, Macworld Italia, Networking Italia, PC World Italia; **JAPAN:** DTP World, Macworld Japan, Nikkei Personal Computing, OS/2 World Japan, SunWorld Japan, Windows NT World, Windows World Japan; **KENYA:** PC World East African; **KOREA:** Hi-Tech Information, Macworld Korea, PC World Korea; **MACEDONIA:** PC World Macedonia; **MALAYSIA:** Computerworld Malaysia, PC World Malaysia, Publish in Asia; **MALTA:** PC World Malta; **MEXICO:** Computerworld Mexico, PC World Mexico; **MYANMAR:** PC World Myanmar; **NETHERLANDS:** Computer! Totaal, LAN Internetworking Magazine, LAN World Buyers Guide, Macworld Netherlands, Net, WebWereld; **NEW ZEALAND:** Absolute Beginners Guide and Plain & Simple Series, Computer Buyer, Computer Industry Directory, Computerworld New Zealand, MTB, Network World, PC World New Zealand; **NICARAGUA:** PC World Centro America; **NORWAY:** Computerworld Norge, CW Rapport, Datamagasinet, Financial Rapport, Kursguide Norge, Macworld Norge, Multimediaworld Norge, PC World Ekspress Norge, PC World Nettverk, PC World Norge, PC World ProduktGuide Norge; **PAKISTAN:** Computerworld Pakistan; **PANAMA:** PC World Panama; **PEOPLE'S REPUBLIC OF CHINA:** China Computer Users, China Computerworld, China InfoWorld, China Telecom World Weekly, Computer & Communication, Electronic Design China, Electronics Today, Electronics Weekly, Game Software, PC World China, Popular Computer Week, Software Weekly, Software World, Telecom World; **PERU:** Computerworld Peru, PC World Profesional Peru, PC World SoHo Peru; **PHILIPPINES:** Click!, Computerworld Philippines, PC World Philippines, Publish in Asia; **POLAND:** Computerworld Poland, Computerworld Special Report Poland, Cyber, Macworld Poland, Networld Poland, PC World Komputer; **PORTUGAL:** Cerebro/PC World Portugal, Computerworld/Correio Informático, Dealer World Portugal, Mac*In/PC*In Portugal, Multimedia World; **PUERTO RICO:** PC World Puerto Rico; **ROMANIA:** Computerworld Romania, PC World Romania, Telecom Romania; **RUSSIA:** Computerworld Russia, Mir PK, Publish, Seti; **SINGAPORE:** Computerworld Singapore, PC World Singapore, Publish in Asia; **SLOVENIA:** Monitor; **SOUTH AFRICA:** Computing SA, Network World SA, Software World SA; **SPAIN:** Communicaciones World, Computerworld España, Dealer World España, Macworld España, PC World España; **SRI LANKA:** Infolink PC World; **SWEDEN:** CAP&Design, Computer Sweden, Corporate Computing Sweden, Internetworld Sweden, it.branschen, Macworld Sweden, MaxiData Sweden, MikroDatorn, Nätverk & Kommunikation, PC World Sweden, PCaktiv, Windows World Sweden; **SWITZERLAND:** Computerworld Schweiz, Macworld Schweiz, PCtip; **TAIWAN:** Computerworld Taiwan, Macworld Taiwan, NEW ViSiON/Publish, PC World Taiwan, Windows World Taiwan; **THAILAND:** Publish in Asia, Thai Computerworld; **TURKEY:** Computerworld Turkiye, Macworld Turkiye, Network World Turkiye, PC World Turkiye; **UKRAINE:** Computerworld Kiev, Multimedia World Ukraine, PC World Ukraine; **UNITED KINGDOM:** Acorn User UK, Amiga Action UK, Amiga Computing UK, Apple Talk UK, Computing, Macworld, Parents and Computers UK, PC Advisor, PC Home, PSX Pro, The WEB; **UNITED STATES:** Cable in the Classroom, CIO Magazine, Computerworld, DOS World, Federal Computer Week, GamePro Magazine, InfoWorld, I-Way, Macworld, Network World, PC Games, PC World, Publish, Video Event, THE WEB Magazine, and WebMaster; online webzines: JavaWorld, NetscapeWorld, and SunWorld Online; **URUGUAY:** InfoWorld Uruguay; **VENEZUELA:** Computerworld Venezuela, PC World Venezuela; and **VIETNAM:** PC World Vietnam. 3/24/97

The Value of Microsoft Certification

As a computer professional, your opportunities have never been greater. Yet you know better than anyone that today's complex computing environment has never been more challenging.

Microsoft certification keeps computer professionals on top of evolving information technologies. Training and certification let you maximize the potential of Microsoft Windows desktop operating systems; server technologies, such as the Internet Information Server, Microsoft Windows NT, and Microsoft BackOffice; and Microsoft development tools. In short, Microsoft training and certification provide you with the knowledge and skills necessary to become an expert on Microsoft products and technologies—and to provide the key competitive advantage that every business is seeking.

Microsoft offers you the most comprehensive program for assessing and maintaining your skills with our products. When you become a Microsoft Certified Professional (MCP), you are recognized as an expert and are sought by employers industry-wide. Technical managers recognize the MCP designation as a mark of quality—one that ensures that an employee or consultant has proven experience with Microsoft products and meets the high technical proficiency standards of Microsoft products.

As an MCP, you receive many benefits, such as direct access to technical information from Microsoft; the official MCP logo and other materials to identify your status to colleagues and clients; invitations to Microsoft conferences, technical training sessions and special events; and exclusive publications with news about the MCP program.

Research shows that organizations employing MCPs also receive many benefits:

- A standard method of determining training needs and measuring results—an excellent return on training and certification investments
- Increased customer satisfaction and decreased support costs through improved service, increased productivity, and greater technical self-sufficiency
- A reliable benchmark for hiring, promoting, and career planning

- o Recognition and rewards for productive employees by validating their expertise
- o Retraining options for existing employees, so they can work effectively with new technologies
- o Assurance of quality when outsourcing computer services

Through your study, experience, and achievement of Microsoft certification, you will enjoy these same benefits, too, as you meet the industry's challenges.

Nancy Lewis
General Manager
Microsoft Training and Certification

FOREWORD TO THE MCSE SERIES

Certifications are an effective way of "selling your skills" to prospective employers because they represent a consistent measurement of knowledge about specific software or hardware products. Because of their expansive product line and tremendous marketing efforts, Microsoft certifications have become the gold standard in the exploding certification industry. As a Microsoft Certified Professional (MCP), you are recognized as a "Subject Matter Expert" as defined by objective standards. As a training organization, we recognize the value of offering certification-level training. In fact, approximately 55 percent of students in our Microsoft classes are working toward certification, and I expect that number to continue to rise.

Studies have been conducted that show increased productivity among Microsoft Certified Solutions Developers (MCSDs) versus noncertified programmers. Additionally, compensation for Microsoft Certified Systems Engineers (MCSEs) and MCSDs averages higher than for those without certification. For individuals looking for a career in these areas, there is no better metric of legitimacy that can be placed on a resume than Microsoft certification credentials.

Information Systems/Information Technology (IS/IT) decision-makers for ExecuTrain clients worldwide increasingly require certifications for their IS employees. Often, individuals are required to be certified or find that certification was their competitive edge in landing the job. Conventional wisdom and every study you read indicates these trends will continue as technologies become more a part of daily business in corporations.

Microsoft recently certified the 100,000th MCP. I expect this number to balloon as corporations make certification part of IS staff job descriptions. I predict certified candidates can expect better-paying jobs and positions with more technical responsibility to match their hard-won certification. Although the number of MCPs rises daily, that population is eclipsed by the more than 200,000 open IT positions reported today. Microsoft tracks these open positions and would like to fill each of them with MCPs. My bet is that if anyone can make the math work, they can.

Kevin Brice
Vice President/General Manager
Technical Training
ExecuTrain Corporation

CREDITS

ACQUISITIONS EDITOR
Anne Hamilton

DEVELOPMENT EDITORS
Suzanne Van Cleve
Tracy Thomsic

TECHNICAL EDITOR
Steve Linthicum

COPY EDITORS
Diane Boccadoro
Tracy Brown

PRODUCTION COORDINATOR
Susan Parini

BOOK DESIGNER
Kurt Krames

GRAPHICS AND PRODUCTION SPECIALISTS
Dina F. Quan
Ritchie Durdin
Mario Amador
Ian A. Smith

PROOFREADER
Annie Sheldon
Michelle Croninger

INDEXER
Sherry Massey

ABOUT THE AUTHOR

William C. Jeansonne is a recognized information systems specialist and Microsoft Certified Professional (MCP) with more than sixteen years of experience in systems integration, financial reporting systems, and microcomputer networks. Shortly after receiving his Bachelor of Science degree in Information Systems Management at the University of Maryland University College in 1989, he founded a systems integration firm. While President and CEO of the firm, he formed a merger with a telecommunications company and led the process to become one of the first Microsoft Solution Providers in the United States. During his five-year tenure at the firm, he wrote numerous articles on information technology trends in microcomputers and elaborated on such issues as software piracy and Microsoft's development in the software business.

After selling his systems integration business early in 1996, he founded IT Recruiters, a personnel recruiting agency based in Bethesda, Maryland, that specializes in the placement of MCPs. He quickly expanded the business to the Internet by creating `IT Specialist.com`. The Web site, aptly named IT Specialist, is an innovative service designed to match MCPs with organizations that need technical specialists. The site also serves as a virtual career development center for MCPs by providing helpful links to Internet resources and by hosting a job and resume bank for organizations and MCPs.

Mr. Jeansonne is currently a member of the Communications Committee at the University of Maryland University College in College Park, Maryland. The committee advises the university on issues such as Internet Web site development and telecommunications. He also is a member of the NT Pro Association based in Washington, D.C.

PREFACE

Welcome to *MCSE Career Microsoft®!* Since the introduction of the Microsoft Certified Professional (MCP) program by Microsoft in 1992, the growth rate of MCPs has been phenomenal. The number of MCPs now stands at roughly 100,000+ individuals. This book aims to educate MCPs in the fine art of career-building within the MCP Information Technology (IT) field and can be used by individuals deciding which MCP career to pursue, or those who know which track matches their interests and talents. Most books covering the MCP program focus entirely on practice exams and their respective subject matter. *MCSE Career Microsoft®!* focuses on the professional characteristics involved with obtaining a Microsoft Certification, as well as on maintaining and advancing your career once you are certified.

This book also provides many practical and essential references to information, training, and tools available to IT professionals, including MCPs and MCP candidates. As the business of professional development moves from the trade journals to the Web, MCPs can look forward to building their careers via the Internet. Distance learning facilities are popping up all over the Web, as are specialist sites devoted to particular niche areas of Microsoft technology. *MCSE Career Microsoft®!* explains and directs MCPs to those sites by providing detailed coverage of sites that are important to MCPs.

MCSE Career Microsoft®! also includes actual interviews with MCPs currently working in the field of Microsoft technology, as well as interviews with some of the industry's leaders. What better way is there to present the realities of what it takes to be a successful network engineer or software developer in the IT field? I hope this book answers those critical issues many of you have when contemplating a career move into an area in which you have little or no experience.

Finally, this book has a very practical step-by-step approach to career planning that you will not find in any MCP exam guide. As some of you may know, obtaining a certificate is only half of the process of becoming a successful certified professional. The other half of the process involves experience and career planning. Most organizations have little resources or the mindset toward helping you build your career. *MCSE Career Microsoft®!* takes the guesswork out of the process by providing many insightful tips, techniques, and resources to help guide you in your career. Last but not least, this book can also be very helpful to those IT individuals who are contemplating a move from the mainframe or minicomputer environment into Microsoft technology.

I hope you enjoy every word of *MCSE Career Microsoft®!* and keep it with you at all times, either as a handy guide on your favorite computer bookshelf or in your notebook computer with the enclosed CD-ROM version of the publication. No other computer book on the market today provides as comprehensive an approach to MCPs and their careers as *MCSE Career Microsoft®!*

HOW THIS BOOK IS ORGANIZED

This book is divided into four parts. Within these parts, each chapter begins with an overview of the topics covered in that chapter. Then pertinent information on each topic is presented, along with additional resources for developing your career as an MCP. A Key Point Summary follows, summarizing the chapter highlights and reviewing important material. This book can be used by individuals deciding which MCP career to pursue, or those who know which track matches their interests and talents.

Part I: The Microsoft Certified Professional Career

The need for qualified MCPs is growing rapidly, and an MCP career is full of opportunity and growth. Microsoft is enticing secondary schools, colleges, universities, and third-party training firms to institute training programs to help meet the incredible demand for MCPs. Recruiting firms are placing MCPs in lucrative and fulfilling jobs, both in corporations and as consultants. Chapters in Part I discuss the MCP careers available and help you assess your specific interests and skills.

Part II: The Microsoft Certified Professional Career Tracks

Becoming an MCP is a challenging road, requiring time to study and learn many skills and technologies. The average completion time for the certification process is roughly six months to a year. Taking the courses necessary to pass the exams is only the beginning. Nearly 60 percent of applicants fail at least one of the certification exams on the first pass, so chances are you will soon be heading back to your own private computer lab and the books after course training. Microsoft's certification tests require hands-on experience to pass the exams successfully. In Part II, you can learn more about a specific MCP career, again referring back to the assessments you did in Part I.

Part III: Opportunities for Microsoft Certified Professionals

Part III reveals opportunities for MCPs, including information to help you decide between a corporate job and life as a consultant. Opportunities abound for MCPs seeking full-time employment with an organization, or opportunities as a contractor or entrepreneur with the small business start-up. With the economy out of the doldrums of the early 1990s, many IT professionals are opting for the independence that comes from being their own boss and prefer to avoid the whims of the corporate world. This part includes information you need to set out on your own, or work in the corporate world.

Part IV: Tools and Information for Microsoft Certified Professionals

Part IV includes useful resources such as Microsoft TechNet and Developer Network CDs to help you launch a successful career. The latter offer quick and reliable access to information on Microsoft operating systems, applications software, and development languages. Other important resources for MCPs can be found on the Internet and in your local area.

Part V: Resources

The supplemental materials in Part V contain a wealth of information. In addition to a detailed glossary and thorough index, you'll find the following information in the appendices: exam study tips, salary negotiation tips, and additional job and consulting resources.

CD-ROM

The CD-ROM included with this book contains the following materials: an electronic version of this book in .PDF format, Microsoft Internet Explorer version 3.01, Microsoft Training and Certification Offline CD-ROM, and an electronic version of three chapters of *Windows NT® 4.0 MCSE Study Guide* (IDG Books Worldwide, 1997).

ICONS USED IN THIS BOOK

Several different icons used throughout this book draw your attention to matters that deserve a closer look:

 **This icon points you to another place in this book (or to another resource) for more coverage on a given topic. It may point you back to a previous chapter where important material has already been covered, or it may point you ahead to let you know that a concept will be covered in more detail later on.**

 I know this will be hard for you to believe, but sometimes things work differently in the real world than books—or software documentation—say they do. This icon draws your attention to the author's real world experiences, which will hopefully help you find or keep that ideal job.

 This icon points out an interesting or helpful fact, or some other comment that deserves emphasis.

This icon indicates an online resource that you can access to obtain products, utilities, and other worthwhile information.

 Here's a little piece of friendly advice, or a shortcut, or a bit of personal experience that might be useful to you.

ACKNOWLEDGMENTS

I'd like to thank all of the people who generously contributed their time and expertise to help me write this book, including Mark Kapczynski of LANTUG, Charles Kelly of NT Pro, Dr. Roy Beasley of Howard University, Dave Harper of Targeted Systems Development, David Fitzpatrick of Client/Server Systems, Inc., Debbie Banik of SS Innovations, Jenifer Wald Morgan of Computer Training & Consulting, Greg Brown of Spring, Texas, Rick Ow of Professional Datasolutions, Inc., Peter Vogel of Champion Road Machinery, Roger Bremer of NCR Corporation, Douglas Koenig of Ford Motor Company, and Michael McDonald of Howard Community College.

I'd also like to give special thanks to my agent, Brian Gill of Studio B/Computer Book Cafe, for his expertise and guidance throughout this endeavor.

Finally, I wish to thank my wife, Angela, for her help in research and the transcription of interviews, and for putting up with all of the commotion that writing a book entails.

CONTENTS AT A GLANCE

TABLE OF CONTENTS

Part III: Opportunities for Microsoft Certified Profesisonals 141

The Microsoft Certified
Professional Career

The explosive demand for Microsoft application and operating systems software has created a tremendous need for qualified Microsoft Certified Professionals (MCPs). Microsoft is enticing secondary schools, colleges, universities, and third-party training firms to institute training programs to help meet the incredible demand for MCPs. It is also working closely with some of the largest recruiting firms in the U.S. to help place MCPs once they are trained and certified. In essence, there has never been a better time to enter this high-technology field of systems and software engineering, technical support, and training.

Whether you're considering a new career in information technology or looking to make a lateral career move from competing technologies, now is the time to act. The opportunities for MCPs are astounding. From network engineering to Web mastering, MCPs find their services in demand the world over.

However, you need to look carefully before you leap. The requirements for becoming an MCP are minimal at best. To successfully be a systems engineer, developer, or trainer, you need to fully understand the skills, training, and professionalism required to succeed as an MCP. You should also make the effort to understand the MCP job marketplace, including employment practices in the information technology industry, in addition to salary structures for the various MCP disciplines. Doing so will significantly enhance your ability to negotiate salaries with prospective and current employers, as well as provide you with the guidance for your career as an MCP.

Introducing *Career Microsoft®!*

About Chapter 1

In this chapter you are confronted with the personal attributes necessary to become a successful Microsoft Certified Professional (MCP). The road to any winning career can be bumpy, but becoming an expert in network engineering or software development can be even trickier. This chapter exposes the essential characteristics that the consummate information technology (IT) professional—particularly the MCP—embodies. This chapter also covers the subject of employment research (job hunting) and the characteristics employers look for in an IT candidate. Finally, this chapter discusses the growing need for MCPs in government.

THE IDEAL MICROSOFT CERTIFIED SYSTEMS ENGINEER (NETWORK ENGINEER)

Microsoft's definition of the Microsoft Certified Systems Engineer (MCSE) is as follows:

"The Microsoft Certified Systems Engineer is qualified to effectively plan, implement, maintain, and support information systems with the Microsoft Windows NT operating system and the Microsoft BackOffice integrated family of server software."

FIGURE 1-1 **The official Microsoft Certified Systems Engineer logo for MCSEs**
(Screen shot reprinted with permission from Microsoft Corporation.)

Overall, Microsoft's description of what an MCSE is capable of performing is accurate. In the real world, however, system engineers typically find themselves working in a heterogeneous computer environment. The trend in most IS shops in this day and age, particularly with Fortune 500 companies, is for multivendor systems integration. In fact, it is not uncommon to find network engineers who have extensive training and experience in UNIX, Novell, and Microsoft network operating systems. In addition to those skills, many network engineers also have experience with specialized computers called routers and Web servers for intranets and the Internet. As a result of this explosion in information technologies, system engineers are expected to work harder and learn faster than ever before. Mastering a network operating system such as Windows NT can take quite a bit of time, energy, and intelligence. Add to that Novell NetWare and maybe a little UNIX, and you can quickly see how many individuals would want to bail out as network engineers.

Surviving in such an overwhelming IT environment as network engineers do today involves a cool head and quick reflexes. System engineers are exposed to numerous urgencies on a daily basis and are expected to respond rapidly. Staying calm and collected during such emergencies requires nerves of steel. On a typical day, a network engineer can expect system hangs (both server and workstation), telecommunication problems, application crashes, and a multitude of peripheral or office automation failures. Remedying all this while trying to maintain system upgrades, respond to end user special requests, and attend meetings can truly tax an individual both mentally and physically. Stamina is very important, as most network engineers work on average from fifty to sixty hours a week, in addition to being on call. As you can see, a career in network engineering requires a great amount of discipline and hard work.

However, many individuals thrive in this type of work environment. If you love day-to-day challenges, varied work assignments, and excellent wages, then network engineering is for you. Many system engineers get to travel the U.S. and abroad and have a great deal of autonomy when it comes to completing projects and tasks. They also get to attend ongoing company-paid training, as well as trade shows and seminars, and to represent their companies to clients in the field by working closely with everyone from executives to the staff in an organization. The network engineer's importance in the IT field is growing quickly due to rapid growth of LANs, WANs, and the Internet. All in all, a network engineer's career can be very rewarding—from both a professional and financial standpoint.

The ideal MCSE, or network engineer, should have a proportionate mix of the following skills:

o Good interpersonal, writing, and speaking skills

o Good problem-solving skills and deductive reasoning abilities

o Good hardware and peripheral systems skills (servers, workstations, network interface cards, and cabling system technology)

o Superb knowledge of Microsoft Windows NT Server/Workstation and/or Microsoft BackOffice (NTS, IIS, SQL Server, Exchange Server, SMS, and so on)

o Good experience with Microsoft desktop operating systems such as Windows NT Workstation, Windows 98, and Windows 3.1

o Good Internet-working skills in LANs and WANs, including routers, CSU/DSUs, modems, and other Internet-working equipment; and protocols such as TCP/IP and IPX/SPX

Microsoft Certified Systems Engineers can work in many different roles in the IT field. For instance, an MCSE may also be a *Certified Novell Engineer* (CNE). Microsoft Certified Systems Engineers can also be program managers of a large project, heads of an entire division that focuses on Microsoft technology, such as an engagement manager, or they can play the role of consultant for a large systems integrator. Whatever their role, MCSEs have a definite future in the IT business. Their growing importance in the field of computers is being felt across all organizations, including government. In fact, MCSEs are in enormous demand throughout the world, due largely to Microsoft's dominance in the software market internationally.

 As a network engineer, it's a good idea to keep your tools of the trade readily available in a large satchel or briefcase ready to go for off-site visits. Flight cases used by airline pilots make an excellent portable carrying case for notebook computers, paperback manuals, compact discs, and other papers necessary while on the job. They are roomy and compartmented, and provide lockable protection for a notebook.

Last but not least, the ideal MCSE needs to be able to cope with pressure and be able to multitask on a personal level. Typically, network engineers are pulled in many directions at once, by their managers, by end users, by vendors and, most important, by their employer's clients, depending on the circumstances. Again, the financial rewards can be excellent, and the career gratifying, as long as you are properly trained, can deal with stress, and are motivated and have the requisite experience.

 Systems engineering is by nature a very dynamic IT field. Most of today's application and operating systems software are in a constant state of flux. Consequently, it is nearly impossible to keep abreast of every application or operating system upgrade or patch. The wise network engineer will always keep a ready resource of technical support telephone numbers on hand from the leading vendors of software and hardware handy in case of emergencies. Even better, the smart thing to do is to keep manuals in CD format and technical support CDs such as Microsoft TechNet on a laptop for quick access while in the field.

THE IDEAL MICROSOFT CERTIFIED SOLUTION DEVELOPER (SOFTWARE DEVELOPER)

Microsoft's definition of the Microsoft Certified Solution Developer (MCSD) is as follows:

"The Microsoft Certified Solution Developer is qualified to design and develop custom business solutions with Microsoft development tools, technologies, and platforms, including Microsoft Office and Microsoft BackOffice."

FIGURE 1-2 **The official Microsoft Certified Solution Developer logo for MCSDs**
(Screen shot reprinted with permission from Microsoft Corporation.)

This description is an excellent summation of the principal skills that a programmer or software engineer of Microsoft technology should possess in the field of software development. However, there are other very important skills that a developer should have to be successful as an MCSD. First is the ability to think in the abstract — to conceptualize processes that a given organization may need to take from a physical state, such as manual bookkeeping, to a completely automated cycle within a computer to produce a data entry system. Also important are math skills, as most experienced programmers attest to, if asked. The reason for the mathematical skills is not so much in the math itself, but a good math foundation helps a programmer with the analytical or logical thinking required when programming. Although high math is important in programming, especially if you are a FORTRAN programmer, the more common nonprocedural languages found in use today require a good understanding of Boolean logic. Finally, a good programmer should be creative.

However, all the programming skills in the world will not make for a successful MCSD. Paramount among the skills of a great developer are those interpersonal skills such as the ability to manage, communicate, and deal with people. Gone are the days of individualism in computing. Most organizations these days expect an individual to be a team player. There are many reasons for this team approach.

According to Jim McCarthy's book *Dynamics of Software Development* (Microsoft Press, 1995), group dynamics play an integral role in today's IT programming shops. McCarthy states, "Everybody on the team must know what the team is trying to do, what the finished product will look like, what the basis of the product strategy is, and when they must deliver the product if it is to have its intended effect. Contradictory visions must be resolved and unified. A harmonious sense of purpose must be achieved." In other words, the author is simply stating that to produce an excellent product or program, everyone in the group must have his or her head in the game. Otherwise, the product will fail to materialize because of an overabundance of competing ideas from the various developers in the group.

The ideal MCSD or programmer/analyst should have a proportionate mix of the following skills:

o Solid interpersonal, writing, and speaking skills, as well as the ability to work well in a team environment

o Excellent logic and deductive reasoning skills

o Intimate knowledge of Microsoft Office (Access and Excel) and Microsoft BackOffice (IIS's IDBC, Windows NTS multithreading processes, SQL Server Scripting)

o Any combination of programming skills in Visual Basic, Visual C/C++, Visual J++ (Microsoft's version of Java), and Java (Sun and others)

o Knowledge of COM and DCOM principals (Inter-process distributed communications)

o Familiarity with the Internet and intranet concepts, planning, and implementation

o Be creative and methodical

MCSDs are employed in various positions throughout the IT world, as well as in private and public organizations. They are working as technical leads (senior programmers), product managers, consultants, software engineers, configuration management, and testers in the design, development, and production of software. The software development industry is booming and will continue to do so for the foreseeable future. Corporate downsizing and cost-cutting measures are just some of the driving forces behind the demand for software products and services. Whatever the case, MCSDs have a rosy future. They can expect to be called upon to do some of the most advanced software projects the world has ever seen, especially with regard to the Internet and intranets. The Internet, particularly electronic commerce on the Net, is poised to explode with opportunities for software developers that were unforeseen just two years ago. Nearly every business that sells goods and services throughout the world is expected to do business on the World Wide Web by early next century. In turn, there will be a great demand for developers to hook those businesses to the Web via systems such as Microsoft Commercial Internet System, Internet Information Server, Proxy Server, and Microsoft Exchange. The future of the MCSD is bright, and the financial rewards for obtaining the MCSD certificate are excellent.

THE IDEAL MICROSOFT CERTIFIED PRODUCT SPECIALIST (SOFTWARE SPECIALIST)

Microsoft's definition of the Microsoft Certified Product Specialist (MCPS) is as follows:

"The Microsoft Certified Product Specialist has demonstrated in-depth knowledge of at least one Microsoft operating system and/or Microsoft application such as Microsoft Windows NT, Windows 95, Word, Excel."

FIGURE 1-3 The official Microsoft Certified Product Specialist logo for MCPSs
(Screen shot reprinted with permission from Microsoft Corporation.)

Microsoft's description of the MCPS is conservative at best. Most MCPSs are certified in at least two or more Microsoft products on average. In fact, quite a few of MCPSs are just a few exams away from becoming an MCSE or MCSD. Consequently, many individuals are MCPSs for the simple fact that they are on their way to becoming an MCSE or MCSD.

Defining the skill set necessary to become a successful MCPS can be difficult, to say the least. Since an MCPS can mean many things from the standpoint of the

MCP program, an attempt is made here to focus solely on the MCP's track as a career in and of itself.

The attributes or qualities that make up a good MCPS start with interpersonal skills and a desire to be one of the best in a given Microsoft product. Given the generalist nature of this professional track in the MCP Program, it is imperative that MCPSs be very good at working with people. It's the nature of the beast, as MCPSs typically find themselves working in support roles, serving as help desk specialists, for example, or training people one-on-one. Another important trait found in successful MCPSs is patience. As a support person, you can expect to be working with untrained and unsympathetic end users. Since this sets up a sometimes acrimonious relationship from the start, it is the duty of the MCPS to calm the end users' fears and be patient with individuals while training them. The ideal software specialist should also have good cognitive skills for determining application errors or system crashes caused by the end user, the operating system, or the application itself. Experience counts under most conditions where the MCPS encounters operating systems and application errors or system hangs. System support knowledge and experience can make the difference in determining the cause of a computer problem instantly within minutes and sometimes days.

The ideal MCPS or software specialist should have a proportionate mix of the following skills:

- Good problem-solving, interpersonal, writing, and speaking skills
- Good hardware and peripheral systems skills (workstations, printer, scanner, and other office automation products)
- Excellent skills with Microsoft Office products (Word, Excel, PowerPoint, and Access)
- Familiarity with local-area networks, network printing, and file-sharing concepts
- Solid experience with desktop operating systems (DOS, Windows 3.1, Windows 95, and Windows NT Workstation).
- Good experience with Internet browser software (Explorer and Netscape)

Microsoft Certified Product Specialists can take on many different roles within the IT industry itself, as well as in organizations such as government and non-profit agencies. They can work as network engineers, programmers, instructors, consultants, salespeople and managers. The main reason for the diversity in the MCPS track is due largely to the fact that the MCPS certificate is actually an entry to all of the other MCP tracks in the certification program. Many MCPSs have backgrounds in IT and experience with such products as Windows 95 or Microsoft Word, so it's only natural that they would want to enhance their careers by becoming an MCP. Some have no real intention of actively supporting others through the program, other than themselves. The certificate is a record of achievement, and they like to see it hanging on their office wall. However, for most MCPSs you will find an individual well on his or her way to a career in networking engineering or programming.

Microsoft Certified Product Specialists can look forward to a healthy job market for years to come. All evidence points to exponential growth in the need for information technologists well into the next century. The fantastic growth in the relatively new field of help desk support alone will create an unprecedented demand for those individuals with careers as MCPSs in Microsoft technology. Most Fortune 500 companies respect the MCPS as someone who has mastered the product. The test is proof that you have mastered it. In fact, most large companies and government agencies will only hire an IT person if he or she is certified in the appropriate systems or applications.

Microsoft has now renamed the Product Specialist to simply, Microsoft Certified Professional.

THE IDEAL MICROSOFT CERTIFIED TRAINER (INSTRUCTOR)

FIGURE 1-4 **The official Microsoft Certified Trainer logo for MCTs**
(Screen shot reprinted with permission from Microsoft Corporation.)

Microsoft's definition of the Microsoft Certified Trainer (MCT) is as follows: "The Microsoft Certified Trainer is instructionally and technically qualified by Microsoft to deliver Microsoft Official Curriculum through Microsoft Authorized Technical Education Centers and Authorized Academic Training Partners."

This description of the MCT is precise. However, there are some very important attributes that an individual may want to consider if deciding on this particular career track of the MCP program.

The single most important aspect of becoming a successful MCT is one of self-confidence. This point cannot be overemphasized. As an instructor and public speaker, you will be scrutinized in ways you have never imagined. From the way you wear your hair to the way you speak, you will be under close inspection as a trainer, at least until your students get to know you. Therefore, confidence plays are large role in your day-to-day life as an instructor in Microsoft technology.

Trainers must also have the skills necessary to speak effectively and present their ideas in a logical and coherent fashion. Public speaking can be one of the most daunting and most humiliating experiences in life if one is not properly prepared for it. Unless you are a journalism major from college or a game show host from TV, you may have little or no experience in public speaking before becoming an MCT. Do whatever you can to get the experience, because without it you are not going to be very successful as an influential instructor teaching Microsoft technology.

Although writing skills are deemed essential in any teaching curriculum, this is not particularly so with the MCT track. The reason is that most of the materials presented to students are somewhat prefabricated, and courses are graded on a pass/fail basis. So although it's good to have excellent writing skills, it is not mandatory.

The ideal MCT or Instructor should have a proportionate mix of the following skills:

- Excellent interpersonal, writing, and public speaking skills
- Superb knowledge of the respective subject matter being taught
- Familiarity with Microsoft-based operating systems and applications
- Familiarity with networking concepts and principals
- Familiarity with Microsoft programming languages
- Familiarity with PC-based hardware and peripherals

Microsoft Certified Trainers typically find work at *Authorized Technical Educational Centers* (ATECs) and *Authorized Academic Training Partners* (AATPs) throughout the U.S. and abroad. The training centers are specially authorized to offer courses in Microsoft technology. The ATECs are privately owned companies that vary in size and scope in their course offerings. Some are franchises, and others are wholly owned subsidiaries of much larger corporations. Nevertheless, they all offer excellent opportunities for MCTs to practice their profession. Authorized Academic Training Partners are typically located within community colleges throughout the U.S. The program is relatively newer than the ATEC program and offers MCTs a chance to teach at the collegiate level.

concept link

The MCT's future is also bright. With the overwhelming success of Microsoft products and services worldwide, MCTs can look forward to teaching students for years to come. Corporations large and small are investing in training now more than ever. Therefore, instructors can anticipate the need for their services and/or career growth to expand rapidly in the near future.

The Ultimate Microsoft Certified Professional—Crosstraining in Microsoft Technology

While it is always a good idea to specialize in your career, more and more IT professionals are opting to branch out in areas closely related to their vocations. The reason for this can be personal, and more often it's a practical choice based on the needs of an individual and a sense of job security and personal growth. Whatever the case may be, it can never hurt an individual's career to have more than one MCP certificate.

FIGURE 1-5 Microsoft's newly redesigned official Microsoft Certified Professional logo for MCPs
(Screen shot reprinted with permission from Microsoft Corporation.)

Microsoft Certified Professionals with more than one MCP certificate have greater flexibility in their careers than single-track MCPs. Holding more than one certificate can also be a plus during times of recession or severe budget cuts on

Capitol Hill. The IT professionals most affected by the cyclical nature of the economy tend to be programmers and trainers. Many instructors and software developers who work on a contract basis are wary of the economy and crosstrain intentionally in order to stay steadily employed.

For example, a solution developer with an MCT certificate can teach *Microsoft Official Curriculum* (MOC) courses in programming languages such as Visual Basic and Microsoft Access at night, while working as a programmer during the day. Or the MCSD can teach during the day on a full-time basis and perform contract development work in the evenings and on weekends. Granted, this individual would not have much of a life if he or she did this, but it definitely has its financial rewards. Most important, an individual who is cross-trained in Microsoft technology would rarely face a day of unemployment, given the current demand for such individuals.

Having more than one MCP certificate can also help you stand out from the crowd when promotions are due at your place of work. Depending on where you look in the IT industry, you will find that IT professionals with multiple certificates (Microsoft and Novell) are either in a managerial position or fast on their way to becoming managers. As most people are aware, education is the path to success, especially in the IT world. Without the right mix of skills and education, the most that you can hope for in the way of a career in IT is the position of network administrator or computer hack. A college degree in information technology never hurt an IT professional's career either, but any kind of degree, including an associate's degree from a junior college, can improve your chances for advancement with your employer.

Although it is unusual, you can find MCPs who are certified in all four certification programs that Microsoft offers. There is no doubt that these individuals are super achievers and have the tenacity and intelligence to successfully command all of the subject matters covered in the MCP program. It is an enormous undertaking from both educational and experiential perspective. However, that's not to say the average person could not successfully achieve the status of MCSE, MCSD, MCPS, and MCT in his or her lifetime. It is definitely doable, but you had better be a fast learner and good test taker to do it within a reasonable time frame.

The main thing that an MCP should keep in mind is carefully tailoring his or her career to the needs of the market. Having two MCP certificates under your belt is more than enough expertise for gainful employment. However, the MCP should also keep in mind where IT is heading. All things in the field of IT currently point to the Internet and intranet technologies. Although an MCT might possess certificates in two or three tracks of the MCP program, he or she is not going to be in demand within the job market if his or her skills are not in demand. It is that simple. Fortunately, most Microsoft technology is in high demand—at least for the time being. However, most MCPs can rest assured that their services are needed, especially if they are solution developers or systems engineers. Ditto if you are a double-major within the MCP program.

Finally, the benefits of becoming an MCP are many, both long-term and immediate. Some of the rewards are listed below:

o **Recognition:** Microsoft Certified Professionals are instantly recognized as experts with the technical knowledge and skills needed to design and develop or implement and support solutions with Microsoft products. Microsoft helps build this recognition by promoting the expertise of MCPs within the industry and to customers and potential clients.

o **Access to technical information:** Microsoft Certified Professionals gain access to technical information directly from Microsoft. Depending on the certification, MCPs also receive a prepaid trial membership to the Microsoft TechNet Technical Information Network or a discount for the Microsoft Developer Network; are entitled to free incidents with Microsoft Product Support Service; and are eligible to participate in the Microsoft beta evaluation program.

o **Global community:** Microsoft Certified Professionals join a worldwide community of technical professionals who have validated their expertise with Microsoft products. Microsoft Certified Professionals are brought together through a dedicated forum on the Web at: www.microsoft. com/mcp; receive a free subscription to *Microsoft Certified Professional*, a career and professional development magazine created especially for MCPs; and, depending on their certification, are eligible to join the Network Professional Association, a worldwide association of computer professionals.

in the real world As with most professional occupations, the more "degreed" a person is in his or her particular field, the better the chances of promotion to the levels of management. While some individuals feel most comfortable in "worker bee" positions for most of their working lives, the majority of career professionals have hopes of obtaining a position in management or executive ranks within a given organization over time. If the former is your goal, you should have at least a bachelor's degree, preferably in computer science or information systems, as well as a proven track record of experience in addition to an advanced degree in your field and/or certification as an MCSE, MCT, or MCSD.

RESEARCHING AND ASSESSING A PROSPECTIVE EMPLOYER

In today's job market, you need to show a potential employer how you can meet his or her needs. This involves having intimate knowledge of both the company and its products, which can only be obtained through basic research of the organization.

There are many different resources in your community that provide company information. This is not an exclusive list—other resources exist that you will find during the job-seeking process. Here are few ideas that will start you on your way.

Library

Start at your local public library—it is a great source of information. Check to see if it has a career or business section; these are particularly helpful to job seekers.

- Check the performance of companies you are interested in by using such standard business references as *Standard & Poor's Register of Corporations, Dun & Bradstreet,* and *Moody's Manuals.*
- If you are unable to find the resources you need, ask for the reference librarian. He or she will be happy to assist you.

College/University

Call or visit your college career center. Most college career centers offer a wide variety of services to their alumni either free or for a nominal fee. The services include such things as:

- Career counseling
- Job postings
- Workshops on such issues as resumes, interviewing, job search strategies, and the like
- Resume referrals to potential employers
- Career fairs
- Practice interview sessions

Chamber of Commerce

Most Chamber of Commerce offices have information on employers in their counties. This is a great way to get basic employer information such as the number of employees a company has, annual sales revenue, how long it has been in business, and the like.

Professional Associations

Find a professional association that has members who perform the job that you would like to do. Telephone the local chapter and try to attend meetings if possible. These individuals will also be able to provide invaluable information on potential employers.

The Internet

There is a wealth of employer information to be found on the Internet. Many companies now carry their own Web sites, which can provide information such as:

- Organizational structure
- Biographical information on management
- Information on current clients and customers
- Products and services

TABLE 1-1 CAREER RESOURCES ON THE WEB		
SITE	*CONTENT*	*WEB ADDRESS*
IT Recruiters, Inc.	Technical recruiting	`http://www.itrecruitersinc.com`
Mastering Computers	Training systems — Microsoft Solution Provider	`http://www.masteringcomputers.com`
Micro Modeling Associates, Inc.	Software development — Microsoft Solution Provider	`http://www.micromodeling.com`
Global Management Systems, Inc.	Systems integrator— Microsoft Solution Provider	`http://www.gmsi.com`
Digex	Internet Service Provider	`http://www.digex.com`
DataFocus	Software development — Microsoft Solution Provider	`http://www.datafocus.com`
FDC Technologies	Systems integrator — Microsoft Solution Provider	`http://www.feddata.com`
Microsoft Corporation	Information technology jobs	`http://microsoft.com/jobs`

Other Resources

Sometimes the obvious resources get overlooked. Hopefully you will find that this list provides you with employer information that is readily accessible to you at little or no cost. These are great resources to utilize in the research process.

For the MCP, or for any professional job candidate for that matter, employer research and assessment can make the difference between a successful career or a working life of spotty employment and discontent. Starting on the wrong track or with the wrong employer can be equally destructive to one's career as an MCP. We hope this portion of the chapter on a career in Microsoft technology will give you new insights on how to effectively screen and scrutinize a prospective employer. Remember, it's your life. So pay close attention and always, always keep in mind that the job search process is a two-way street, that is, as the employer scrutinizes you, so should you scrutinize the employer.

THE JOB MARKET FOR MICROSOFT CERTIFIED PROFESSIONALS

Given the size and scope of the MCP program, it's only natural that some of the largest and most specialized IT companies and IT departments are now seriously considering MCP candidates to fill their ranks. Microsoft's push into the enterprise market has created a wealth of new opportunities for MCPs throughout the United States and abroad. As a result, system integration firms and Microsoft Solution Providers (MSPs) in particular are finding it increasingly difficult to find qualified MCPs, due to the exponential growth and demand of Microsoft products worldwide.

The hunt for qualified MCP candidates by the major IT organizations will continue well into the year 2000. Currently, many IT firms are in the process of ramping up their base of Microsoft troops for the coming onslaught of service demands brought on by the use of Microsoft products. Many large IT shops are also bringing in MCP recruits for training in their newly created consulting and service unit groups. These specialty divisions in particular are placing huge demands on the market for qualified MCPs across the U.S.

As a result of the pent-up demand for MCPs, many of the larger IT organizations are scrambling to find and retain just about any MCP they can get their hands on. They are looking past the warts and all, and are retraining when necessary. As a result, many IT organizations are picking up the bill for further certification and general IT training for individuals lacking skills in certain areas of Microsoft technology. That's good news, of course; free education is always a good thing when you can get it. However, getting additional training in Microsoft systems and applications is usually not enough for your career as an MCP, especially if you're working for a large systems integrator or an MSP.

Today, MSPs and big system integrators mostly look for experience in a candidate. Education is a definite plus, but it will not guarantee you a job with the big players in IT. They typically screen first for experience, then consider education credentials. As discussed earlier in this chapter, other attributes that an MCP should possess are interpersonal, writing, and speech skills. Such skills are important, but not as important as having hands-on, bare-knuckle experience with Microsoft systems and applications. So much of Microsoft technology is new that it can be next to impossible to get the experience you need unless you get some type of training or tinker with the technology in your spare time. Nevertheless, plenty of MCPs are getting the hands-on field experience and classroom training they need to get in with the larger IT organizations and departments.

Some of the major MCP job roles and functions are described here. The information should give you a realistic idea of the type of person that the IT industry wants, as well as the job functions you can expect to encounter as an MCP.

Typical Microsoft Certified Professional Job Titles and Functions

A **network administrator** is responsible for the entire network or networks within an organization. This includes all hardware such as servers, workstations, printers, faxes, telephone PBXs, and other office automation equipment hooked to the local area network. They are often responsible for vendor relations as well (for example, purchasing of equipment and supplies). Network administrators can be CNEs with an MCPS certificate, but can also have an MCSE certificate as well.

DILBERT reprinted with permission of United Feature Syndicate, Inc.

A **network engineer** is responsible for all aspects of local-area network design, installation and configuration. Duties may include network architecture planning, network traffic analysis, and diagnostics. Additional duties typically include router installation and configuration, as well as some telecommunications planning and installation for wide area networks. Network engineers are typically MCSEs, CNEs, or both.

A **software specialist** is responsible for training users in a one-on-one relationship in desktop operating systems and applications. Specialists may also work as help desk technicians, supporting end users in applications and stand-alone operating systems. They also assist end users with light programming tasks, such as in the development of macros (scripts) in Word or WordPerfect. Software specialists are an excellent match for the MCPS program.

A **trainer** is responsible for training individuals in a classroom setting. Trainers, often referred to as instructors, teach classes in a multitude of subjects ranging from Microsoft Word to Windows NT. They may also train users on-site at client offices and in some cases perform training in a one-on-one setting. Trainers are certified as MCTs, but can also teach other curricula from competing software vendors, such as Novell or Sun Microsystems.

A **developer** is responsible for the design and creation of executable software code. Developers often code specific subroutines (dynamic link libraries, DLLs) during all phases of a software development project. They write or code software in development languages such as Visual C/C++, FoxPro, and Visual Basic. They may also develop databases and corresponding screens in relational database management systems, such as SQL and Microsoft Access. Developers who work with Microsoft programming languages are often certified as MCSDs.

A **technical lead** is responsible for a small group of programmers or developers who specialize in a specific language and/or product within a development group or division. The lead programmer's duties often include providing escalation support to the group, as well as providing assistance to the program manager to help keep the project on schedule. They may also have such esoteric duties as helping keep the lid on secret projects and boosting the morale of the group from time to time. Technical leads are often certified as MCSDs.

A **product manager** is responsible for the overall project and developer group within an organization. Duties often include budgeting, hiring and firing, and other general administrative tasks for a project and/or department. A product manager's duties often transcend boundaries within a technology group, and he or she can be held responsible for the management of all types of IT professionals within the group or division. He or she may manage personnel from administrative assistants to senior-level programmers. Program managers are often accomplished individuals with more than one Microsoft certification, such as an MCSE and MCSD or MCT.

A **consultant** is responsible for determining the client's or customer's IT needs. There are actually two roles a consultant can take on: that of a developer consultant or, in the case of a systems engineer, that of an engagement consultant. Both roles have similar duties in that you are expected to work closely with clients or customers in determining the data processing needs. The role typically requires an advanced degree, familiarity with leading methodologies, and excellent interpersonal skills. The employer usually requires certification, and the consultant is expected to have either the MCSE or MCSD certificate.

A **technical salesperson** is responsible for supporting the sales staff with product/service technical information. Duties typically include on-site sales presentation support for clients and customers. The sales support representative also has full technical knowledge of a product or service and backs up the lead salesperson for Q&A by the client or customer. Other duties include setting up computers, projection systems, and other visual aids for the lead salesperson in a product or service demonstration. Technical sales individuals are often certified as MCPSs or MCSEs, and a small percentage are certified as MCSDs.

A **project manager** is responsible for managing the specification, development, quality assurance, and delivery of a proposed solution. The project manager is the single individual responsible for the successful implementation of the proposed system by managing all phases of a project. As such, the project manager serves as the sole point of contact and responsibility with the customer, and closely tracks all tactical issues and problems related to the systems deployment and delivery until the project is signed off by the customer. Project managers often have multiple certifications, such as a CNE or an MCSE, in the technologies of such vendors as Novell and Microsoft.

A **practice manager** is responsible for an entire department's or division's operation, from budgeting to hiring and firing. The practice manager directs all projects, oversees training for his or her employees, and guides all marketing and sales activities within the division. The title *practice manager* can sometimes be used interchangeably with *program director*, depending on the size of the business unit. Practice managers are often well-educated individuals with a minimum of fifteen years' experience in the IT field. A practice manager often has more than one Microsoft certification, such as MCSE, MCPS, and MCT certificates.

MICROSOFT CERTIFIED PROFESSIONALS IN GOVERNMENT

As the popularity and early adoption of Microsoft technology in business continues to grow, federal agencies including state and local governments are following suit. With federal agencies such as the U.S. Post Office and the IRS in the lead with the installation of some of Microsoft's latest systems, such as Exchange and Windows NT, MCPs will soon be in high demand there, too. While many government agencies in Washington, D.C. hire outside consulting firms and systems integrators to do the initial planning and installation of their computer systems, MCPs can expect the need for their skills to increase in the coming years within federal government.

Many of the federal jobs for MCPs will most likely be located in Washington, D.C. The federal government employs thousands of individuals in and around the nation's capital. However, many military installations located across the U.S. and abroad are rapidly adopting Microsoft technology and will need individuals to support products such as Windows NT and Exchange. You don't have to join a military service unit to get these jobs. Quite a few of the armed forces branches employ U.S. civilian citizens as an alternative to enlisted men and officers.

In any case, MCPs can expect to be paid a lot less for their efforts at a government institution. The budgets of IT departments at federal agencies do not support the freewheeling salaries the private sector of the economy offers. However, an MCP can expect better job security, as well as exposure to large and varied system projects that he or she may not see while working for a small Microsoft Solution Provider or privately owned company.

KEY POINT SUMMARY

In summary, you should now understand the key attributes necessary to becoming a successful MCP in the IT industry. In addition, you now understand how MCPs are employed by organizations ranging from government to private industry and what roles the MCP can expect to perform while employed by such organizations. Finally, you should now know how to research and assess a prospective employer before taking the plunge as an MCP.

The following are some important points of the chapter that should be kept in mind:

- A career as an MCP is both demanding and rewarding.
- Multiple certifications can enhance your prospects for being hired.
- Microsoft Certified Professionals are employed throughout the industry as network engineers, programmers, software specialists, and instructors.
- You should carefully research and assess a prospective employer before accepting a job.
- The growing need of MCPs in local, state, and federal governments.

Personal Assessment and Career Planning

About Chapter 2

In the previous chapter you learned of the ideal traits that a Microsoft Certified Professional (MCP) needs to possess in order to succeed in the workplace. In this chapter you'll learn how to identify and quantify your skill base in order to determine the best MCP track for your career. Taking it a step further, you are also asked to accurately and honestly assess your skill base so that you can set a realistic career path that leads to success. All too often in the computer industry, you find individuals who have no conceptual framework of what it takes to survive in the computer industry. The information technology business, in particular the microcomputer field, is fraught with change and is not a place for the faint of heart. If individuals do not maintain their career focus in this environment, they will fall into a trap of generalization and, perhaps, unemployment. People who are not focused typically end up becoming jacks-of-all-trades, and lend truth to saying "a master of all is a master of none."

On the other hand, some individuals, typically computer hackers, believe that, because they are good at playing computer games or know Windows 95 and are labeled "computer geniuses" by their friends and family, they would necessarily make good network engineers. They are known as a *wannabes,* and the information technology field has only limited space for those individuals with no formal training. This chapter will also help you with the process of matching your specific skills to one of four certified professional tracks offered through Microsoft. Finally, this chapter discusses career planning and how to stay abreast of developments in your profession once your career is on track.

SELF-ASSESSMENT

The first step in the career-planning process involves self-assessment. Self-assessment involves taking a long, hard look at yourself and asking the tough questions. What is important to you and why? What are your likes and dislikes? What do you need that will give you satisfaction on the job and in your career? It is only by answering these kinds of questions that you can answer two very important career questions: What do you want to do, and where do you want to do it?

Self-assessment begins by acquiring basic knowledge about yourself. You need to know about your own personal traits—your interests, abilities, skills, and values. Interests are defined as the things you like to do. Abilities are things you may be able to do, but in which you have no training or work experience. Skills are things that you have now and can do well. Values are the things that are important to you that have been gained through life experience.

This overview has given you a basic understanding of what self-assessment entails. "That's fine," you say, "but how can this information be applied to career planning?" There is an exercise that will take you through this process step by step, and allow you to answer these questions.

Step 1: Write Down Information About Yourself

In order to be effective in the self-assessment process, the first step involves writing down on paper the basic information about yourself. Without this information, it will be difficult at best to assess yourself accurately. This information should include, but is not limited to the following:

Work experience

1. **Company information:** company name; employment dates; title of your position; position responsibilities; job accomplishments (such as awards); special skills, knowledge, and abilities used; reason for leaving.

Education/training

1. College/university, enrollment date, major, degree, graduation date
2. Other training
3. Honors/commendations/awards/scholarships
4. Extracurricular activities

Personal activities

1. **Professional:** organization memberships, positions held, awards, and so on.
2. **Community/volunteer:** civic, political, other memberships, offices held, and so on.

Step 2: Build on Your Foundation

The basic information above has given you a clearer picture of your career, training, and personal activities. Continue to build on that foundation. You will need to examine your life in three separate time periods: childhood, adolescence, and adulthood. Think back and recall some of your past accomplishments, including things you liked and felt good about.

 tip *Consider This:* **What natural talents have you had since you were a kid? What is it that you *know* you are good at? Mechanical skills? Math? Writing? Are you at ease with adults, superiors?**

Try to write down a minimum of three accomplishments for each age group. This process may take some time — be patient. Keep a log or journal and write down the things that come to mind.

Once you have compiled this information, you will want to develop a simple chart. In the first column, list your age at the time of the accomplishment. In the second column, describe what you did to make this experience happen. In the third column, write down why you felt you were successful.

Next, analyze this information. When you look at these stories, you should begin to see a definitive pattern, which utilizes the same values, skills, and interests. These are the things that motivate you — it is what you like to do and what keeps you going.

Now reread the information you wrote, but begin to ask specific job-related questions, such as:

1. What specific skills were used in this accomplishment?

2. What are the interests focused on? People? Things? Numbers?

3. What was the end result of this accomplishment? What did you hope to achieve?

Step 3: Examine Your Values

The next step in self-assessment is one that is often overlooked but is critical. You need to write down and examine your own values. You may *think* you understand your own values, but it is helpful to write them down, as values can change over time. What was important to you when you were twenty may not be important to you when you are forty.

For this step you will need to do several things. First, brainstorm and come up with a list of values that are important to you. Next, rank each value on the following scale:

1. Very important

2. Important

3. Somewhat important

4. Not at all important

Then examine all the values you ranked number 1. Of these responses, you will want to take your top five values and rank them 1–5, with 1 being the most important.

This exercise can be extremely important, because it may or may not reflect what you expected. You may have thought money was most important to you, when actually independence was higher on your list. This exercise helps clarify your values and determine what is most important to you.

Step 4: Brainstorm About Your Strengths and Weaknesses

You have now compiled the basic information about yourself, your accomplishments, and your values. This invaluable information reveals much about you, and will be helpful in Step 4 of the process.

You now need to sit down and brainstorm about your strengths and weaknesses. List as many things as you can. The list can include examples from both your personal and professional experiences. You can be general or specific in your responses. Don't worry about right or wrong answers—the goal is to list as much information as possible.

Step 5: Analyze Your Data

During this process, you have learned a lot about yourself. You now have a lot of information, and it may seem a bit overwhelming or intimidating. This next procedure will help you to analyze and understand the data that you have.

Create a table that has the following categories:

1. **Accomplishments:** What have you done successfully?

2. **Personal interest:** Is there a special significance to the activity? Why did the activity interest you?

3. **Role:** What role did you play? What strengths did you capitalize on?

4. **Values/needs:** What was important to you? Why was it important?

tip *Consider This:* **What are your major accomplishments in life? (Hint: Graduation from college? Winning a science award for best project?) What are your deep personal interests? (Hint: Seeing things to completion? Working with your hands? Problem solving?) What roles have you eagerly taken on in life? (Hint: Team captain, quarterback, foreperson, manager, or supervisor?) What values are most important to you? (Hint: Hard work, a sense of fair play, honesty?)**

Now look at the information you have for Step 2. Put the information for each accomplishment in this table. You should be able to discern some type of pattern, which reveals what you like and what you dislike. Congratulations! You have now completed the critical first step: self-assessment.

However, self-assessment is only part of the career-planning process. Now that you know about yourself, you need to identify specific job-related skills. This is the next part of the process: skills assessment.

SKILLS ASSESSMENT

The assessment process is twofold: The first part is self-assessment, which you completed in the previous section. The next step in the career-planning process is skills assessment. Skills assessment involves examining yourself in relation to the skills you will be able to offer a potential employer. This means focusing on yourself and asking relevant questions such as: What skills do I currently possess? What skills do I want to have? What skills will be necessary for me to have in the future? The answers to these types of questions will help you in both your career planning and career advancement.

Skills assessment begins with taking inventory of all the things you have to offer an employer. This includes identifying your skills, abilities, knowledge, and experience. Remember that skills can be obtained through a variety of ways: work experience, life experience, volunteer work, and so on.

When you go through this process, keep in mind that skills generally fall into one of three broad categories:

1. **Specific knowledge skills,** which require specialized knowledge or training, such as learning a foreign language or computer program.

2. **Functional skills,** which enable you to relate to people, information, or things, such as analytical or technical skills.

3. **Management skills,** which show how you manage the day-to-day activities of your position, such as meeting deadlines.

"This information is great," you say, "but how do I make sure I uncover the skills that are relevant to an employer?" The next section covers the skill discovery process.

Step 1: Brainstorm About Your Skills

You should begin the process by brainstorming about your skills. Think of every skill that you possess. Write down everything—do not rule anything out. You possess many more skills than you might think. You may discover during this process that you have a skill that is invaluable to an employer.

This can be a difficult process, but do not be discouraged. If you are having difficulty coming up with a skills list, you may want to look at something called an action word list such as Table 2-1. Action words are what employers like to see on a resume, as they tell what you actually did on the job. For example, you administered (administration skills), analyzed (analytical skills), researched (research skills), communicated (communication skills), etc. You get the idea.

Step 2: Divide Your Skills

You should now have a complete list of skills. Take this list and divide it into the three categories that were discussed previously. This is a little tricky to do but not impossible. This step will give examples of each category.

tip *Consider This:* **What are your specific knowledge skills? What are your functional skills? What are your management skills?**

TABLE 2-1 ACTION WORDS				
achieved	controlled	facilitated	judged	outlined
acted	converted	finalized	launched	oversaw
administered	conveyed	fostered	learned	persuaded
advised	corrected	founded	lectured	planned
analyzed	counseled	generated	led	prepared
applied	cut back on	guided	logged	processed
approved	decided	handled	maintained	published
arranged	defined	headed	managed	purchased
assisted	delivered	helped	measured	qualified
attended	demonstrated	hired	merged	recruited
balanced	determined	identified	modernized	refined
bought	diagnosed	implemented	modified	reorganized
budgeted	directed	improved	motivated	represented
built	distributed	improvised	negotiated	restored
centralized	edited	increased	observed	set up
changed	encouraged	initiated	obtained	studied
coached	established	innovated	opened	taught
compiled	evaluated	instituted	operated	trained
computed	expanded	integrated	organized	upgraded
conceived	expedited	invented	overhauled	worked

Specific knowledge skills

These are the technical skills that relate to a specific field, job, or subject. To figure out what skills you may possess, examine what you do daily on the job and in your leisure time. Examples include the following:

- Computer programming
- Internet Web design

o Local-area networks

o Microcomputer hardware/peripherals

Functional skills

These are the skills you use to deal with people, information, or things. Functional skills are sometimes called transferable skills, because they can be transferred to different office settings and fields. These are the skills you want to stress if you are changing fields and/or careers. Examples include the following:

o Problem-solving skills

o Design skills

o Consultation skills

o Integration skills

Management skills

These are also known as your personality traits because they show how your personality will impact the day-to-day responsibilities of getting the job done. Examples include:

o Competency

o Industriousness

o Logicality

o Precision

Step 3: Group Your Skills

You have come up with a list of skills and have identified which general categories they go under. It is now necessary to take this information and put it in a format that speaks to an employer. This process is called skill grouping. Skill grouping involves taking all your skills and putting them into broader categories. These categories would include the following:

tip **Consider This:** (1.) Name at least three specific knowledge skills that you possess. (2.) Name at least three functional skills that you possess. (3.) Name at least three management skills that you possess.

- **Leadership:** Actual skills are leading, motivating.

- **Advocacy:** Actual skills are negotiating, implementing.

- **Teaching/training:** Actual skills are influencing, designing.

Step 4: Consider Your Accomplishments

Now you have not only identified the skills you possess, but have put them under general skill areas that employers will want to see on your resume. However, it may seem like you have a lot of information and are uncertain what to do with it. At this point you may want to simplify the process. Think about the accomplishments that were discussed in the self-assessment section.

tip *Consider This:* **Name an important functional skill you think would be important in the IT field. Name a specific knowledge skill that would be important for a network engineer. Name an important management skill that would be absolutely necessary to be a successful IT manager.**

On the table that you initially created, add the following categories:

1. **Personality traits:** What traits did you exhibit that allowed you to achieve your accomplishment?

2. **Specific knowledge skills/functional skills:** What special knowledge or skills enabled you to accomplish these goals?

At this point in the process, you have a wealth of information at your disposal. You have performed two critical assessments: one of yourself and one of your skills. These assessments must be made before you can proceed with planning your career. Career planning is a lifelong and continuous process. As you will see in the next section, planning your career is vital to your success as an MCP.

MATCHING YOUR PERSONAL SKILLS TO A SPECIFIC CAREER TRACK

Now comes the easy part, matching those essential skills and personality traits of yours to a career in Microsoft technology. The first step in the matching process would be to try to leverage your existing skills by selecting an MCP track that closely matches your technical abilities. For example, if you're mechanically inclined and enjoy working with your hands, you would most likely be happy in a career as a network administrator. Another example would be taking a personality trait and comparing it to one of the four MCP tracks in the certification program at Microsoft. For instance, if in the process of identifying your interpersonal skills you named communication as one of your strengths, you might want to consider a career in teaching as a Microsoft Certified Trainer. As you can see, the process of matching is fairly simple and straightforward, albeit important.

If you want to have a successful and satisfying career in IT, you must be honest and straightforward in your approach to career planning. Just because you think you might be good at a particular job doesn't mean you would necessarily be successful at it. In other words, don't be a dreamer when it comes to something as serious as the IT business. If you know, for instance, that you work well under pressure, you would most likely do well in a career as a network engineer or computer consultant. If you don't work well under stress, then a career in systems integration is definitely out of the question, and you probably would do better as a software developer or an instructor in a classroom setting, because these disciplines can be less stressful.

The choice is ultimately yours when it comes to career planning, so don't be shy about asking for help when you need it. There are plenty of career centers on the Internet (as well as colleges and trade schools) that can help you with the matching process. Table 2-2 offers some insight into the matching process.

TABLE 2-2 MATCHING YOUR SKILLS TO MCP CAREERS	
SKILLS	*CAREER*
Good math skills	Developer, network engineer
Personable	Trainer, software specialist
Mechanically inclined	Network administrator
Good analytical skills	Programmer/analyst, developer
Good writing skills	Technical proposal writer, computer sales
Good leadership skills	Program manager, director of IT

By now you get the picture, so try to match your skills and personality traits as best you can. In the long run, you will be a happier and more successful IT professional.

PLANNING YOUR CAREER AS A MICROSOFT CERTIFIED PROFESSIONAL

Congratulations! You have now completed the assessment process that will enable you to develop a concrete career plan. Career planning is by no means an easy process, but it is necessary to do continuously throughout your career. There are three steps involved in the career-planning process. The first step involves examining specific criteria; the second is consideration of career issues; and the last step is career plan development.

Step 1: Criteria

The first step is examining the specific criteria that are involved in the career-planning process.

There are three primary criteria that you should consider in the career-planning process to ensure that you are in a job that suits your skills, interests, and needs. These criteria are as follows:

Job content

What are the activities that you do on a daily basis? You need to pursue a job and career that entails tasks and responsibilities you enjoy doing, and that will keep you continually challenged. Many individuals have dreamed about pursuing a specific career only to find that the daily routine of the job was not for them.

Environment

What type of environment will allow you to be productive and do your best work? When examining potential employers, consider the following factors when making a decision: work location, schedule flexibility, the type of people you will work with, and so on. You will be able to focus more on your job if you are in an environment that is compatible with your needs.

Salary

Everyone states that they want a lot of money. However, money is not the only factor to consider in your career plan. Ask yourself what kind of salary you need. Do your homework and know what you are worth to a potential employer.

By examining these criteria and answering some basic questions about yourself, you will be able to go onto the next stage of developing your career plan.

Step 2: Issues

This part of the process involves examination of several different key job components. As you progress throughout your career, your circumstances will change. As a result, you will probably examine these issues more than once. They include, but are not limited to:

Education

How much education do you currently have? How much education are you willing to get for a particular career? Do you need to go back to school and either upgrade your skills or train for a new career? If you are not willing to go to school for a long period of time, you should not choose a career that requires extensive schooling.

Personal disposition

Your disposition affects your personality. People who find work that is compatible with their disposition are more likely to be happy on the job. For example, if you prefer working alone, you may not do well working on a team.

Aptitude

Aptitude is defined as a person's natural ability to learn and acquire new skills. Today's job marketplace is skill oriented. What skills have you learned and acquired? What skills are you willing to learn? What skills can you acquire that will make you more valuable to an employer?

Future career outlook

Research your field and know what the predictions are for the future and how they can impact your career. Are jobs likely to increase? Decrease? Stay the same?

Work hours/travel

Some jobs require extensive hours or travel. This could severely impact your lifestyle. Are you able to work long hours or travel frequently if the job requires it? If not, you may want to rethink your job choices and find a job that has more regular hours.

Step 3: Career Plan Development

The last stage of the career-planning process is the development of an actual action plan. The action plan is a proactive process that allows you to be in control of your career. The outline of the action plan is as follows:

Establish short-term and long-term goals

It is important to your career that you establish both short- and long-term goals. You cannot achieve your goals if they have not been set and defined. Goals must be defined; they will provide a focus for everything you do related to your career. Identify your goals and develop a strategy that will allow you to achieve them.

Marketplace research

It is essential that you remain continually aware of what it may take to be marketable in your profession. This is a rapidly changing society. Know your profession, and also be aware of the changing business climate and how that may affect your potential career opportunities and advancement.

Assess your current job situation

Research and analyze how to get to the next stage in your career. Are you happy in your current job? If not, why? Do you need to change your job? If so, what does this involve? Acquiring new skills? You may have to consider such ideas as going back to school, leaving your present company, or changing careers altogether. Identify where you need to go and how you plan to get there.

Identify barriers to your plan

Are there any barriers that can prevent you from implementing your plan? If so, can you overcome them?

Identify resources that will help you implement your plan

More than likely, you will need help in the development of your action plan. Identify what or who can help you get where you need to be.

Implement your action plan

You finally have the components in place to implement your plan. Do not wait too long to activate your plan—you need to make sure that your plan is relevant to the current marketplace.

Research and analyze your progress

Your plan needs to meet your original goals. If your plan is not addressing your goals, it will not be effective. Monitor your progress on a regular basis—this will ensure that you are on track with your career path.

Evaluate your plan

Once your plan has been implemented, evaluate the results. If the plan did not meet its objectives, you may need to develop another action plan that will enable you to proceed on your career path.

How to Stay Abreast of Developments in Your Field as a Microsoft Certified Professional

Staying current in one's field is becoming more and more difficult, especially in the information technology business. The Internet in particular is spawning whole new technologies unforeseen just two years ago. Information technology professionals are striving to keep up with the head-spinning pace of Microsoft and other major players. However, many IT professionals manage to survive and stay on top of their careers by using the many channels of support that are available to them both on the Internet and in the IT community.

Nearly every computer trade journal in existence now has a version of the magazine or periodical on the Internet for easy access to information concerning an IT professional's specialty. They also offer electronic forums for discussion groups on subjects ranging from Windows NT networking to Visual Basic.

Another way of staying current in your area of specialty is to join a local user group or *special interest group* (SIG). These groups offer a wealth of resources and support for IT professionals that is unmatched in the industry.

One of the all-time best means of keeping current in your field is attending trade shows and seminars. They offer you the opportunity to meet with your peers to discuss the latest breakthroughs and advances in IT. They also offer you the chance to build a network of contacts and associates, which is definitely a necessity in the ever-changing IT field.

Whatever your particular interests are in the IT field, it is important that you stay current with the latest developments in technology, especially with regard to the Internet. The Internet is your future, whether you like it or not. It is here to stay, and all roads now lead to it no matter what area of IT you specialize in.

Key Point Summary

In summary, this chapter helped you identify and quantify your skills. You learned of the three major skill sets: functional, specific knowledge, and management skills. You then learned how to match those skills to specific categories of IT in order to find the best fit for a career in computers. You learned about self-assessment, which can help you begin the process of finding a suitable career in any field. This chapter also gave excellent examples of how to stay current in the IT field. Finally, you learned how to plan your career by assessing your current employment situation, identifying barriers to promotion, and then implementing the results of research into an action plan.

- **Self-assessment:** Start by identifying your most basic skills and attributes, such as personality, education, and training.

- **Skills assessment:** Identify the three types of skills that employers look for in a candidate (specific knowledge, as well as functional and management skills).

- **Career matching:** Once you have identified your skills base, you need to match those attributes and skills to a career in IT that will allow you to succeed.

- **Career planning:** Plan your career by carefully assessing where you want to be in five, ten, and fifteen years.

- **Staying current in your field:** Join user groups, attend seminars and conferences, and network, network, network!

The Ultimate IT Award –
The MCP Certificate

About Chapter 3

At first glance, the Microsoft Certified Professional (MCP) program can seem daunting, perhaps as complex as sitting for the bar exam or for certification as a public accountant. However, to most information technology (IT) professionals, especially programmers and network engineers, the certification process is just another career milestone, albeit a significant one. One of the most difficult problems with obtaining an MCP certification (or passing the exams) can be in finding adequate training materials and courses in Microsoft technology. This chapter describes in detail the many sources for MCP training that are available to computer professionals, such as Microsoft Authorized Training Centers (ATECs), computer-based training systems (CBTs), online distance learning facilities based on the Internet, and various other instructional materials. This chapter also discusses the actual certification requirements necessary to become an MCP. Finally, the first few pages of this chapter will cover Microsoft's MCP Web site on the Internet. The MCP Web site is fast becoming the central point for dissemination of information concerning the MCP program. In fact, Microsoft is drastically cutting back on most, but not all, printed matter for the MCP program in the interest of cutting costs. Therefore, the MCP Web site will inevitably become the most important source on the Web for the most up-to-date information on the MCP.

THE CERTIFICATION PROCESS

In Chapters 1 and 2, you learned some of the preliminary steps that must be taken prior to undertaking a specific career track in the MCP program. A broad outline of the certification process, from start to finish, is listed below. It includes important contact numbers and Web address information for you to begin the process of becoming an MCP, or simply pick up where you left off with your last MCP exam.

MICROSOFT CERTIFICATION PROCESS OUTLINE

1. Go to Microsoft's Training & Certification Web site at `http://www.microsoft.com/train_cert` for the most up-to-date information on the MCP program, or call 800-636-7544 to receive a copy of their Training & Certification Web site on CD-ROM.

 The Training & Certification Web CD requires an installed Internet browser as it is in HTML format. The CD is available at no charge for anyone interested in the MCP program.

2. Prepare for the exam(s) by referring to the numerous training courses and materials available on videotape, CD-ROM, disk, and the Internet, and so on, in the next section of this chapter.

3. Once you are prepared to take an exam, call Sylvan at 800-755-EXAM (U.S. and Canada) for the nearest Drake PROMETRIC Authorized Testing Center. Outside the U.S. and Canada, contact your local Microsoft subsidiary. The Sylvan PROMETRIC registration center will ask you for your name and Social Security number and when you would like to schedule an appointment to take an exam. Sylvan accepts Visa, MasterCard, American Express and personal check for payment. The Drake PROMETRIC Authorized Testing Centers are open Monday through Friday, and some Saturdays and Sundays.

 You have up to the day before the exam (up to 7 p.m.) to cancel your exam appointment. If you wait until the last day you will forfeit any fees paid for the exam and will have to reschedule for another time.

The cost is $100 for each exam. However, there are many incentive coupons offered through Microsoft and Microsoft Solution Providers (MSPs) for up to 50% off the normal price of an exam. So if you work for a MSP, be sure to check with the

person in charge of the Solution Provider Monthly mailing from Microsoft to see if there are any coupons for MCP exams included in the box.

4. Show up for the exam! Also, bring a photo ID, such as your current driver's license, and another form of signature ID such as a credit card or your Social Security card for identification purposes. The testing center provides all scratch paper, pencils, and computers for the examination. You are not allowed to take any calculators, papers, notes, pagers, or any other electronic devices into the exam booth at the time of examination. The time varies for each exam, but on average you have anywhere from an hour to a hour and a half to take the test. All examinations are conducted via computer and are somewhat similar to Microsoft's practice assessment exams (discussed in the next section) both in format and in types of questions posed to the test taker.

Your exam results are automatically printed out at the end of the test. Ask your examiner for the Score Report once you exit the exam booth. If you passed an exam for the first time, you will receive a welcome kit four to six weeks from the date of the examination. The kit includes a Certificate of Excellence award certifying you as Microsoft Certified Product Specialist (MCPS) in the MCP program, as well as a wallet card identifying you as an MCPS with your member ID imprinted. You also receive an MCP logo sheet and digital logo diskette for use on your business cards. In a separate mailing you will receive a free year's subscription to the *Microsoft Certified Professional* magazine in hard copy, and a free TechNet CD.

If you fail the exam, you are allowed to take the test over as many times as you like. A modest percentage of individuals fail the MCP exams for the first time due to a lack of preparation and command of the subject matter. Whatever the reason, you should take the time to get the experience in a particular subject, as many of the MCP exams test one's actual expertise based on hands-on training. As discussed later in this chapter, there are multitudes of resources for gaining the requisite experience in order to pass the MCP exams.

It is also important to keep in mind that once you decide on a particular MCP track, make sure you select the proper version of exams that you are most comfortable with, especially with regard to Windows NT. Currently, Microsoft offers two different tracks for certification in Windows NT — Windows 3.51 and 4.0. Although Windows NT 4.0 is a relatively new and revamped version of NT, many IT shops are still running NT 3.51, mainly because of its maturity and stability. However, Windows NT 4.0 with its new Windows 95-style graphical user interface (GUI) is getting rave reviews in the IT press, and its early adoption by the IT industry is causing many MCPs to take notice. So the call is yours when it comes to selecting the course of study that you want to pursue, but just keep in mind that older operating systems get dropped from the MCP curriculum eventually, which could force you to recertify later on, or sooner than expected.

MICROSOFT TRAINING AND CERTIFICATION WEB SITE

Since Microsoft instituted its certification program over four years ago, over 100,000 individuals have become MCPs. With the astounding growth in the number of MCPs in 1996 alone (some 65,000 people were added to the ranks), the MCP program reached a threshold of dominance in the IT industry. Leaders in the IT industry are quickly recognizing the significance of the program and MCP certificate holders as well. Thus, the need for certification is becoming readily apparent with hiring managers, recruiters, and personnel departments in the U.S. and abroad. Therefore, understanding the requirements of the program and preparing for the exams is extremely important if you expect to succeed in becoming an MCP.

The first step you can take in understanding the requirements is visiting Microsoft's Microsoft Training & Certification Web site on the Internet. The Web site, shown in Figure 3-1, offers ample information about the requirements for the various MCP tracks that lead to certification in Microsoft operating systems and applications. In 1998 the Training & Certification Web site will be drastically overhauled, providing links to hundreds if not thousands of new ATECs throughout the world, as well as improvement to the layout and design of the site.

FIGURE 3-1   The Microsoft Certification & Training Web site as shown above offers the latest information on the MCP program. The Web site also contains important links to other sites at Microsoft. You can visit the site at `http://www.microsoft.com/train_cert`.

(Screen shot reprinted with permission from Microsoft Corporation.)

The Web site could definitely benefit from some of Microsoft's own technology, such as wizards. A definite plus for the site would be for Microsoft to develop a wizard that queries the user on his existing skills, including exams he has already taken, and then plots an optimum path for obtaining a Microsoft Certified Systems Engineer (MCSE) or Microsoft Certified Solutions Developer (MCSD) certificate. It can be difficult determining the requirements for becoming an MCPS that specializes in the Internet or Microsoft Exchange based on the site's layout. The specialist requirements are buried in the pages of the Training & Certification site. Overall the Web site does a good job of answering frequently asked questions (FAQs) and provides information on every aspect of the MCP program. The Training & Certification Web site is in the process of being redesigned as of this writing. In fact, according to Microsoft representatives, the entire Training and Certification Web site is due to be replicated and published on CD, thereby replacing the older RoadMap CD they used before to explain the MCP program.

ASSESSMENT AND PRACTICE EXAMS

Assessment exams offer students an excellent way to determine deficiencies in their knowledge of a subject matter, and practice exams provide test takers with a competitive edge in *how* to take an exam. While neither type of test taking provides the answers to the actual examinations administered by Drake Testing Centers, they can help a student determine areas of weakness in a particular subject matter. Practice exams in particular can help a student understand prior to test taking the format, length of time, and types of questions that will be posed to him while under examination. This can significantly improve scores of students, especially for those test takers who are apprehensive about taking any sort of exam. This section on assessment and practice exams sets out to inform readers about the options available to them for test preparation for the MCP program.

Microsoft Assessment Exams

Microsoft's practice assessment exams are intended for use as a preparation tools. The assessment exams are limited to older versions of their products such as Windows NT 3.51 and Windows for Workgroups. Microsoft is no longer producing any new assessment exams. However, there are a number of third-party vendors that produce practice tests for exam preparation (see next section for details). The older practice assessment exams are currently available for download at no charge on the Microsoft Training & Certification Web site. You can also order the offline version of the Training & Certification Web site, which also contains the assessment exams, if you have no connection to the Internet, at 800-636-7544. Figure 3-2 shows the MCSE assessment exams' main menu.

Overall, the practice exams offer a good sampling of the actual exams downloaded to the Drake PROMETRIC Authorized Testing Centers when you take your test. It is a good idea to take the assessment exams only once, as they are intended to test your knowledge of the fundamentals of a particular subject matter. The score report generated after each test will indicate your proficiencies and deficiencies in a bar chart format on a scale of 1 to 1,000. A score of 80 percent is needed to pass. You should analyze your results of the exam carefully and take the appropriate action based on those results. Also, When taking the practice test, understand *why* a certain question was asked; the same question may be asked a different way on the real test. Understand the concepts that the question is asking, not the question itself. Look at the correct answer, but also understand why certain incorrect questions were asked.

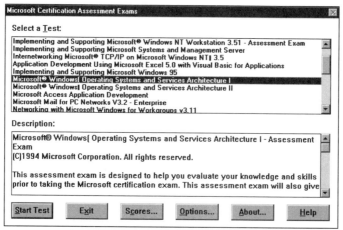

FIGURE 3-2   The Microsoft certification assessment exams' main menu. The assessment exams are an accurate sample of the exams given at Drake PROMETRIC Authorized Testing Centers.

Self Test

Self Test offers prep exams in some of the latest Microsoft operating systems and applications. It currently offers free demo exams directly from the Microsoft Training & Certification Web site (see previous section). Although the demo exams are free and are only a sampling of the full-blown prep exams, the price charged per test is moderate.

A sampling of some of Self Test's prep exams include:

- Windows 95
- NT Workstation 3.51 or 4.0
- NT Server 3.51 or 4.0
- TCP/IP
- Networking Essentials

- Exchange

- SQL Administration and SQL Server

Figure 3-3 shows Self Test's Web site. For more information on Self Test's full line of prep exams call 800-200-6446.

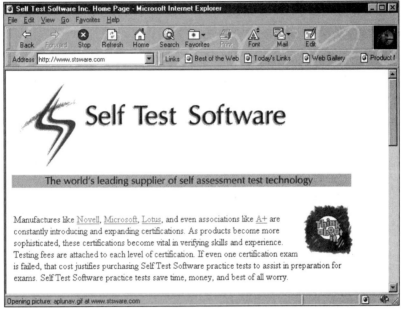

FIGURE 3-3 Although Self Test's Web site is simple in design, its exams are not! It is busy building some of the latest prep exams for the Microsoft certification series of exams. You can see for yourself at `http://www.stsware.com`.

Transcender's Certification Solution Exams

Transcender Corporation is a leading provider of quality prep exams for both network engineers and developers. It offers a full array of tests that simulate the real thing when it comes to BackOffice certification and developer mock exams. Its software packages provide predictive simulations of the essential Microsoft exams. Figure 3-4 shows Transcender's home page.

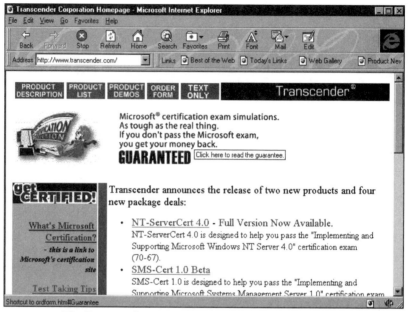

FIGURE 3-4   The Transcender Corporation's home page. Transcender's certification demo exams are available for download from its Web site, located at `http://www.transcender.com`.

- Each product contains several timed exam simulations similar in difficulty and nature to the certification exams.

- The products provide analysis of exam results and identify the areas in which additional study is needed.

- The programs also provide explanations of the correct answers and valuable references to selected Microsoft study aids and documentation.

- Their products include study outlines to aid in your preparation.

Transcender was one of the first software vendors to offer an alternative to Microsoft's practice certification exams. It is experienced in the development of quality precertification exams. Transcender Corporation can be reached at 615-726-8779 for more information on its products.

Microhard's Quest Series of Exams

Microhard's MCSE Quest exam is considered one of the toughest certification tests in the industry. Its newly revised MCSE Quest exam, previously known as Q:CSE, contains hundreds of questions covering the following exams:

- NT Server 3.51

- NT Workstation 3.51

- Windows 95

- Networking essentials

- Implementing a database design on system administration for MS SQL Server

- TCP/IP using MS Windows NT

- Windows 3.1

Figure 3-5 shows Microhard's MCSE Quest practice exam. For more information on Microhard Technologies exams, call 800-266-7648.

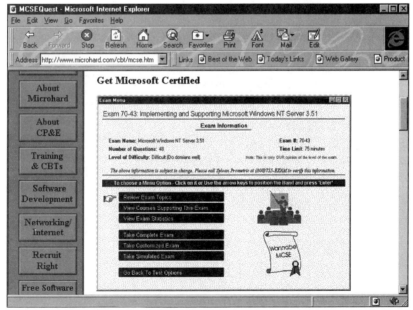

FIGURE 3-5 Microhard's Technologies MCSE Quest practice exam as depicted above is for the MCSE career track. A demo of the exam is available for download at http://www.microhard.com.

MICROSOFT TV SEMINAR SERIES

Microsoft TV (MSTV), shown in Figure 3-6, offers viewers a multitude of taped and live shows such as seminars, case studies, and presentations from speakers as high up in the company as Bill Gates. The shows air on cable and satellite broadcast. On cable the shows can be found on the Jones Computer Network and the Mind Extension University. Ask your local cable operator if your cable company offers either of the two networks. If it doesn't, tell them it should!

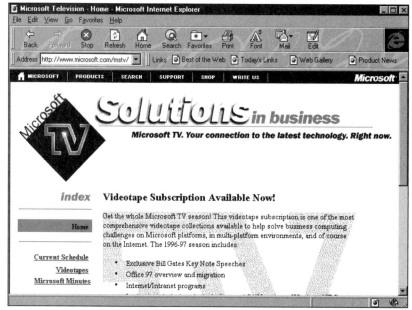

FIGURE 3-6 Microsoft TV's Web page has the latest show times for its videotaped seminar series available on Cable Television. The Web page also offers the full line-up of taped seminars for sale at http://www.microsoft.com/mstv.
(Screen shot reprinted with permission from Microsoft Corporation.)

A sampling of past broadcasts includes:

- Deploying Windows NT Workstation 4.0
- Inside Microsoft Office
- America at work: customer, inventory and employee tracking

- America at work: information sharing made easy
- Publishing information on the Internet

MSTV also offers most of its broadcasts for sale as videos. To order videos, call 800-369-5718; outside the U.S., 805-295-0504.

MICROSOFT PRESS BOOKS, TAPES, AND CDS

The Microsoft Press Web site, shown in Figure 3-7, offers an impressive array of books that rival some of the largest computer book publishers on the planet. The site contains an online bookstore that you can browse freely and even download some freebie software and sample code. It also publishes a full-color catalog once a quarter.

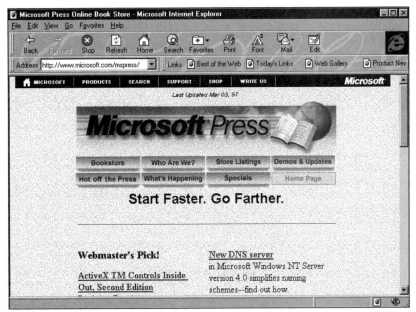

FIGURE 3-7 Microsoft Press's Web site offers a multitude of titles for the beginner through advanced Microsoft professional. Their bookstore also offers sample code and demos for immediate download at http://www.microsoft.com/mspress.

(Screen shot reprinted with permission from Microsoft Corporation.)

A sampling of Microsoft Press's books include:

o *Microsoft Mastering Series CDs for Developers*

o *Windows 95 & Windows NT Resource Kits*

o *Self-Paced Training Kits for Windows NT, IIS & SQL Server*

o *Learn Java Now — Visual J++ instructional book*

o *Communications Programming in Windows 95*

o *Client/Server Programming w/Visual Basic*

For more information call Microsoft Press at 800-MSPRESS.

MICROSOFT ONLINE INSTITUTE

The Microsoft Online Institute (MOLI) offers what is termed as distance learning. Students can register and attend courses over the Internet on their own time and at their own convenience. For some folks this is the future of education; for others it's seen as just a fad. Microsoft has poured an enormous amount of time, money, and talent into making this the number one place to get a Microsoft education online. Actually, the MOLI began on The Microsoft Network some years back but was moved to the Internet because Microsoft views the Internet as the future of remote computing and learning, among other things. Figure 3-8 shows the MOLI Web site.

 Microsoft is currently in the process of phasing out MOLI and will fold all of MOLI's instructional classes into the Microsoft Training and Certification site beginning in 1998. Microsoft is restructuring its distance learning facilities to become a more distributed educational center on the World Wide Web, authorizing ATECs from around the world to conduct training classes virtually through their Training and Certification Web sites.

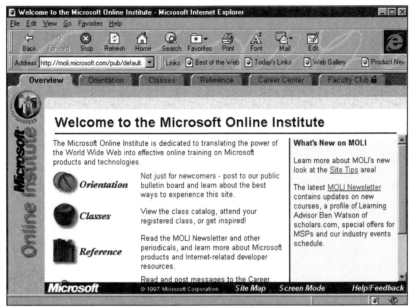

FIGURE 3-8 The Microsoft Online Institute's Web site is a full-blown educational center in its own right. Also known as "MOLI," the institute offers full distance-learning services especially suited for MCPs and people studying for certification. The site can be found at: http://www.moli.microsoft.com/pub/default.htm.
(Screen shot reprinted with permission from Microsoft Corporation.)

MOLI offers more than just an education. There is a career center, reference library, and an orientation center for students. Some of MOLI's course offerings are:

- Fundamentals of Visual Basic 4.0
- Implementing a Database Design using Microsoft SQL Server
- Interactive Web Development with VBScript and ActiveX
- Internet Application Development
- Intro to Programming using Microsoft Access VBA
- Supporting Windows NT 3.51

All MOLI courses are taught by third-party Microsoft ATECs (see next section for details). Classes combine self-paced learning materials with live instructor guidance to allow you to both work at your own pace and learn in a class environment.

SELF-STUDY KITS

Self-study kits offer users or students a self-paced method of learning that is better suited for those individuals who do not have the time or budget to attend certification training in a classroom. The training vendors listed offer a multitude of training products that range from computer-based training (CBT) in CD-ROM format to videotaped classes on just about every subject you could possibly need to become an MCP. Many of them also offer study guides that either complement the other training tools that they are bundled with or are intended as course-specific training in such topics as Windows NT or Windows 95 certification training. Some of the study guides are also Microsoft Approved Study Guides, which Microsoft has given as its stamp of approval for meeting certification training requirements for the MCP Program. Prices for study kits and guides range from about $50 all the way up to $2,000 depending on the vendor. Overall, the kits and guides offer an affordable alternative to classroom instruction and do so admirably.

IDG Books Worldwide

IDG Books Worldwide is publishing the MCSE Study Series, certified and approved by Microsoft. The books are written by expert authors with MCT, MCSE and MCSD credentials. The books include companion CDs with test assessment software, a full HTML version of the book, and the *Microsoft Road Map to Certification.*

In addition to the book that you're reading, titles include:

- *MCSE TCP/IP*
- *MCSE IIS and Proxy Server*
- *MCSE MCIP*
- *MCSE Windows 95 and Networking Essentials*
- *Windows Architecture I & II*
- *Windows NT*

Figure 3-9 shows IDG Books Worldwide's Web site. For more information on IDG Books Worldwide call 415-655-3000.

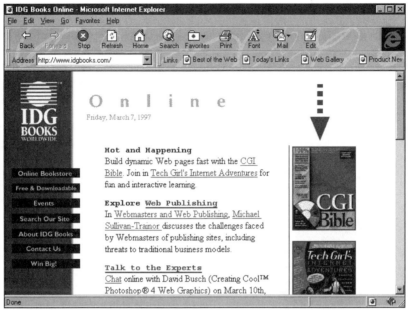

FIGURE 3-9 IDG Books Worldwide is renowned for its superb line of books on information technologies. Its new book series on MCSE certification has gained considerable attention in the IT press. IDG Books Worldwide's Web site is easily accessible at `http://www.idgbooks.com`.

Learnkey

For those individuals who prefer to study at their own pace as opposed to classroom instruction, Learnkey has the training materials you are looking for. Its outstanding line-up of CDs, videos and study guides are the some of the best in the market. Its training materials can also be used as learning aids for classroom training as well.

A quick overview of training products is outlined below:

- Comprehensive CBT training CDs and videos
- Microsoft-approved study guides
- Full line-up of Microsoft certification courses
- Windows 95 Certification Series
- Access Developer Series
- Visual Basic Series

- Windows NT 4.0 Certification Series
- TCP/IP Certification Series
- Intranet—Building an Intranet
- And many more series (call Learnkey for a catalog)

Figure 3-10 shows Learnkey's Web site. For more information on Learnkey's training products, call 800-865-0165.

FIGURE 3-10   The Learnkey Web site is an excellent resource for state-of-the-art learning materials for any MCP. Its wide assortment of books, videos, and CDs is currently unmatched in the IT industry. The Learnkey Web site is located at `http://www.learnkey.com`.

CBT Systems

CBT's computer-based training CDs are intelligently designed and offer users a very elegant approach to computer-based training. During a training session on the computer, users are taught in increments and are then queried for appropriate responses before reaching the end of the training session. So if they do not comprehend the subject matter they can step back and go over the topic again. This way the session creates a more interactive approach to learning, and retention of the subject matter is much higher with each user. CBT's training CDs are the most elegantly designed training programs in the market, offering users a near 3-D viewing session. This is particularly helpful when describing physical environments such as network and workstation processes. You have to see them to believe them — and make sure you use a high-quality monitor. Figure 3-11 shows the CBT Systems Web site.

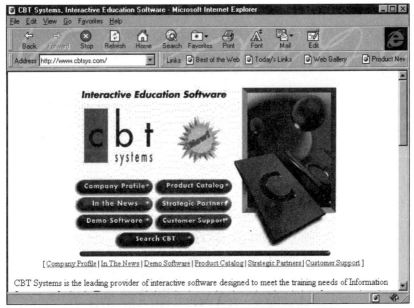

FIGURE 3-11   The CBT Systems Web site reflects the elegant design of its CD-based training products. CBT offers a wide assortment of training courses for the MCP program. The Web site address is http://www.cbtsys.com/cbt/index.html.

For more information on CBT's products and services, call 415-614-5900.

Keystone Learning Systems

Keystone Learning System's specialty in the self-study market is training videos. Keystone offers a full line-up of training tapes for the MCP program. Many of Keystone's instructors are highly trained in the various Microsoft technologies such as Exchange, Windows NT, and Office. Keystone offers over 400 videos in all and is priced well below its competitors. Overall Keystone offers a good product at affordable prices. It also has training workbooks that complement its full line of training videos.

A partial list of Keystone's course offerings are listed below:

o Windows 95 video training set

o Access 95 and 97 video training sets

o Visual FoxPro video training sets

o Visual Basic Power Packs

o Visual C++ 4.x video training set

o Windows NT 4.0 video training set

o Exchange Server video training set

o SMS video training set

o TCP/IP video training set

Figure 3-12 shows Keystone's Web site. For more information on Keystone Learning Systems training products call 800-748-4838.

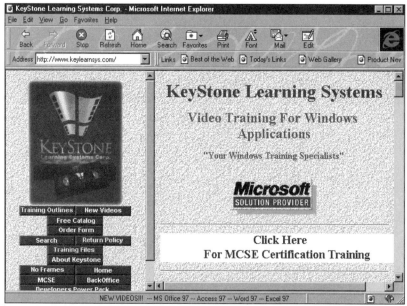

FIGURE 3-12   The Keystone Learning Systems Corp. Web site is easy to navigate. It also allows you to order Keystone's full line of training videos for the Microsoft professional directly online. The Keystone Learning Systems Web site is accessible at http://www.keylearnsys.com.

Wave Technologies

Wave Technologies offers Microsoft-approved study guides for MCP programs. It offers a Microsoft Certified Systems Engineer self-study program that includes an impressive array of study guides for the following exams:

- Windows 95 — Prep guide for core exam #70-63
- Networking Essentials — Prep guide for core exam #70-58
- Windows NT 4.0 Workstation — Prep guide for core exam #70-73
- Windows NT 4.0 Server — Prep guide for core exam #70-67
- Windows NT 4.0 Server and Enterprise Implementation — Prep guide for core exam #70-68
- Microsoft TCP/IP — Prep guide for core exam #70-53
- SQL Server 6.x Administration — Prep guide for elective exam #70-26

Wave offers other specialized elective kits for the MSCE track. It also has a self-study program for the Microsoft Solution Developer track.

Figure 3-13 shows the Wave Technologies International Web site. For more information on Wave Technologies products and services, call 800-828-2050.

AUTHORIZED TECHNICAL EDUCATION CENTER

Authorized Technical Education Centers are commercial technical training organizations that are MSPs (also known as value-added resellers or VARS) and are authorized by Microsoft to deliver courses to computer professionals on the full range of Microsoft products, including the Windows and the Windows NT operating systems, the Microsoft BackOffice family server software, and Internet and platform development products such as Visual Basic and Visual C++. Microsoft ATECs use Microsoft Official Curriculum (MOC) courseware delivered by Microsoft Certified Trainers (MCTs) at Microsoft-approved training facilities.

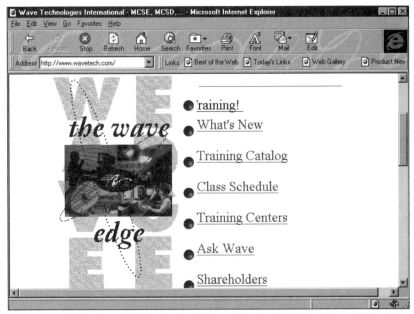

FIGURE 3-13   The Wave Technologies International Web site offers both self-study kits training materials as well as classroom training for the Microsoft professional. The Wave Technologies Web site is located at `http://www.wavetech.com`.

Currently there are thousands of ATECs located around the world. The majority of ATECs are small and serve mostly local or regional markets across the U.S.; they number between 1,400 to 1,500. The larger ATECs typically are international and offer a broad array of Microsoft courses. All ATECs offer what is termed as MOC which can be instructor-led training (ILT) and/or self-paced training (SPT). Courses at an ATEC are typically held during normal business hours since they are privately owned and operated. The cost of an average course depends on the number of days the course is taught. The price for a typical five-day course at an ATEC is approximately $1,895, but the price may vary depending on the ATEC, so shop around. A small sampling of some of the course offerings available at ATECs are listed below:

- Windows NT 4.0 Server and Workstation
- Windows 95
- Excel
- Microsoft SQL Server

- Internet Information Server
- Visual Basic

Authorized Technical Education Centers are an excellent source for quality hands-on training in Microsoft technologies. An IT professional considering a career as an MCP should consult with a local ATEC for advice and guidance on the best approach to becoming an MCP.

Global Knowledge Network

Global Knowledge Network (GKN) is the largest Microsoft ATEC in the world, according to GKN. Its estimate is based on the number of students trained and certified training locations that the company operates internationally. GKN offers a multitude of training programs both for students and its larger clients. A partial list of GKN programs is outlined below:

- Lecture/lab programs—single- and multiple-day programs taught by certified, professional instructors at 23 fixed U.S. and 45 international certified locations
- Self-paced and multimedia programs—over 220 programs are available in interactive CD-ROM, videotape, audio tape programs
- On-line programs—the company offers a range of online/on-demand programs

Figure 3-14 shows GKN Web site. For more information on GKN products and services call 617-788-8600.

AUTHORIZED ACADEMIC TRAINING PARTNER

Authorized Academic Training Partners (AATPs) are not-for-profit schools or institutions that offer MOC in a traditional academic environment. The number of AATPs that exist today is in the hundreds. Eventually the number of AATPs is expected to grow, as Microsoft has recently revamped the program by changing the requirements for qualifying as an AATP.

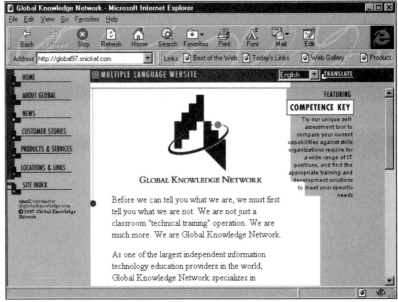

FIGURE 3-14   The GKN Web site offers course listings for instructor-led classes as well as for self-paced CBT held in-house. The GKN Web site can be accessed at
`http://www.globalknowledge.com.`

Howard Community College

Howard Community College (HCC) is small state-funded community college based in Columbia, Maryland. It is currently the only academic institution in the state of Maryland that is an AATP. Howard Community College's IT department is very innovative in its approach to providing quality hands-on training for students interested in obtaining skills in the latest technologies, such as Microsoft, Novell, and Cisco. Howard Community College can be reached at 410-992-4800. Figure 3-15 shows the HCC Web site.

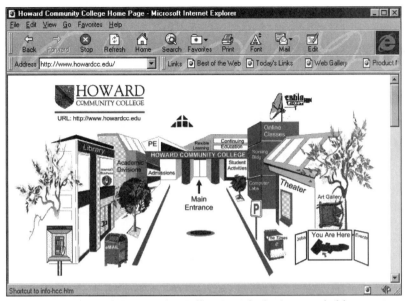

FIGURE 3-15 Howard Community College's Web site is remarkably easy to navigate given its metaphorically designed home page. The Microsoft AATP is located in Columbia, Maryland, which is a planned community designed by James Rouse. The Web site is located at `http://www.howardcc.edu`.

INTERVIEW: MICHAEL MCDONALD, HOWARD COMMUNITY COLLEGE AUTHORIZED ACADEMIC TRAINING PARTNER PROGRAM ADMINISTRATOR

Michael McDonald is the Industry Certification Program Administrator at Howard Community College. He was instrumental in the development of HCC's Novell and Microsoft Certification Programs. He can be reached via e-mail at mmcdonal@ccm.howardcc.edu.

Q: Why did Howard Community College decide to enter the Microsoft AATP program?

A: Howard Community College had been a Novell Education Academic Partner since spring 1993 and had enjoyed great success with its students getting jobs in this field. When Microsoft started the AATP we took a look at it and decided that that was what our students needed to stay current in this field.

Q: As a Microsoft-approved AATP, what advantages does your institution have to offer to MCPs over a privately owned and operated ATEC?

A: The difference between us and an ATEC is that we take the same curriculum, taught by the same instructors, and using the same student materials, and we deliver it in a traditional education format instead of the corporate seminar format of the ATEC. This allows the student time to absorb that material over two to three months instead of one week. We can therefore take a lower level of experienced students and spend more time bringing them up to speed in the field.

continued

continued

Q: Does the student get the essential hands-on training through lab exercises that he or she would receive at an ATEC?

A: Yes. We add at least one extra day's worth of time to each of these classes, and the student is always in front of his own Pentium machine. We have added lab time, and even other labs where the students can work till as late as 11:00 p.m. on their own.

Q: How successful is your AATP program at the college?

A: Depends on how you gauge success. We have technical headaches we normally wouldn't have with a homegrown effort, but our students are very happy with the instruction and curriculum, and are out there getting real jobs. That is the best measure—the students' success in the real world, and in that sense I would say we are getting more and more successful all the time.

Q: Does your college offer other IT certification programs?

A: Yes, we are a Novell Education Academic Partner (NEAP) and support CNA and CNE in NetWare 3 and 4, we have an A+ certification program, and a Smalltalk certification program that we developed with Dr. Adele Goldberg and ParcPlace. We are also in negotiations to bring authorized Cisco training in, and we are looking at Lotus.

Q: Do you encourage students to get Novell certified as well? If so, why?

A: Yes we do, for several reasons, depending on the students' skill levels and where they are working. If a student is currently working in a Microsoft NT environment, we recommend that he stay with Microsoft to start. If the student is not in a networking job and has little or no networking experience, we generally recommend some Novell training at least in conjunction with Microsoft training. The reason is that Microsoft training focuses primarily on the operating system and what one can achieve from the console, whereas Novell does that but has a lecture series on the field of networking, and a hands-on technical course where the students build networks all day. (Basically, the MCSE curriculum assumes that a CNE has been there and built your network first.) Plus, Microsoft will acknowledge the CNE as meeting the Networking Essentials exam component, but Novell does not reciprocate. Also, until Microsoft comes out with Active Directory, the large networks around this area will be primarily using Novell NDS with Microsoft subnets. Having both is therefore essential.

 note   An important factor in determining whether you should attend either an ATEC or AATP is the level of experience and education that you currently have in IT. If you are in the process of changing careers and you are contemplating entering systems engineering or software development, you would be wise to attend classes at your nearest AATP. AATPs offer extended courses in IT along with ample lab time, which is absolutely necessary in order to become a successful MCSE or MCSD. ATECs are an excellent source of training for seasoned technology professionals who need to quickly come up to par on the latest technologies from Microsoft.

Study Groups

In addition to all of the various training centers, self-study kits, practice exams, and distance learning facilities come study groups. Study groups are really nothing new, but they seem to be catching on in the IT community, especially with various Windows NT user groups located around the country. The Windows NT user groups encourage individuals to form small groups to help strengthen their chances of passing the rigorous certification exams developed by Microsoft.

 concept link **For more information on study groups, see Chapter 12.**

KEY POINT SUMMARY

This chapter explained the initial steps necessary to begin the process of becoming an MCP. The chapter also covered the multitude of technical resources available to MCP candidates that can assist them in their endeavor to be certified professionals. Beginning with Microsoft's own Training & Certification Web site, the chapter disclosed information on Microsoft's own assessment exams, in addition to the many third-party exam preparation tools for test taking available to prospective MCPs. Finally, the chapter covered ATECs, as well as the newer AATPs currently emerging on college and university campuses throughout the U.S. and abroad.

- Use Microsoft's Training & Certification site to stay abreast of the latest developments and requirements for the MCP program.
- Take full advantage of the third-party practice exams, study kits, and training videos and CDs for preparation in taking the actual certification exams at Drake.
- Attend classes at ATECs and AATPs depending your academic needs, including joining study groups.

Microsoft Certified Professional
Career Tracks

Becoming a Microsoft Certified Professional (MCP) is not easy. The average completion time for certification is six months to a year. Taking the courses necessary to pass the exams is only the beginning. With a failure rate of near 60 percent for the certification exams, chances are you will be heading back to your computer lab and books after course training. Unlike Novell NetWare certification exams, which require book knowledge of a subject matter to pass, Microsoft's certification tests require hands-on experience. However, if you're committed to becoming the consummate information technology (IT) professional and are willing to train hard, the rewards for becoming an MCP are many.

Microsoft Certified Professionals are becoming a recognizable force in the IT community. Many organizations now insist on certification as a qualification for employment. Hiring managers are aware of the level of mastery required for becoming an MCP. The MCP certification is also in big demand, which means higher salaries for all certified professionals.

Other benefits are more intangible. For instance, one benefit is an autonomous working environment whereby you are trusted to make critical decisions regarding the company's or client's information system. Another intangible benefit is the personal creativity allowed on the job solving complex information systems problems. Finally, the sense of self-worth and accomplishment one obtains by becoming an MCP is one of the greatest benefits derived by many IT professionals the world over.

Developing Your Career as an MCP

About Chapter 4

The first three chapters of this book focused on what it takes to become a successful Microsoft Certified Professional (MCP); in this chapter you'll explore the multitude of sources on the Web that can help you *build* a successful career as a certified professional in Microsoft technology. While the World Wide Web may be considered by some to be in its infancy, there are many formidable sources for enhancing your career as a certified professional on it. Some of the most promising Web services for training on the Net are called distance learning facilities (DLFs). They provide anyone who has a multimedia PC, a modem and an Internet connection with the ability to participate in seminars or training classes located anywhere in the world. Some of the largest DLFs or Authorized Training Education Centers (ATECs) will provide MCPs with a host of continuing education services.

Other sources of information on the Web for MCPs can be found in online trade publications, specialist forums, and sites that focus on career building and employment. Finally, there are various other products and services that an MCP can use to enhance his or her career. Interactive computer-based training (CBT) is growing in popularity and is an effective means of training and continuing one's education. Other sources include television or cable TV, as well as Internet news groups and list servers.

ONLINE RESUME AND JOB BANKS

While job and resume banks may not seem relevant to career development on the Internet, many of them provide valuable links and information to resources that do make for career building. Nearly every employment-related site on the Web offers some sort of career center to help individuals find jobs and grow their careers. Most Web sites found on the Net are non-specialized and offer all types of jobs from advertising to sales. Other sites are completely specialized and take a career approach to the job search process. Nevertheless, most of the online job centers on the Internet offer job seekers a fast and efficient means of finding gainful employment and none should be overlooked. Listed here are just a few of the Web sites mentioned previously that offer job opportunities and career-building or career-planning services.

tip

Some of the hottest and most innovative job banks on the Web for MCPs are "specialist" sites that concentrate on specific fields in information technology (IT). Instead of having to wade through a morass of jobs from auto mechanics to zoologists typical on some of the larger employment Web sites, job seekers can find what they are looking for in a matter of seconds. One of the first specialist employment sites on the Web was IT Specialist.com, which boasts an online job bank specifically for MCPs.

IT Specialist

IT Specialist is a Web site that specializes in recruiting and job placement for MCPs. The Web site is international in scope with job and resume listings from the world over. The resume bank on IT Specialist offers MCPs a free resume listing in an abbreviated format (no contact information is divulged about the candidate). Organizations scanning the database of resumes for possible job candidates can request information by clicking on a candidate's MCP code (not MCP ID!) for more information. Likewise, organizations that list jobs in the IT Specialist job bank, as shown in Figure 4-1, offer MCPs a convenient method for job hunting. Candidates can simply review jobs and click on the appropriate hyperlink to gain access to more information about a particular job opening. IT Specialist also offers a virtual career center for MCPs. There are hyperlinks to news organizations, trade magazines, and user groups located throughout the U.S. and abroad.

FIGURE 4-1   **IT Specialist sports a virtual career center for MCPs as well as job and resume banks for both organizations and MCPs, respectively. The IT Specialist Web site is located at** `http://www.itspecialist.com.`

For more information on IT Specialist's recruiting services, call 301-913-0233.

Monster Board

Monster Board is one the Net's first major online resume and job banks offered to the general public. The site boasts a career center, job/resume bank, and a virtual open house for individuals interested in finding out the details of a prospective employer. Many companies now operate a virtual recruiting center through the Monster Board, shown in Figure 4-2, offering a plethora of jobs from academia to zoology. Employers are organized into communities to facilitate local job searches. The Monster Board has also gone international and has job listings from Australia to the United Kingdom. Job seekers can use Monster Board's resident monster agent to search for jobs in the Monster database, or they can find the latest information on career fairs located throughout the U.S. and abroad.

FIGURE 4-2 Monster Board is by far one of the largest resume and job banks found on the Internet today. Monster Board is located at `http://www.monsterboard.com`.

The Riley Guide

The Riley Guide, while not an online job or resume bank itself, provides valuable links to job resources on the Net. It also provides extensive help on the job-search process itself. The Riley Guide, shown in Figure 4-3, was founded by Margaret Riley back in 1995 and is one of the first major resources for job information on the Internet. Her Web site has won several awards based on its content and free services. For anyone who is initiating a job search on the Internet for the first time, The Riley Guide is a necessary first stop.

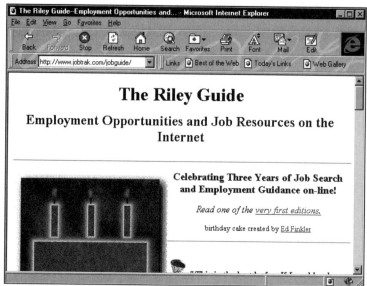

FIGURE 4-3   The Riley Guide is a Web site that focuses exclusively on job resources on the Internet. The Riley Guide is located at `http://www.jobtrak.com/jobguide`.

PROFESSIONAL DEVELOPMENT WEB SITES

The classrooms of tomorrow may very well be your living room or den. Distance learning facilities are popping up all over the Internet, and Microsoft and others are taking the lead. They hope to be the future facilitators of education on the Internet by providing the systems and infrastructure necessary to host classrooms on the Web. Some of these companies also want to be teachers too. Whatever happens, they most likely will succeed because of the incredible popularity of the Internet.

The Internet offers an unbelievable amount of flexibility and convenience to most users. Where else can you surf the world from an armchair? So why not sit back in the comfort of your own home and take a class whenever you want, instead of trudging across a mile-long parking lot in the freezing rain to attend a one-hour class in programming. You get the picture. It's only a matter of time before a large percentage of the population takes to the Internet for classroom instruction, especially with videoconferencing just around the corner. So see for yourself in the following paragraphs what awaits you in the online classroom of today.

Microsoft Online Institute

The Microsoft Online Institute (MOLI) began back in 1995 on the Microsoft Network but has since moved to the Internet. The site boasts virtual classrooms that are hosted mostly by ATECs. The site has the metaphorical design of a group of files that enclose a Career Center, Classes, Orientation, Reference and Faculty Club. The Faculty Club is open only to faculty members and may be of some use to Microsoft Certified Trainers who happen to work for one of the ATECs that sponsor courses at MOLI. The rest of the site is open to all individuals interested in classes and information on Microsoft technology.

There are currently 16 MOLI Training Partners (MTPs) throughout the U.S. and Europe that offer classes on MOLI. The MTPs were hand-selected by Microsoft from the former MOLI on the old MSN campus. They are companies that have proven that online training is a viable market and training solution. MOLI, shown in Figure 4-4, is in the process of decentralizing (moving from MSN hosting) its services to allow MCPs the ability to host classes directly from their own Web servers. This will allow for greater participation in the MOLI Web site and therefore lead to better competition and ultimately lower prices for classroom instruction for all.

Beginning in 1998 Microsoft will completely revamp MOLI as it is now known. Nearly all of the existing ATECs will be offering courses through the Microsoft Training & Certification Web site. Instead of a small group of select ATECs, MCPs will be able to select from a wide variety of training organizations (both public and private). The main benefit to current subscribers will be the incredible choice of classes available, including meeting times and, of course, pricing. However, with the multitude of new training sources that will be available through the Microsoft site, it is important to research the training vendor before proceeding with registration for courses.

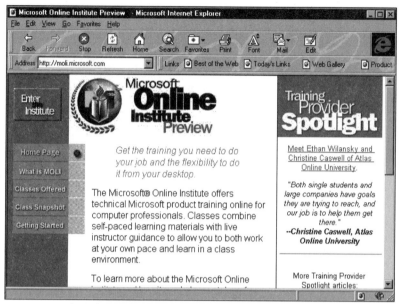

FIGURE 4-4   The Microsoft Online Institute is a virtual training center for ATECs the world over. The MOLI Web site can be found at `http://www.moli.microsoft.com`.

ZD Net University

ZD Net University (ZDU) offers online computing classes and seminars taught on private, moderated message boards for a very modest fee. The online university, shown in Figure 4-5, also has an alumni lounge where students can hang out after class to discuss subjects taught at the school. Students can actually earn credit for courses taken at ZDU by registering with the National Registry of Training Programs and by taking and passing ZDU's classes on computer technology. Credits earned by the students can then be applied toward a certificate issued by the American Council on Education.

ZD Net University also houses a campus book store and library as well.

A sampling of some of the courses taught at ZDU includes:

- C++ for Beginners
- Introduction to Java Applets
- Beginning Delphi
- Java for Managers

- Lotus Notes 4.0 for Executives
- Build Your Own Duke Nukem 3-D Level
- Build Your Web Page with Hot Dog Pro
- How to Code with HTML

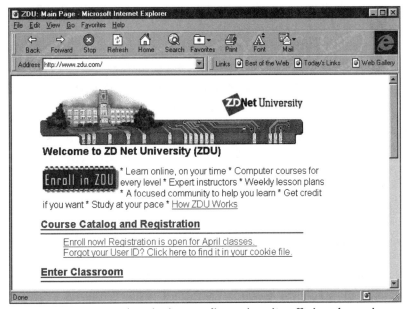

FIGURE 4-5   ZD Net University is an online university offering classes in continuing education in IT. ZD Net University is located at `http://www.zdu.com`.

ONLINE TRADE MAGAZINES

Nearly all of the hard copy trade magazines based on Microsoft technology such as *Windows NT* and *Microsoft Certified Professional* are now published on the Web. The reason for this trend is easy to understand: The World Wide Web has basically reinvented the printing press and turned traditional publishing on its head. For the avid reader of trade magazines this has been a boon. Not only does the subscriber get a hard copy of his favorite magazine, but he also gets a companion Web site to go along with the publication, which is usually more up to date.

Most of the Web sites covered in this section offer a plethora of information on Microsoft technology. From online forums to job banks, they all have valuable and very timely information for the Microsoft professional. Some of the sites go beyond just reporting the latest breakthroughs and advancements in third-party applications designed for Microsoft systems. They sponsor technical conferences and seminars throughout the U.S. All in all, the Web versions of trade journals are here to stay. It may not be too long before we see the end to some of these publications in hard copy form. With the increased cost of printing and postage and the relatively inexpensive price tag for designing and publishing a Web site, it's no wonder so many of the publishers of magazines and other periodicals are eyeing the Net for major cost savings for their operations. Further, advertisers are beginning to spend more money on Web advertising.

 tip **The best trade magazines or journals are the ones that maintain a companion Web site and target a niche within the IT industry. Some of the first and most authoritative online magazines are *Microsoft Certified Professional*, *Windows NT*, and *BackOffice*.**

Windows NT

Windows NT was one of the first magazines written exclusively for Microsoft professionals. The magazine's focus is on administrators and managers of large to small organizations that use Windows NT. The Web version of the magazine, shown in Figure 4-6, is basically an electronic version of the periodical but with late-breaking news in the Windows NT industry. *Windows NT* also produces a series of Windows NT technical conferences held around the U.S. for IT professionals who specialize in NT.

For more information on the Windows NT Professionals Conference, e-mail Dennis Martin at dennism@winntmag.com.

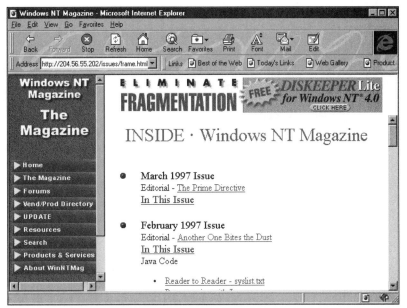

FIGURE 4-6   *Windows NT* offers MCPs an electronic version of the hard copy
that is published monthly. The Web site is located at
`http://www.winntmag.com`.

Microsoft Certified Professional

The *Microsoft Certified Professional* Web site, shown in Figure 4-7, offers the best
of both worlds when it comes to MCPs. The site contains the hard copy version of
the magazine as well the latest editorials and articles on certification exams and
the MCP program itself. This magazine also contains a special search tool for finding MCP training centers closest to you, as well as a forum and book store. The
site is one of the most comprehensive trade magazine Web sites on the Net. The
magazine hard copy is a bimonthly publication with pertinent articles covering
every conceivable aspect of the MCP program. The hard copy version of the magazine is free for one year to all new entrants to the MCP program, as well as to qualified subscribers.

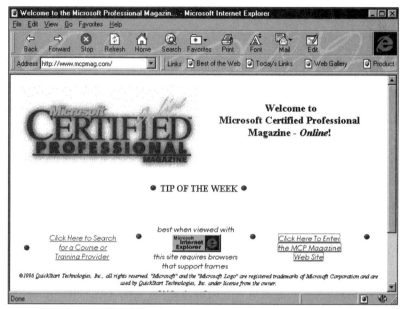

FIGURE 4-7 *Microsoft Certified Professional* is specifically targeted to MCPs. The MCP Web site is located at `http://www.mcpmag.com`.

For more information on *Microsoft Certified Professional* please e-mail the publication at `mail@mcpmag.com`.

BackOffice

BackOffice is written and published for the systems and IT professional. The magazine covers topics from Exchange Server to SQL Server. Many of the articles focus on systems programming and systems management. The articles are very technical in nature and require at least an intermediate level of comprehension in Microsoft systems technology. Its companion Web site, shown in Figure 4-8, is basically a rehash of the hard copy but with added features and a special download area. The Web site is also for the serious-minded Microsoft systems professional. No room for fluff on the *BackOffice* Web site, as systems implementation and management is no place for wimps! ☺

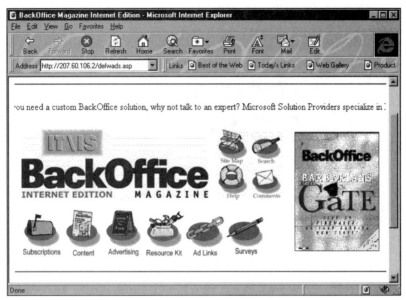

FIGURE 4-8 *BackOffice* **is dedicated to Microsoft systems professionals. The** *BackOffice* **Web site is located at** `http://www.backoffice.com.`

For more information on *BackOffice*, e-mail the publication at `info@` `backoffice.com.`

NT Specialist

NT Specialist, shown in Figure 4-9, is an electronic publication devoted to the professional development of Windows NT specialists. The magazine is published monthly on the World Wide Web at no charge to readers. The magazine (Web site) offers articles on career planning and development, as well as editorials and stories from MCPs actively working in the field of Microsoft technology. The magazine also covers training systems vendors and ATECs involved with the professional development of MCPs, both online and in the classroom. Finally, the site offers a forum for MCPs, which focuses strictly on career development of Windows NT professionals such as trainers, solution developers, and systems engineers.

FIGURE 4-9   *IT Specialist* **is devoted to Windows IT professionals. The Web site is located at** http://www.itspecialistmag.com.

For more information on becoming a contributing author for *IT Specialist*, please e-mail the publication at authors@itspecialistmag.com.

SPECIALIST WEB SITES

The previous section discussed generalist or trade Web sites that cover the entire spectrum of the MCP program. In this section, specialist sites on the Web that focus on specific MCP tracks such as systems engineering and database development are featured. In a sense, these and other specialist Web sites are like special interest groups (SIGs), in that they offer systems development specialists and programmers tools and forums to help them do their jobs better. While there are no specific specialist Web sites for trainers on the Net, there are dozens of sites devoted to network engineers, programmers, and software specialists. Just a few of the many specialist Web sites on the Internet are discussed here.

Microsoft Site Builder Network

This Site Builder Network run by Microsoft wins hands down for Internet Web design alone. As the name suggests, the site is devoted to Webmasters who develop Web sites based primarily on ActiveX technology. ActiveX technology is a powerful alternative to Java, and Microsoft makes no bones about it on the Site Builder Network. In fact, much of the Site Builder's Web site is constructed using this state-of-the-art Web programming technology.

The site has three levels of membership for users of the site. Level 1 is fairly simple to join—just sign the membership form, place a few logos on your home page, and you're in! Level 2 requires that you put at least one ActiveX component on your home page along with the Microsoft Internet logo. Level 3 requires you to build and deploy at least three "ActiveX-exploitive" sites and pay an annual membership fee.

The Web site, shown in Figure 4-10, has a workshop that contains a gallery for ActiveX components developed by Microsoft and other ISVs. The workshop also contains authoring, design, programming, server, and Intranet sections for the Webmaster/developer. One of the site's best features is the download area for

FIGURE 4-10   **Microsoft's Site Builder Network is an excellent source for Webmasters in need of Internet programming tools and support. The Web site is located at**
`http://www.microsoft.com/sitebuilder.`
Screen shot reprinted with permission from Microsoft Corporation.

members only. You can download free demos and trial software from the hottest vendors in Web technology, including Microsoft's own Merchant Server system software. This is definitely one of the hottest Web sites on the Net for ActiveX developers and Webmasters.

Microsoft Access Developer Forum

The Access Developer Forum, shown in Figure 4-11, is more than just a forum for meeting and discussing Access programming techniques. The forum provides Access database developers with valuable technical information about the latest add-ons to the product as well as third-party vendor utilities designed to work with Access. The forum also offers case studies of actual Access implementations and a Special Focus section providing support on upsizing issues and other important Access version information. The Access Developer Forum has a Resources and Events section, which provides links to training events and conferences held in the U.S. and abroad. There is also a freebie section for downloads, which contains at least 25 utilities designed by Microsoft to enhance the Access product.

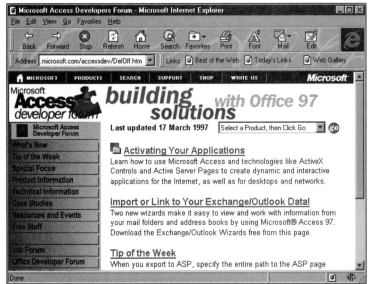

FIGURE 4-11   The Microsoft Access Developer Forum on the Web offers database design experts a specialty forum like no other. The Access Developer Forum is located at `http://www.microsoft.com/accessdev/defoff.htm`.
(Screen shot reprinted with permission from Microsoft Corporation.)

Finally, there is an Access Job Forum within the Access Developer Forum that boasts a "Jobs Available Bank" and a "Jobs Wanted Bank" for Access developers.

Microsoft Systems Pro Web Site

The Systems Pro Web site is dedicated to systems engineers and specialists who need active support from the many systems put out by Microsoft. The site has a direct connection to an online version of the TechNet program CD, named TechNet Reference Desk, for support on just about every product developed by Microsoft. You can get immediate access to system knowledge bases, FAQs, online support wizards, and support programs offered through Microsoft. The Systems Pro Web site also has an abundance of articles relating to systems integration and the Internet. The site is a must for the Microsoft Certified Systems Engineer.

FIGURE 4-12   The Microsoft Systems Pro Web site offers the latest news and support for Microsoft systems engineers and specialists. The Systems Pro Web site is located at http://www. microsoft.com/syspro.

(Screen shot reprinted with permission from Microsoft Corporation.)

CNET ActiveX.com

CNET's ActiveX.com, shown in Figure 4-13, is a Web site where developers, Web authors, and programmers can find and download ActiveX products while keeping up-to-date on the latest developments surrounding Microsoft's Active Platform. The site's user interface is replete with sophisticated search facilities, a featured ActiveX control of the week, and an information desk where users can be directed to additional ActiveX resources available on the Internet.

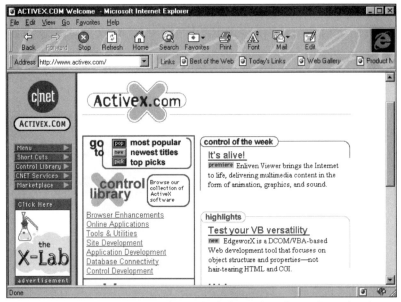

FIGURE 4-13   CNET's ActiveX Web site is dedicated to the ActiveX developer community. ActiveX is located at `http://www.activex.com`.

ActiveX.com is designed to accommodate the needs of the developer community in one comprehensive site by offering features, component software, and links to additional CNET resources, including NEWS.com and DOWNLOAD.com.

A sampling of some of the valuable resources on ActiveX.com is listed below:

o A comprehensive library of downloadable ActiveX components, updated on a daily basis, which includes freeware, shareware, demos, fixes, patches, and upgrades

- A platform for developers to showcase the latest and greatest ActiveX components through the CNET Premiere Program

- Timely information about the issues that affect ActiveX developers, like security, standards, and interoperability

- An easy-to-use online service for developers to add new controls to the ACTIVEX.com repository

MICROSOFT'S MASTERING SERIES CD

The Mastering Series CD was designed by Microsoft to help developers master the tasks and concepts they need to develop sophisticated solutions using Microsoft technology. Most of the Mastering Series CDs are for intermediate to advanced developers. The CDs offer a comprehensive learning system with modular interactive lessons, flexible searching, sample code, and technical articles on object-oriented programming concepts and tasks, such as how to use ActiveX automation to integrate existing applications for the Web.

Some of the titles currently offered in the Mastering Series are:

- *Mastering Internet Development with Microsoft ActiveX Technologies*

- *Mastering Microsoft Access Programming*

- *Mastering Microsoft Visual FoxPro*

- *Mastering Microsoft Visual C++ 4*

To really maximize the training experience on the Mastering Series CD, shown in Figure 4-14, it is highly recommended that you have a full multimedia PC. Each chapter has an introduction that uses sound and animation to describe concepts and tasks to be completed in each chapter.

FIGURE 4-14   **Microsoft's Mastering Series CDs offer users a multimedia training experience. Subjects from ActiveX controls to Visual C++ are available from Microsoft Press.**

(Screen shot reprinted with permission from Microsoft Corporation.)

For more information on the Mastering Series CD's call Microsoft Press at 800-MSPRESS. You can also visit the Microsoft Press Web site at http://www.microsoft.com/mspress/.

MICROSOFT PROFESSIONAL SEMINARS

During the year Microsoft holds numerous technical conferences ranging from Developer Days (DevDays) to TechEd. These and other conferences offer developers, software specialists, and systems engineers a wealth of seminars on Microsoft technology. Developer Days is a technical conference for Microsoft programming language experts and TechEd is for software specialists and systems engineers. The conferences usually begin on a Tuesday and end on a Thursday. They are held all over the U.S. and sometimes abroad. There is no one single Web site or home page on the Microsoft Web site that covers all of the conferences. For instance, to find information on DevDays, you need to visit the Microsoft Developer Network home page, and for the TechEd conference you need to visit the Systems Pro home page. As for the other conferences, you need to either visit the Microsoft Web site on a regular basis or join one of Microsoft's many programs for IT professionals.

Developer Days

At DevDays, more than 45,000 developers worldwide learn about the latest versions of Microsoft's Visual Development tools, like Visual Studio 97, Visual Basic and Visual C++. Keynote speakers like Microsoft executives Bill Gates and Steve Balmer kick off the technical conference, with product managers leading technical sessions throughout the week. Attendees of the conference typically receive the latest beta software under development by Microsoft, as well as T-shirts, knapsacks, tools, and lots of food and drink.

The conferences are very lively and offer developers an excellent opportunity to network with their peers. Microsoft invites many third-party language and tools vendors to the technical conference, who usually put on a pretty good show themselves. There are many different tracks in the seminars depending on your specialty or programming background. All in all, DevDays, shown in Figure 4-15, is an excellent technical conference for developers who code in Microsoft programming languages.

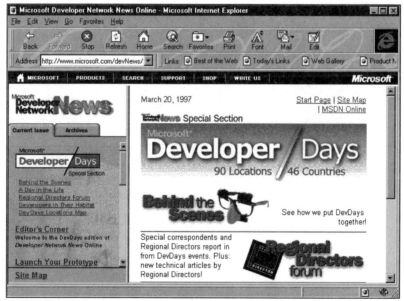

FIGURE 4-15   **Information on DevDays can be found on the Microsoft Developer Network located at** `http://www.microsoft.com/msdn`. (Screen shot reprinted with permission from Microsoft Corporation.)

MICROSOFT AT THE MOVIES

Microsoft at the Movies, shown in Figure 4-16, offers developers a neat way to keep up in their field. The shows are beamed to movie theaters around the U.S. in a live format. The fee is modest and includes free giveaways such as evaluation software and sample training tools. The topics usually covered are the Internet and intranets. The shows usually last all day, with time for lunch in between.

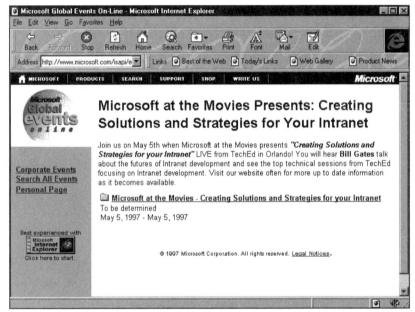

FIGURE 4-16 **Microsoft is now holding technical seminars at a movie theater near you! For information on the latest show times, visit the Web site at** `http://www.microsoft.com/events/msmovies/`.

(Screen shot reprinted with permission from Microsoft Corporation.)

NEWS GROUPS AND LIST SERVERS

Usenet news groups, or simply news groups as they are referred to today, offer users quick and efficient access to information on a wide variety of topics.

Currently there are over 25,000 news groups, possibly more, on the Internet. Some are moderated, but most are not. Often you can find postings or submissions that are seemingly unrelated to the main discussion and the source can be traced to what is termed as Spamming in the industry. Spamming is the unwarranted or unsolicited posting of information that is sometimes totally irrelevant to the subject matter of the news group. Spamming is also associated with e-mail that is also unwarranted or unsolicited, in other words, junk mail. Users have to sift through the garbage of spams to get to the answers they need, which can be annoying at times. However, the advantages that news groups offer far outweigh any of the minor annoyances that may occur with using them.

List servers or mailing lists offer users a way to keep current in their fields. The process of signing up for a mailing list is fairly easy and straightforward. The user simply creates an e-mail with an address to the list server and enters "subscribe" in the subject field or body of the e-mail message. From that point on the user will receive a copy of every posting or submission to the list server, including any messages he may have posted himself. One of the drawbacks to joining mailing lists is that you can clog your e-mail in-box with messages that you may or may not be interested in receiving from day to day.

Both systems are early remnants of the Internet. List servers and news groups have existed on the Net for many years, long before the World Wide Web was invented. However their use is still strong and they can offer MCPs access to cheap, albeit valuable, information and help on just about any topic in IT.

Microsoft News Groups

Microsoft currently has over 250 news groups, some of which are shown in Figure 4-17, for its products. However, most MCPs will only need access to a minimum of 10 or so depending on their specialties. In order to access the news groups you will need a news group reader. Microsoft offers a free news and mail reader that is available for free download at www.microsoft.com/ie. You will also need access to the news groups via your Internet Service Provider (ISP). Most ISPs provide this news group service access free of charge.

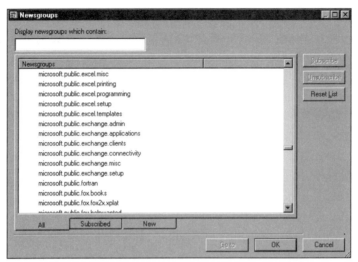

FIGURE 4-17   **Microsoft has nearly 250 Usenet groups for just about every product it sells. Microsoft offers a free news browser at** http://www.microsoft.com/ie.
(Screen shot reprinted with permission from Microsoft Corporation.)

Mailing Lists

The following lists a few of the mailing lists that specialize in Microsoft technology. To subscribe to the lists, simply type in the address listed below in the "To" field in your e-mail message and then type "subscribe" in the "Subject" field of the message. If that does not work try typing the word "subscribe" in the body of the message. To end your subscription to any mailing list, simply perform the same steps as above but type "unsubscribe" instead.

 note   **Be careful not to subscribe to too many list servers at any one time, as you can overload or clog your e-mail box, possibly missing important messages in between, in addition to causing information overload on yourself, too!**

Here is a sampling of a few mailing lists on Windows NT:

o nt-info@huearn.staki.hu is an unmoderated discussion list run by the San Diego NT Users Group. The list covers topics on Windows NT.

o windows-nt@mailbase.ac.uk is a mailing list that focuses on such topics as BackOffice, Windows NT and LAN Manager.

- `winnt-1@peach.ease.lsoft.com` is an open unmoderated forum on the Windows NT operating system.

- `ntdev@atria.com` is a mailing list that hosts Windows NT developer interests.

Mailing lists exist all over the Internet, and finding an appropriate one can sometimes be difficult. To find a mailing list that you may be interested in joining, try using Yahoo or some other search engine on the Net. You should also try your local user group or SIG for an address to a mailing list that specializes in your field.

KEY POINT SUMMARY

In summary, this chapter included valuable links to information on the World Wide Web that can help you enhance your career as an MCP. You learned of some top online trade magazines like *Windows NT* and *Microsoft Certified Professional*, two excellent sources for MCPs. This chapter also covered some of the "specialty" Web sites for MCPs, like NT Specialist, an employment Web site dedicated to MCPs. Other Web sites referred to in this chapter focus on systems engineering, such as Microsoft's Systems Pro Web page, or software development, like CNET's ActiveX.com Web site. Finally, this chapter offered information on some of the top mailing lists on the Internet that are dedicated to MCPs.

- Online trade magazines found on the World Wide Web offer a substantive alternative to their treed cousins.

- Specialist online job banks offer MCPs a fast and efficient means of locating a good job via the Internet.

- List servers and news groups offer a great way for MCPs to stay abreast in their field.

- Microsoft offers professional development seminars throughout the year for MCPs.

MCSE Career Track Revealed

About Chapter 5

In this chapter you will discover how a Microsoft Certified Systems Engineer (MCSE) works as a professional in the world of information technology (IT). You will also learn through interviews with real systems engineers the responsibilities and issues one can expect to encounter working as a systems professional. In addition, this chapter discusses the expected salary ranges for MCSEs throughout the United States, as well as where and how to find a job as a network engineer.

BECOMING A MICROSOFT CERTIFIED SYSTEMS ENGINEER: RECOGNITION AND REWARDS

Opportunities for MCSEs are wide open. Never before has the MCSE enjoyed such a wealth of job openings from employers the world over. The MCSE can expect to find ample opportunity and work well into the next century. On the other hand, MCSEs can also expect to be challenged with duties by their employers in keeping up with IT. As a systems engineer you will have to keep pace with the extraordinary growth of Internet and intranet systems technology. As you work in the capacity of an MCSE, your employer will expect above-average performance on the job and with your career overall. You will be expected to maintain your career by attending trade shows, technical seminars, and hands-on training all while doing your job.

However, the financial rewards for becoming an MCSE are well worth it. Average salaries for a certified systems engineer range anywhere from $45K a year, all the way up to $125K, depending on the capacity in which you are employed as an MCSE. Every aspect of the MCSE career track is discussed in detail to give you a better understanding of the opportunities for and responsibilities of the MCSE.

The Benefits of Becoming a Microsoft Certified Systems Engineer

As you can discern from the chapter introduction, the benefits of becoming an MCSE can be both tangible and intangible. The tangible benefits are obvious: good pay, a certificate with Bill Gates' signature, and cash bonuses for a job well done. However, it's the intangible benefits that many IT professionals look for in a job as opposed to just pay and bonuses. Systems professionals in particular look for challenging IT environments where can they get maximum exposure to the latest technologies, such as Internet and intranet systems software. They also look for many other hidden benefits that may or may not be so obvious to the novice who is just entering the field of systems engineering.

Some of the major benefits awaiting the active MCSE are listed below.

Challenging Work Environment

Anyone who follows today's headlines is aware of the enormous pace that IT is currently undergoing, especially with respect to the Internet and World Wide Web. MCSEs are expected to keep pace with emerging intranet and Internet technologies, and in doing so they reap the rewards both intellectually and financially.

Work Autonomously

Systems engineers by the very nature of their jobs are typically required to work under their own direction. Local- and wide-area networks are distributed by their inherent design, and as such systems engineers can easily find themselves working alone in many instances. For some, this is an added bonus of the job — not having the boss looking over one's shoulder all of the time.

Travel

Depending on whether you like to travel or not, network engineers are typically required to do light to medium travel, especially if they are working for a Microsoft Solution Provider (MSP) or Fortune 500 company. Today's MCSE can easily find himself all over the globe if he is working for the big organization like Microsoft or one of the large MSPs.

Work with Cutting-Edge Technology

Systems engineers who work for MSPs can expect to work with most of Microsoft's latest systems technology. All MSPs are participants in Microsoft's beta program. Any systems professionals working for an MSP will naturally get advanced exposure to the latest systems from Microsoft. Some of the Fortune 500 companies are also members of Microsoft beta program, so network engineers at those organizations have the opportunity to gain advance knowledge of the systems coming out of Redmond, Washington.

Skills in High Demand

With the explosive growth in demand for Microsoft Certified Professionals MCPs), in particular MCSEs, many systems engineers can expect a rewarding career, both financially and professionally. Salaries for MCSEs are well above average throughout the U.S. and abroad. Also, with the MCSE's skills in high demand, systems engineers can maintain a certain level of job security for the future.

Management Opportunities

Microsoft Certified System Engineers who take their jobs seriously and continue with their professional development by staying abreast with technology can expect a promotion into the ranks of management. Some of the management positions that an MCSE network engineer can aspire to are program manager, engagement manager, and director of IT.

HOW TO KEEP YOUR MICROSOFT CERTIFIED SYSTEMS ENGINEER CAREER IN FOCUS

Some of the toughest jobs that most people have keeping up with are personal finances and their careers. Setting career goals and keeping them in focus can be very difficult to do on top of raising a family and performing well on the job. However, doing so isn't as painful as you may think and it can even be fun. Listed here are just a few of the steps you can take to enhance your career opportunities, both professionally and financially.

tip One of the hottest new methods of staying on top of your career is to subscribe to an electronic newsletter. These electronic news briefs allow you to keep an up-to-date pulse in your particular niche of IT. For example, Sunbelt Software (http://www. ntsoftdist.com/) frequently sends out electronic alerts and a newsletter informing network engineers and Windows NT specialists of the latest developments with Windows NT implementations in the real world.

Read Trade Journals

Magazines that focus on professional development such as *Windows NT*, *BackOffice*, and *Microsoft Certified Professional* offer readers the latest news and information on a wide variety of topics concerning system engineers.

Attend Technical Seminars

Some of the best technical seminars are held annually by Microsoft. TechEd and Developer Days are two of the largest conferences held in the U.S. for software developers and engineers, respectively.

Continue Your Education

Authorized Technical Education Centers (ATECs) and Authorized Academic Training Partners (AATPs) are excellent sources for hands-on technical training. They are located throughout the world and on the Internet. Microsoft Certified Trainers versed in the latest systems and applications from Microsoft teach classes both in a classroom setting as well as online via the Internet's World Wide Web.

 concept link For more information on ATECs and AATPs see Chapter 3.

Network with Peers

Interact with people, not machines! One the best tried-and-true methods of staying abreast in your field is through friends and acquaintances in the industry. It is difficult at best to try to master it all, so build a network of people in your field— you can actually learn a lot from them.

Join User Groups

No amount of training can replace the value of becoming a member of a user group or special interest group (SIG). These associations offer individuals the best help and guidance found anywhere. Some of the largest IT user groups in the nation are Rocky Mountain NT in Denver, Colorado and LANTUG, the Los Angeles NT Users Group. They also have SIGs within these groups such as the Exchange Specialist User Group and Internet Systems User Group.

 concept link More information on user groups and SIGs can be found in Chapter 12.

Set Career Goals

If a manager or superior has the time or inclination, he or she should be helping you attain your career goals by providing you with the proper training and guidance. Unfortunately, many managers don't have the time or budget to look after a subordinate's career. Often it is up to the individual to set his or her goals for a successful career. Anyone who is serious about career development should set realistic goals from time to time through careful planning and analysis.

Find a Mentor

This is one person often overlooked by IT professionals. With the busy, hectic life that a typical systems professional leads, it's often difficult to bond with one particular individual for help and guidance with your career. Systems professionals often report to many different superiors because of downsizing and flatter management structures in organizations. Systems professionals need to actively pursue and find a mentor to help them grow professionally. Start with the nearest manager or supervisor who you see eye to eye with.

 tip Mentoring is often a very subtle process, which takes time and is built on trust. Most highly motivated individuals such as upper management or supervisors often seek out individuals much like themselves to assist them with their occupational objectives. Therefore, it's not easy to strike up a mentoring relationship as a subordinate, rather the mentoring process always starts from the top. However, you can enhance your chances of gaining a mentor by being a responsible, industrious and honest worker.

ENGAGEMENTS FOR MICROSOFT CERTIFIED SYSTEMS ENGINEERS

Depending on the vernacular you use to distinguish the type of projects you work on, the term engagement is used more often for external projects that a systems engineer may work on. An engagement is a more inclusive or comprehensive term because it takes into account every aspect of an encounter with a client from start to finish; in other words, the entire life cycle of a system installation from sales to customer sign-off of the implementation. However, MCSEs also work on traditional systems integration projects within IT departments as well. The typical MCSE can find himself in either context, especially if he is working for a large systems integrator or MSP. In either case, the systems engineer is expected to perform well in either environment and do so professionally.

The MCSE is typically called on to perform a multitude of tasks, which may or may not be considered to be pure network engineering. In fact, an MCSE can rightfully expect to be asked by his employer to do hands-on manual labor in addition to his normal systems engineering duties. Unlike programming, where you have a well-defined discipline, in systems engineering there are many gray areas with regard to duties and responsibilities. Listed here are just some of the engagements and/or projects an MCSE can be expected to perform on the job:

- **Local-Area Network Installation and Configuration:** Installing network operating systems (NOSs) software and configuring the server. This also includes loading desktop operating systems software such as Windows 95 and Windows NT Workstation. Additional duties may include configuring printers, fax, and scanner, and installation of Network Interface Cards.

- **Wide-Area Network Installation and Support:** Installing and configuring specialized computers known as routers for internetworking, intranets, and the Internet. Other duties may include configuring CSU/DSUs and ISDN equipment for specialized telecommunications services.

- **Internet/Intranet Server Installation and Configuration:** The installation of Internet and intranet Web servers for hypertext transfer protocol for Web hosting, as well as internal intranets and/or extranets. For the client side, installation of a Web browser such as Microsoft Internet Explorer or Netscape Navigator.

o **Network Management and Design:** Monitoring networks through traffic analysis and diagnostics with products such as Microsoft Systems Management Server (SMS) or Hewlett-Packard's OpenView network monitoring and management software. Systems engineers may also design or plan networks from scratch using a design tool such as Visio from Shapeware Corp.

o **Network Maintenance (Upgrades, Patches and Fixes):** Upgrading NOS server software and workstation clients on the network by applying version upgrades and patches or fixes for bugs in the software.

o **Parallel Conversions/Migrations:** Performing a system migration from one NOS such as Novell file and print network operating system to a Windows NT application server system. Duties may also include providing assistance with the migration of a financial reporting system from one platform such as a mainframe or UNIX to Windows NT.

o **Telecommunications:** Installing and configuring fax/modem cards or modem banks for remote access services. Additional duties may include installing network hubs and computer-telephony equipment such as phone system PBX interface.

o **Backups:** Performing crucial backups to all mission-critical applications and data on a regular and prescribed basis.

This list is by no means comprehensive, but it does include a majority of the types of jobs and functions that an MCSE is capable of doing. Many smaller companies may require a systems engineer to perform all of these functions, while larger organizations may have many different network engineers on staff tending to each of the areas outlined.

INTERVIEWS WITH MICROSOFT CERTIFIED SYSTEMS ENGINEERS IN THE FIELD

Given the diversity of jobs for MCPs out in the field, this author has taken the liberty of interviewing a few MCSEs to find out just what they are up to in their profession. These are candid interviews with some of the more experienced systems engineers who are actively working on systems engineering projects and/or engagements.

INTERVIEW: DOUGLAS KOENIG, SYSTEMS ANALYST AND MCSE AT FORD MOTOR COMPANY

Douglas Koenig is a Systems Analyst and MCSE at Ford Motor Company. He has over 20 years of experience in information systems technology. His background includes six years in metallurgical engineering, 10 years in consulting/management, one year of freelance consulting in systems administration, and the last three years in IS project management at Ford.

Q: What is the nature of your work, duties, and responsibilities? What do you do during an average work day?

A: I work for the Ford Motor Company in an in-house information systems development group. Our department (Engineering Information Systems) is responsible for development of applications in support of business practices that are used by our end users (Ford Product Design Engineers). We have 65 programmers and analysts teamed up in six sections, which act more or less independently insofar as their planning and people resources for development. Our department reports to the Systems Office, which claims about 3,600 people in Ford worldwide.

We have recently migrated our entire development platform to Windows NT 4.0 (server and workstation) from OS/2 servers and Windows 3.1 clients. Our end user environment tends to be 80% PC platforms (Windows 95 and Windows 3.1) and 20% high-end UNIX CAD/CAE workstations.

Within our department, I have three sets of responsibilities, with several activities:

a) Manage application development projects for our section (Engine Test Data Management)

i) Provide project management as required for application development efforts including support for system

design, module design, coding, testing deployment, and support according to the prevailing project methodology

ii) Guide project selection and development in a manner consistent with corporate directions and objectives (at least as they are defined to the department in which I work)

iii) Support system design efforts such that they are compliant with local office deployment and design criteria and with corporate architectures

b) Provide long-term departmental architectural development strategies department-wide

i) Strategies are based on *n*-tier client/server/server architectures

ii) Front-end development is based on VB and Web clients, with back-end support from Oracle and UNIX servers. Middle server layer is not standardized but is becoming a mix of Microsoft BackOffice applications (transaction server, NT, IIS, SQL Server) and Netscape ONE

c) Support local office technical requirements department-wide and beyond as required

i) In conjunction with local technical support services, support deployment of Windows 95 systems and associated applications in support of developers

ii) Provide beta test sites, people, and systems for new software and for in-house or external applications. On an average day I spend about 20% of my time in support of the department (answering questions, supporting resolution of problems that cannot be resolved by first-level services); 20% in meetings of various sorts; 20% in long-term architectural planning; and 40% in project management. I am sure that my participation and eventual leadership in the process of architectural development for the department is a direct result of my having the MCSE. To be truthful, the MCSE did not give me any more knowledge, but it is a symbol that people can trust when they are considering who might have relevant skills to be utilized. A similar reaction was observed when my Digital CAE customer base realized that I was a certified CIM technologist.

Q: Why did you decide to become an MCP?

A: Two things: First, experience with Microsoft while I was employed at Digital Equipment Corporation (until 1992) led me to respect Microsoft as a company with outstanding potential and incredible enthusiasm for the technology. Understanding the technology in depth was measured by the exams; I wanted to prove, to myself as much as anyone, that I was able to grasp, appreciate, and work with these technologies.

Second, gaining exposure to the process, to the world outside of Digital and the competitive nature of the industry, and to the demand for MCP and MCSE certification in particular led me to want to have the certification as a measure of my expertise in relationship to the rest of the world. I would not have followed through with just one of these reasons, but I needed both to motivate me to get through the rigor of the MCSE.

Q: What is your working environment like? Deadlines, stress, workflow, hours, etc.

A: We have launch dates and plans to which we must adhere. We generally do not work excessive hours, although they are appreciated by management if we do.

Q: What do you like about this field?

A: Change. And the technology. In fact, as I prepare for another stab at management, this time at Ford, the one fear that I have is that I will lose track of the advances. I have five computers at home, a dual Ethernet network (TP and Thinwire) throughout the house, a Windows NT Server, Web pages and network printers, and on and on . . . so I am a technology junkie!

Q: What kind of person do you feel would do well in this job?

A: This job (my job) requires an ability to see the details in the scheme of getting the job done (for effective project management), and to see the big picture (for effective planning on long-term horizons). Enjoyment of the technologies should be assumed, with drive to keep up with them. But, focus too . . . I find myself constantly battling to stay "appropriately" involved. I have too much inclination to read everything, download everything, install everything, then end up able to do nothing!

Q: What are the advantages/disadvantages of your job as an MCP?

A: Being an MCSE suggests to some that I really know what I am talking about. I can be assumed to have at least some span of limited knowledge, which is accurate. Of course, only history tells if I use the accurate parts inaccurately!

Also, being an MCSE means that some people resent the time spent, the certification gained, or the assumption by others of innate knowledge; they are jealous. Can't help that, but it is a fact, and does get in the way. Not much.

continued

continued

Probably the key advantage for me right now as I am interviewing for management openings is that I don't have to tell anyone I am knowledgeable; I just show them the certification, and during the interview, most of the technical questions stop. We can concentrate on the business drivers that make the job a fit or not.

Q: What knowledge, skills (for success), and abilities are required for this type of work?

A: I think I covered most of this. I would like to add that just taking the exam is possible, and you might even pass it. However, the TCP/IP exam is an example of how work pays off . . . half of the exam can be "guessed at" from the NT exams. Subnets can't be guessed; you have to understand them or not. I studied for two weeks, trying out every possible combination, testing them on my systems, eventually understanding subnetting. I got 100% on the section and passed the test. Great, but even better, when I got back to work, the *next day*, we had a problem with a group of Windows 95 systems, which I could now correctly diagnose and follow up by suggesting a technical services repair approach. We got the systems back on the network, limited the downtime and effect on program efforts, and were greatly successful.

I *needed* the IP subnetting knowledge. It pays off to study, work with the product, and use it.

Q: What are the advancement opportunities and outlook for this field?

A: Within Ford, the MCSE is not appreciated as a corporation. We are appreciated within the department, but there is not a formal recognition nor advancement criteria that certification completes.

However, it is useful to have within my department sphere of influence. More interestingly, it gives me a chance to work with other professionals and MSPs (in my spare evening time). This gives me the chance to stay up on the technology, keep supplemental income coming in, and keep knocking around with my peers who are not trapped in the large company bureaucracy!

INTERVIEW: ROGER BREMER, SOLUTIONS ENGINEER AT NCR CORPORATION

Roger Bremer is Solutions Engineer at NCR Corporation. He provides support to customers around the world pertaining to all Microsoft operating system environments and hardware support for NCR Corporations multiprocessor server systems. He also works closely with NCR's global network of systems engineers and other support professionals who provide technical assistance to the company.

Q: What is the nature of your work, duties, and responsibilities? What do you do during an average work day?

A: Over the course of an average day I spend quite a lot of time on the telephone answering questions from around the globe on the NCR Windows NT Global Support Hotline. These questions run the gamut, from straight software problems to performance issues to hardware and software interaction issues. Also, I consult with a number of the internal hardware and software development teams to provide in-depth support and troubleshooting for newly developed products, with regard to the way that these products interact with various Microsoft applications. Another of my roles is to serve as the Global Support Knowledge Domain Owner, which is essentially a champion for creating and maintaining support-related knowledge pertaining to several of the high-performance machines in NCR's line of multiprocessor Pentium and Pentium Pro servers. I also assist other support professionals worldwide in configuring, tuning, and troubleshooting these systems, both on-site and as a remote resource expert.

Q: Why did you decide to become an MCP?

A: It became clear to me a few years ago that Microsoft had the resources and desire to make Windows NT the premier operating environment for business. With the proliferation of Windows-based applications and services, in both the home and office arenas, it seemed to me that it was practical to get to know as much as I could about Microsoft's products and services. Along the way, I had the opportunity to speak with a Microsoft representative at the Windows World trade show. This individual was promoting the MCP program. I was impressed with the fact that Microsoft intended the MCP program to be a true measure of skills and abilities, and not just an indicator of the fact that certification tests had been passed. I'm sure that just about everyone knows a "paper CNE," that is, someone who has passed the tests to become a Certified Novell Engineer but who really has no practical knowledge of how the operating system really is used. The MCP program is a much more accurate measure of an individual's true knowledge and ability, and as such it is a significantly more valuable credential, both for a computer professional to hold, and for an employer to look for. The more I learned about the MCP program, the more I realized that it would become a significant benchmark of professionalism in the computer industry. And I knew that I had to be a part of it.

Q: What is your working environment like? Deadlines, stress, workflow, hours, etc.

A: I work in a 24-hour-a-day, seven-day-a-week global support center. Although my primary hours are 8 a.m. to 5 p.m., Monday through Friday, I periodically rotate through a series of off-hours shifts, which allows me to experience the kind of issues that are raised by customers from all of the areas of the globe. (Obviously, we get a lot more calls from Australia at 2 a.m. than we do from Nebraska!) Our support workflow is essentially the same, regardless of where the call comes from. We take the call, identify the problem, research the problem (if necessary, including building test systems to duplicate the customer's problem or issue), formulate a solution to the problem, and follow up to make sure the customer is pleased with the solution and with our performance. This work is totally customer-oriented. We have only one deadline: "ASAP." We know that the customers are counting on us to get them the right answer as quickly as possible, and we take our responsibility to them very seriously. In cases when a customer's system is down, we concentrate all necessary resources to get them back up as quickly as possible, including other analysts in the Global Support Center, hardware engineers, and any of the thousands of available field engineers and customer engineers around the world. Approximately 90% of our Global Support Team consists of MCSEs, and nearly all of the remaining 10% are MCPSs.

Q: What do you like about this field?

A: Every day, there's a new challenge. This work is never dull. It's also a good feeling to know that you can directly impact the customer's satisfaction through your skills and abilities. Plus, we get the opportunity to use and support state-of-the-art equipment, and we keep up-to-date on all the Microsoft products.

continued

continued

I feel that we're in the best possible position to benefit from Microsoft's research and development, both individually and as a company. As the industry grows, I'm confident that the demand for MCPs will grow as well.

Q: What kind of person do you feel would do well in this job?

A: Probably the most important trait that is vital for success, both in the NCR Global Support Center and as an MCP in general, is a strong desire to help the customer. If someone isn't customer-oriented, he should probably do something else for a living. There is a significant amount of outward pressure to make things right quickly, and to be sure the customer is pleased. Anyone who isn't customer-oriented probably would not enjoy this kind of work, or at least wouldn't enjoy it as much as someone who is customer-oriented.

Q: What are the advantages/disadvantages of your job as an MCP?

A: One significant advantage of being an MCP is the instant respect that you get from customers and colleagues. The requirements to become an MCP are becoming better known as time passes, and people who are familiar with the MCP program know that someone who has passed MCP tests knows the subject matter very well. Ultimately, that allows you to spend more time getting down to business and less time convincing the customer or client that you're able to do what you say you can do. MCP certifications are also in high demand by employers, which is another significant advantage in an increasingly volatile business environment. Although I'd be pretty hard-pressed to name a specific disadvantage of my job as an MCP, I would say that occasionally I encounter someone who wants to classify me as "a Microsoft guy." That is, since they're aware that I

have invested the time and effort to become Microsoft certified, once in a while, someone will think that I am some kind of "Microsoft evangelist," ready to force-fit a Microsoft solution into every situation. Others might overlook the fact that much of my work is hardware-related and tend to classify me as a "software guy." I'm not sure that these are really "disadvantages," but I will admit that these misperceptions can be difficult to overcome.

Q: What knowledge, skills (for success), and abilities are required for this type of work?

A: More than anything else, I would say that the ability to think analytically is vital. Certainly, familiarity with current trends in computer technology is important. Also, as I mentioned, customer focus and orientation is necessary to succeed. And knowledge of the fundamentals of computer science occasionally comes in handy.

Q: What are the advancement opportunities and outlook for this field?

A: Judging by the current number of job postings in newspapers and trade magazines and on the Internet, the current opportunities for advancement in Windows NT and other Microsoft-related installations are impressive. Because of this, employers are making extra efforts to retain current employees who are MCPs. Since nearly all of the significant computer-related publications now acknowledge that Windows NT is becoming the primary operating environment in the business world, and more companies are migrating to NT every day, that will necessarily translate into more opportunities for highly trained and skilled computer professionals. Since the MCP certifications are the best way to demonstrate those highly sought skills, I think that the future looks bright for MCPs.

INTERVIEW: RICK OW, DIRECTOR OF IT FOR PROFESSIONAL DATASOLUTIONS, INC. (PDI)

Rick Ow is Director of IT at Professional Datasolutions, a Partner Level member of the MSP program and MCSE. Rick's primary duty as IT Director for the company is to seek and deploy the latest Microsoft software offerings for the company's clients. In essence, PDI is the MIS department for most of its clients, and Rick's job is to oversee recommendations and implementations of that technology to the firm's customers. Rick is also responsible for all internal corporate software and systems deployment for PDI.

Q: What is the nature of your work, duties, and responsibilities? What do you do during an average work day?

A: I am the manager of the IT department. I'm responsible for all computing and data communications within the company, defining corporate policy on information systems, and technology research and integration within the company. An average work day is a mystery to me as well, but here is a rough outline.

My typical work day includes something like this: Get update from team members on their projects and duties (software deployment projects via SMS, SQL Server status, database integrity checks, PC staging and deployment, help desk calls, and other projects); check state of our Web server; process orders for new systems and software; investigate on the Internet new technologies (streaming video, Internet security to connect our company to the Internet, Zero-Administration Initiative progress); visit Microsoft's Web site for latest developments; visit Microsoft Premiere Web site for the latest news to MS Solution Providers; test new technologies (currently I'm testing Exchange Server 5.0) for deployment to our company; test new technologies that are in beta.

Q: Why did you decide to become an MCP?

A: I saw the benefits of having industry recognition and being able to quantify my credentials, in addition to maintaining my life-long pursuit of higher education. The program was the best, most pertinent, and stringent testing sequence I ever saw, and I knew that it carried respect along with the title of MCSE.

Q: What is your working environment like? Deadlines, stress, workflow, hours, etc.

A: As with all the respondents, my environment is extremely stressful with deadlines that are constantly missed due to other "higher-importance" projects. Managing in an environment, especially one that is dedicated to instituting new software and systems as soon as they become products, is absolutely crazy. Hours fluctuate from 40 to 60 per week, depending on what is happening. The demand for newer, better, and faster is always present, which drives me to seek out the latest technologies for deployment.

Q: What do you like about this field?

A: The rapid changes that have been happening. For example, software versions typically had a two-year lifespan. Now, it is typical to see a six-month to one-year life cycle of a version of a product. This, by the way, is also the thing I find the most challenging about this field: You can never become complacent with your level of knowledge; you always need to seek more and more.

Q: What kind of person do you feel would do well in this job?

continued

continued

A: Someone who can juggle many jobs at one time, can handle office politics, and has a firm moral foundation. For example, I can never stay focused on a single project nor can I ever say I'm going to work the entire day on one task. You need to be able to manage many projects, handle multiple deadlines, and be used to being responsible to many folks, not just your boss. This person would need to be thick-skinned as well, since everyone is your critic. You also need to be as technically competent and up-to-date on *all* technologies, as proficient as the best IT person you manage. Nowadays, the manager is expected to have answers any time, anywhere, on any subject that relates to computers or data communications. Concerning a firm moral foundation, this person is the key to the company. He can make or break a company (more likely break a company). He needs to have the intestinal fortitude to look someone in the eye and say, "This is wrong, we need to fix it," or more important be able to say, "With the knowledge I had at the time, this was the smartest technical direction to go toward. Six months later I see that it wasn't the best decision. I'll fix it and get us on track." Passing blame or pointing fingers cannot be the answer to this person. He must be able to take responsibility for all actions that happen in IT.

Q: What are the advantages/disadvantages of your job as an MCP?

A: I think I've discussed the advantages. The only disadvantage I can think of is that people label me as a "Softie," in other words a Microsoft devotee. Which for the most part is correct!

Q: What knowledge, skills (for success), and abilities are required for this type of work?

A: Maybe I'm being too lengthy in my answers. I think I answered this question under "What kind of person do you feel would do well in this job?"

Q: What are the advancement opportunities and outlook for this field?

A: Advancement opportunities are awesome. Outlook for this field is wonderful. There is demand for MCPs like I've never seen before. I started my MCSE certification process when Windows NT was still on version 3.1. That was a long time ago. I looked at their program and weighed it against the others out there and saw that this was going to be *big* one day. It didn't have all the glitz and glory when I started the program, but one day I knew that it would be the "golden key" that employers would look for in judging one's technical competence. I constantly get called by recruiters even though I'm not employed by one of the big consulting firms or blue chip companies. I believe that my reputation has helped, but the buzzword that is attracting recruiters is spelled out in the four letters, M–C–S–E.

WHAT YOU CAN EXPECT TO EARN AS A MICROSOFT CERTIFIED SYSTEMS ENGINEER

While the MCSE is commanding ever-higher salaries, which is due largely to the popularity of Microsoft technology, all MCSEs are not necessarily enjoying increases in pay. Salaries vary widely by region of the U.S., as denoted in Table 5-1. Salary bases also vary among employers, so it all depends on whom you are working for and where your employer is located. Finally, salary ranges depend on your experience, education and, most important, your track record as an IT professional.

Tables 5-1 and 5-2 show salary ranges.

TABLE 5-1 MCSE SALARY RANGES BY REGION

REGION	SALARY RANGE
Northeast	$65K–$125K
Midatlantic	$55K–$95K
South	$42K–$75K
West	$50K–$68K
Midwest	$55K–$70K

TABLE 5-2 MCSE SALARY RANGE BY EMPLOYER TYPES

EMPLOYER TYPE	SALARY RANGE
Private company	$42K–$125K
Government	$22K–$58K
MSPs	$55K–$90K

IT Recruiters Inc. (http://www.itrecruitersinc.com) conducted the salary survey informally and at random. As indicated in Tables 5-1 and 5-2, the MCSE salaries can vary widely by region, country and employer.

WHERE TO FIND A JOB AS A MICROSOFT CERTIFIED SYSTEMS ENGINEER

Although there are many jobs for MCSEs in the U.S. and abroad, many of them are not so easily found. Compiled here are some of the major sources for jobs on the

Internet that reside in job and resume banks. Their names and Web addresses are listed for your convenience:

- Yahoo! Job Guide—www.yahoo.com./business/employment
- IT Specialist.com—www.itspecialist.com
- Monsterboard—www.monsterboard.com
- Career Path—www.careerpath.com
- Career Magazine—www.careermag.com/index.text.html
- Online Career Center—www.occ.com/occ/
- Career Web—www.cWeb.com
- Job Web—www.jobWeb.com
- Career Net—www.careers.org
- The Riley Guide—www.jobtrak.com/jobguide/
- Job Bank USA—www.jobbankusa.com
- FedWorld—www.fedworld.gov

The job and resume banks listed constitute an ever-growing presence on the Web for opportunities in IT. However, the Web is not by any means the only source for jobs in the IT industry. Listed here are some of the more traditional sources for job information and opportunities.

Newspapers, Periodicals

While not the best method for job hunting, many individuals prefer this method of searching for employment to any other. Note: Many of the trade magazines and newspapers are online now and offer a much faster and more sophisticated way of hunting for jobs through the use of search engines on their Web sites.

Networking

Socialize with your peers as often as you can. Friends and associates in your field can often be the best source for a good-paying job. Also, don't forget about trade fairs; they are excellent way to meet new people in your field.

Informational Interviewing

Ask for an interview with some of the biggest companies in the IT industry and you would be surprised by the response you get—usually positive. This method of interviewing can sometimes lead to an immediate job offer.

Although there are many methods of job hunting available to IT professionals, none beats the often free and easy access to jobs on the World Wide Web. Many employment Web sites are now becoming specialized and are catering to niche job markets, such as IT Specialist does. The IT Specialist Web site focuses entirely on MCPs. Newly certified network engineers, software specialists, trainers, and developers can post their resumes on the Web site, as can seasoned veterans of the MCP program.

KEY POINT SUMMARY

In summary, this chapter covered the benefits of becoming an MCSE, such as high pay, a challenging work environment, and respect within the IT community. You learned tips and techniques to keep your career on track and how MCSEs are employed in the field. You also were shown how to find a job as a systems engineer and what salaries you can expect to make as an MCP. Most important, you gained insights into how actual MCSEs in the business of supporting information systems work from day to day in the field of information technology.

- It's always a good idea to specialize in your field and keep your career in focus.
- Network, network, network—make the effort to meet and greet your peers in the field of systems engineering. You can never have too many technical contacts in the field of information technology.
- Find a mentor to help your career along. It can make the difference in your salary and position in the organization.
- Use every available source at your disposal to find the job you are qualified for — including the World Wide Web.

MCSD Career Track Revealed

About Chapter 6

I n this chapter you will discover how a Microsoft Certified Solution Developer (MCSD) works as a professional in the world of information technology (IT). You'll also learn through interviews with real developers the responsibilities and issues one can expect to encounter working as an MCSD. In addition, this chapter discusses the expected salary ranges for MCSDs throughout the U.S., as well as where and how to find a job as a programmer.

BECOMING A MICROSOFT CERTIFIED SOLUTION DEVELOPER: RECOGNITION AND REWARDS

Microsoft Certified Solution Developers are in high demand these days. Never before has the MCSD enjoyed such a wealth of job openings from employers the world over. The MCSD can expect to find ample opportunity and work well into the next century. On the other hand, MCSDs can also expect to be challenged with duties by their employers in keeping up with IT. As a developer you will have to keep pace with the extraordinary growth of Internet and intranet systems technology. When you're working as an MCSD, your employer will expect above-average performance on the job and with your career overall. You will be expected to maintain your career by attending trade shows, technical seminars, and hands-on training, all while keeping up with projects at the office.

However, the financial rewards for becoming an MCSD are well worth it. Average salaries for a software developer range anywhere from $48K a year, all the way up to $125K, depending on the capacity in which you are employed as an MCSD and where you live in the U.S. or abroad. Every aspect of the MCSD career track is discussed in detail to give you a better understanding of the opportunities and responsibilities of the MCSD.

The Benefits of Becoming a Microsoft Certified Solutions Developer

As you can discern from the chapter introduction, the benefits of becoming an MCSD can be both tangible and intangible. The corporeal benefits are obvious: good pay, a certificate with Bill Gates' signature, and cash bonuses for a job well done. However, it's the intangible benefits that many IT professionals look for in a job as opposed to just pay and bonuses. Software developers in particular look for challenging IT environments where can they get maximum exposure to the latest technologies, such as ActiveX and Java. They also look for many other hidden benefits that may or may not be so obvious to the layman or novice who is just entering the field of software development.

Some of the major benefits awaiting the active MCSD are listed here.

Challenging Work Environment

Anyone who follows today's headlines is aware of the enormous pace that IT is currently undergoing, especially with respect to the Internet and World Wide Web. MCSDs are expected to keep pace with emerging intranet and Internet technologies, and in doing so they reap the rewards both intellectually and financially.

Creativity

Developers are often placed on development projects that require them to create applications from scratch. Depending on the scope of a project, a programmer may be required to design and code an application. With today's Internet programming languages such as ActiveX and Java, the software developer is often expected to be both designer and coder. A coder-designer is formally known as programmer/analyst, or PA for short. However, the term developer is rapidly becoming the de facto name for programmer/analysts or software engineers.

Travel

Depending on whether you like to travel or not, developers are typically required to do some light travel, especially if they are working for a Microsoft Solution

Provider (MSP) or Fortune 500 company. Today's MCSDs can easily find themselves all over the globe if they are working for a big organization like Microsoft or one of the large MSPs.

Work with Cutting-Edge Technology

Software developers who work for MSPs can expect to work with most of Microsoft's latest programming languages such as Visual Basic and Visual C++. All MSPs receive the latest software development kits (SDKs) from Microsoft on a monthly basis. Any MCSD working for an MSP will naturally get advanced exposure to the latest versions of development languages from Microsoft. This gives developers the opportunity to gain advance knowledge of the latest scripting engines and programming languages coming out of Microsoft.

Skills in High Demand

With the explosive growth in demand for Microsoft Certified Professionals (MCPs), in particular MCSDs, many developers can expect rewarding careers, both financially and professionally. Salaries for MCSDs are well above average throughout the U.S. and abroad. Also, with the MCSD's skills in high demand, they can maintain a certain level of job security.

Management Opportunities

MCSDs who take their jobs seriously and continue with their professional development by staying abreast with technology can expect promotions into the ranks of management. Some of the management positions that a Microsoft Certified Solution Developer can be prompted to are program manager, product manager, and director of software development.

HOW TO KEEP YOUR CAREER IN FOCUS

Keeping your career on track may not be as difficult as you imagine. There are many channels open to you as an IT professional that can help you grow your career. For example, networking—with people, not machines—has taken on many new forms in the '90s. From trade associations to user groups, the opportunities abound for you to learn and grow professionally. Much of the microcomputer industry is still fairly nascent, especially the World Wide Web, which means greater leadership opportunities for those interested in becoming a voice in an exciting industry. As with college or school, it's what *you* make of it that really counts. Take the lead and there's no telling what opportunities will arise for you now and in the future.

tip **User groups or trade associations are an excellent source for networking in the '90s. Join as many as possible and try hard to attend. You would be amazed at the level of access that you have to industry leaders in the IT business. You would also be impressed with the number of leadership opportunities open for IT professionals within these groups.**

Read Trade Journals

Magazines that focus on professional development, such as *Microsoft Systems Journal, BackOffice*, and *Microsoft Certified Professional*, offer readers the latest news and information on a wide variety of topics concerning software development.

Attend Technical Seminars

Some of the best technical seminars are held annually by Microsoft. TechEd and Developer Days are two of the largest conferences held in the U.S. for developers and engineers, respectively.

Continue Your Education

Authorized Technical Education Centers (ATECs) and Authorized Academic Training Partners (AATPs) (see Chapter 3) are excellent sources for hands-on technical training. They are located throughout the world and on the Internet. Microsoft Certified Trainers versed in the latest systems and applications from Microsoft teach classes both in a classroom setting as well as online via the Internet's World Wide Web.

Network with Peers

Interact with people, not machines! One the best tried-and-true methods of staying abreast in your field is through friends and acquaintances in the industry. It is difficult at best to try to master it all, so build a network of people in your field. You can actually learn a lot from them, and they can help grow your career.

Join User Groups

No amount of training can replace the value of becoming a member of a user group or special interest group (SIG). These associations offer individuals the best help and guidance found anywhere. Some of the largest IT user groups in the nation are Rocky Mountain Windows NT User Group in Denver, Colorado, and LANTUG, the Los Angeles NT Users Group. There are also SIGs within these groups such as the Visual C++ User Group and SQL Server. More information on user groups and SIGs can be found in Chapter 12.

Set Career Goals

If a manager or superior has the time or inclination, he or she should be helping you attain your career goals by providing you with the proper training and guidance. Unfortunately, many managers don't have the time or energy to look after a subordinate's career. Often it is up to the individual to set his own goals for a successful career. Anyone who is serious about his career development should set realistic goals from time to time.

Find a Mentor

This is one person often overlooked by IT professionals. With the busy, hectic lives that a typical developer leads, it's often difficult to find a particular individual for help and guidance with your career. Programmers often report to many different superiors because of downsizing and flatter management structures in organizations. Software engineering professionals need to actively pursue and find mentors to help them grow professionally. Start with the nearest manager or supervisor who you see eye to eye with.

Engagements for Microsoft Certified Solution Developers

Most software developers work on what is termed as a project. The project often has a leader who is called the technical lead or program manager, depending on the type of project the group is undertaking. The group is usually composed of three to five programmers/analysts who each specialize in a particular language and/or segment of the development process. For example, you may have one to two developers who code, one or two who design, another who tests and debugs the application, and yet another who writes the technical documentation for the product. Again, the division of labor depends on the size, scope, and type of software development work being performed by the group. Developers often work on site for the employer's clients or customers. Space is usually allotted for the developers at the client's place of business so that they can work closely with end users and attend meetings with management from time to time to make sure the project is on course and within budget.

Microsoft Certified Solution Developers also work on traditional systems integration projects within IT departments as well. The typical MCSD can find themselves in either context, especially if they are working for a large systems integrator or MSP. In either case, the software developer is expected to perform well in either environment and do so professionally.

Listed here are just some of the projects and/or components of a project an MCSD can be expected to work on.

Visual Basic Applications

The Visual Basic for Applications (VBA) developer works on projects such as screen development for back-end relational database management systems like Microsoft SQL Server and Microsoft Access. The VBA programmer/analyst (PA) may also work on the development of small control programs that tie Microsoft Office applications, like Access and Excel, together to create a small custom application. In addition, the VBA developer may write object linking and embedding (OLE) controls for use in a C/C++ application or full-blown Visual Basic application.

C/C++ Projects

C developers or programmers often work on many diverse projects ranging from subroutine development such as dynamic-link libraries (DLLs) to communications applications that utilize remote procedure calls or RPC. They may also develop full-blown applications that are designed for niche markets like the financial and insurance industries. Other projects that a C programmer/analyst may work on include shrink-wrapped applications for Windows 95 and Windows NT Workstation desktop markets. C/C++ is a very powerful programming language that can be used to develop programs for popular computing platforms like Windows NT and UNIX. Therefore, a programmer who specializes in C can expect to work on just about any type business or scientific application imaginable depending upon where they work.

ActiveX Controls

Many MCSDs are hard at work retooling existing applications for the Internet by developing ActiveX controls. ActiveX is basically OLE, which has be redesigned for developing distributed computing applications for the World Wide Web and intranets. Thousands of companies and organizations across the U.S. are extending their legacy applications to enable them to conduct business on the Web. Developers who specialize in Web site design and development can expect a very bright future, especially if their focus is ActiveX control development.

SQL Development

Projects that SQL programmers work on involve coding or scripting SQL statements for large databases. The projects themselves vary according to the application being developed. SQL Server is rapidly becoming important for handling transactions over the Internet because of its secure and robust processing capabilities. Many SQL programmers are developing SQL scripts that connect new and legacy databases to World Wide Web sites for all types of organizations around the world. SQL programming projects are not limited to the Web by any means. MCSDs also work as database administrators for large to medium-sized businesses that require constant modifications to applications that access a SQL database. Other SQL programmers work on projects like document imaging or banking applications for ATMs.

MS Access Projects

Microsoft Access's popularity with small- to medium-size businesses has led to a proliferation of opportunities for Access developers (see the job bank on the Access Developer Forum on the Microsoft Web site for an idea of the demand for Access programmers). Access projects are typically small by nature but can extend for months or even years depending on the number of individuals developing the application. In fact, the majority of vertical market Access applications that are developed are done by in-house IT professionals who are not even programmers by trade, such as software specialists and technically proficient staff members. Nevertheless, there are many programmers who make a living at developing applications for many different businesses and organizations on a contractor basis. Therefore, as with C programmers, the projects on which an Access developer may work can vary widely since Access is such a robust relational database management system for small- to medium-size businesses or departments at the enterprise level.

FoxPro Projects

While the level of projects or assignments for FoxPro developers is diminishing, there is still a huge installed base of Xbase applications in need of support by MCSDs and Xbase programmers alike. FoxPro developers work on myriad projects just as Access and C programmers do. However, they typically code in DOS or command-prompt environment. Projects typically range from small database development and maintenance to migration of existing data (export), from legacy apps to newer, faster graphical-based DBMSs like Access and SQL Server.

Testing and Debugging (Quality Assurance)

In the larger software houses or IT departments, developers often specialize on development processes like testing and debugging for a product or project. Quality assurance programmers run a particular application through its paces by stress testing the program to its limits. This process helps reveal any obvious or major flaws in the design and coding of the application being developed. Quality assurance technicians often use specialized tools that help them scrutinize code that may number in the millions of lines. Although testing and debugging help expose serious flaws in an application, no amount of testing can make an application foolproof.

Technical Documentation

Often programmers or developers who have excellent writing skills are encouraged to help write technical documentation for products and/or special projects. The documentation may be for the end user or it may be documentation for the actual code, depending on the situation.

This list is by no means comprehensive, but it does include a majority of the types of jobs and functions that an MCSD is capable of performing. Many smaller companies may require a developer to perform all of these tasks, while larger organizations may have many different software developers on staff tending to each of the areas outlined.

INTERVIEWS WITH MICROSOFT CERTIFIED SOLUTION DEVELOPERS IN THE FIELD

Given the diversity of jobs for MCPs in the field, this author has taken the liberty of interviewing a few MCSDs to find out just what they are up to in their profession. These are candid interviews with some of the more experienced software developers who are actively working on software projects and/or products.

INTERVIEW: PETER VOGEL, MCSD

We begin our first interview with Peter Vogel, an MCSD. He is the Applications Supervisor at Champion Road Machinery, which is located in Ontario, Canada.

Q: What is the nature of your work, duties and responsibilities? What do you do during an average work day?

A: This is a difficult question to answer because my job has changed radically since I started working on my certification two years ago. When I took my first test I was supervising a team of developers building LAN, client/server, and AS/400 applications for a heavy equipment manufacturer. In that job I spent about a third of my time writing code and another third exploring new technologies or consulting with users. The final third was spent managing employees, developing company IT strategy, and working with the company's departments to set priorities. It was a neat job because, while I could still write code (something I enjoy doing) and deliver applications, I was also having an impact on the way the department's work was done and the direction of the company. Getting the certification really

continued

continued

cemented my reputation at work as someone "who knows how this stuff works." It also helped me fill in some holes in my knowledge of the Microsoft tools and broadened and deepened my understanding of some of the fundamental principles that all this technology was based on. I also acted as a role model, leading one of my staff members to start seeking her certification.

At least in part because of the knowledge I acquired in getting certified, I started writing articles for various computer magazines. I think by now that I've written for almost every magazine that covers programming with VB and the Microsoft Office products (*Visual Basic Programmers' Journal, Smart Access, Visual Basic/Access Advisor/VBA Advisor,* etc.) and a couple of the business-oriented magazines (*Information Week* and *Datamation*). This, again, exposed me to another set of people and opportunities, which led me to presenting at a Visual Basic conference (VBTeach in Toronto, Ontario). Being able to put the MCSD at the end of my name was, I think, a big help, as people assumed that I wouldn't say anything obviously stupid in an article or presentation. It was also a minimum requirement for writing for *Microsoft Certified Professional,* which led to a contact with Macmillan Publishing asking if I was interested in participating in writing a book for its Que imprint.

Presenting at the conference was so much fun that, based on it (and 10 years of teaching night school), I applied to Learning Tree International to develop courses. They weren't interested in me for that but were keenly interested in having me teach – but they wanted me for six or more weeks of the year. Again, my certification assured them that I knew what I was talking about for a set of courses they needed instructors for (VB, Access, Microsoft Office). Part of the process of certifying to teach a course includes being interviewed by the course author. None of these interviews have been as grueling as the certification exam (and one author remarked that since I was certified, the interview wasn't going to be about my product knowledge).

Since I couldn't stay in my job and do the teaching, I quit and set up a consulting firm. Fortunately, I was immediately hired back for 52 weeks over two years by my old company. I also contacted a local software development firm about doing work for them and they not only wanted me on board but offered me a partnership. We're still working out how we'll work together.

What does my work day look like now? With my old employer we've changed to this new "consulting" relationship by eliminating most of the programming from my old job to concentrate on helping to shape strategy, developing staff members, exploring new tools, providing knowledge about new technologies, and setting department direction. I continue to write for the computer magazines but do it during the day instead of nights and weekends. One week a month I'm on the road, teaching for Learning Tree. I also spend time looking for a second major consulting client, finding ways to expand the writing side of the business, looking for a chance to present at one of the "name" conferences, and publicizing the business. (I'll be starting a one-page, monthly VBA e-mail newsletter this month; contact `peter.vogel@ odyssey.on.ca` for a free subscription.)

Q: Why did you decide to become an MCP?

A: I took my first exam because I was going to TechEd and they were offering certification exams for half-price. More as a lark than anything else I took the Access exam. I had done very little preparation because, after all, I had been using Access for over three years. Well, more by luck than smarts I squeaked through and passed the exam. That exam made me realize how much I didn't know about this product. I realized that anyone who did well on this exam would be someone who really knew the tool— someone who would be very valuable to any organization. I then explored the whole certification program and realized that this was true of the entire MCSD certification: Someone with this certification would really know something. So I put together a training plan to ensure that I would ace the next exams I took because I knew my stuff. And I did.

Q: What is your working environment like? Deadlines, stress, workflow, hours, etc.

A: Working for my old employer consisted of delivering applications as soon as we could while remaining responsive to our users (i.e., answering questions whenever the phone went off). I spent a lot of time either at my desk, at the desk of one of our users, or talking with the other members of the team. If I was at my desk I was mostly typing, either code or documents. About 50% of the coding work we did was maintenance: 50% of it with an indefinite deadline and 50% with a "we need it now" kind of deadline. In my new job I spend a lot more time talking to people or sitting in meetings, listening. Deadlines around deliverables are still tight. The teaching doesn't really have a deadline, but I'd better make sure that I'm in the classroom when I'm supposed to be. Deadlines around the article writing tend to be flexible with the smaller magazines and tighten up with the larger ones. I try to get any writing work done before it is expected. It gives me more time to polish or get it off my desk so that I can start a new project.

With sharing my resources among so many people, scheduling becomes important. I have to know what I'm doing when if I'm going to balance my family, my work, my training, and developing the company. I don't intend to miss

any commitments, and only good scheduling will prevent that. Fortunately, I have an excellent general manager (my wife, Jan).

Q: What do you like about this field?

A: The variety of stuff you can use and do. Using my career as an example: I'm creating client/server programs, shaping development techniques for an IT department, shaping IT strategy for a Volvo subsidiary, building/designing Intranet applications, playing with new tools, teaching, writing articles ...

In the last two months I learned about HTML-Help (so I could write an article on it), implemented it on an intranet I'm building for my major client, and rolled it into a class I was teaching on VB5. I'm part of the Microsoft beta program and got to work with VB5 two months before it was generally available. That set me up to teach classes on VB5 the week it came out. I'm also reviewing software for various magazines, so I am constantly getting new toys that I can use to build new applications and deepen my understanding of how all this technology works. I meet a huge number of people in the classes I teach, from private industry to utility companies to the military to not-for-profit organizations. Thanks to the articles I've written, I get e-mail from people in the Ukraine, Crete, and Korea; one person at a candy company I helped sent me 25 pounds of chocolate. If I can expand my client base the same way, I'll be very pleased.

Q: What kind of person do you feel would do well in this job?

A: Smart people who like variety and aren't afraid of learning new things (or just trying new things). People who can work well with other people will really succeed. By that I mean the ability to really listen deeply to other people and understand what they want and need. If you can

continued

continued

leave yourself at the door to concentrate on what's important to the other person (in any activity you are engaged in), you're halfway there. If you can then bring to bear all your knowledge, experience, smarts, humor, and whatever resources you have, you can do anything. I really believe that you can have whatever you want if you help enough people get what they want.

Q: What are the advantages/disadvantages of your job as an MCP?

A: Advantages/disadvantages really depend on what your point of view is. One person's sushi is another person's cold, raw fish, after all. If you are looking for a job where you can learn one set of technical skills and stay with them forever, this isn't the life for you. Of course, I'm not sure that life exists anywhere anymore. If you are a person who likes to learn new things this is a great job.

If you want a very regular job with predictable activities, the career I've followed is obviously a poor choice. On the other hand, if you enjoy a variety of activities, a certain number of surprises, and the opportunity to do new things, then the water's fine.

I also like my work and that's good because I probably do too much of it. I think that's the really important thing: Get into doing something you like and then you don't mind doing it. That makes the question of the advantages/disadvantages of a job disappear. It would be like asking, "So, what are the advantages/disadvantages of living?"

Q: What knowledge, skills (for success), and abilities are required for this type of work?

A: I don't think I've mentioned the ability to learn and, especially, to learn quickly on your own. I can, and that's been a tremendous advantage to me. If you've got the commitment to listen to people and the desire to learn, nothing beats a solid technical understanding of the tools that people want you to use. The trick is to find a toolset you feel comfortable using that matches what people are currently demanding. I'm keeping my head up about Java, for instance, and have started working with intranet applications. There's lots of stuff I've explored that didn't pan out (AI leaps to mind, for instance), but the commitment I made to Microsoft's application development tools has paid off handsomely. The ability to talk to people in their own terms is another valuable asset, but I think that falls out of listening to them. If not, a course in teaching adults can do a world of good in this area. It did for me, at any rate.

Another worthwhile ability is to be able to figure out some way to get paid for what you want to do anyway. The software reviewing I do, for instance, means I get paid for working with lots of different software packages. I'd probably pay to do that (don't tell the magazine editors). Also, finding ways to get paid to learn is a useful ability. By teaching at a community college I was able to suggest new courses to them about stuff I wanted to learn. I would use the fee for the course to pay for my training and then pass that on to the students. I did some low-fee work for not-for-profit organizations on the understanding that I didn't know what I was doing (which is why my fee was so low), but I would guarantee them a finished product. While the money wasn't much, it paid for my training. And so on.

Finally, you've got to have an unswerving dedication to putting your customers' needs first. If you aren't going give your customers more than they want then don't start. Any particular skill set, knowledge base, or technical knowledge will be out of date tomorrow and so it isn't really a key to success. Four years ago I was doing well because I was a wizard PL/1 and Rexx mainframe coder. Eight years ago I was making a very good living as a wizard DL/1 database guru. And so it goes. For eight years I got by without knowing much about the businesses I was supplying services to. Now I consider it essential, but the businesses I'm working for now are very different from the ones I worked for three years ago.

I think a fundamental understanding of how computers and operating systems work won't do you any harm, but I'm not sure how much good it does. I think it does me a world of good, but I may just be justifying the time and energy I spent on it. When I'm hiring someone, I hire someone smart first, someone who knows the toolset I'm using second, and someone with a computer science degree third.

Q: What are the advancement opportunities and outlook for this field?

A: Excellent, I think. There's still a North American shortage for application developers. You can see that in the rush to outsource, to buy third-party packages, and to develop more powerful tools for end users. I think that the more powerful tools for users just frees us developers up to work on more interesting things. While I don't see this letting up in the next 10 years, I do think fewer and fewer of us will be working for the companies running our code, and more and more of us will be working for organizations supplying IT services to those companies. I think that's too bad, but I also think business will need more and more of us every year. When you have eliminated the impossible, whatever remains, however improbable, must be the truth.

INTERVIEW: DAVE HARPER, SENIOR TECHNOLOGIST AT TARGETED SYSTEMS DEVELOPMENT

The next interview is with Dave Harper. He is a Senior Technologist at Targeted Systems Development in Ossining, New York. He has broad experience in multiple hardware and software platforms, including hands-on experience in all phases of client/server project design, staffing, software/hardware selection, and programming.

Q: What is the nature of your work? What do you do during an average working day?

A: I run a small software development, consulting business (Targeted Systems Development Inc.) that specializes in leading-edge, Internet/intranet and client/server applications. We use JAD (Joint Application Development) and RAD (Rapid Application Development)

techniques to ensure our projects are completed on time and as defect-free as possible.

My daily duties vary but almost always include a combination of the following activities:

- Software development
- On-site
- Off-site
- Looking for skilled senior technologists to work with me (they're not plentiful!)
- Seeking new projects and clients
- Reading computer-related and business publications
- Networking with business clients and technologists

continued

continued

Rapid Application Develop-ment, or RAD, is a term commonly used in programming circles that refers to rapid prototyping of application design. It is an iterative process of design and analysis done in conjunction with programming tools such as CASE, Visual Basic, and/or DBMSs. It allows developers to design, code, and deliver applications faster than through typical manual structured design methods.

Joint Application Development or JAD is a requirements-definition and screen design methodology in which end-users, management, and developers attend highly focused meetings to work out systems details.

The net effect is to produce a system or application, faster, cheaper, and more precise than could be achieved by traditional systems analysis and design methods.

Q: Why did you decide to become an MCP?

A: Several nationally recognized certifications are available to technologists. My feeling is that these certifications beneficially serve those technologists who become certified, the firms that employ these technologists, and the organizations that create and sponsor the certification exams. From the applicant's viewpoint, certification provides an objective means of judging his knowledge compared to that of his peers. Certification standards that are published by sponsoring organizations normally provide a bibliography and recommended coursework for passing a particular exam, thus giving an applicant an excellent educational framework.

Firms that employee certified technologists recognize that these technologists have at least a minimal level of training and experience. Certification also indicates that a technologist has the dedication and motivation necessary to spend time outside normal work hours studying and reviewing course material to pass required exams. Sponsoring organizations can ensure that those who claim to be are successful technologists.

It's also important to note that some of the most successful, creative people in this field come from somewhat unusual backgrounds. I, for instance, started out as a history and philosophy major. I think this field requires a lot more creativity than the average person is aware of, and as a result some people with unexpected backgrounds end up being very successful software developers.

Q: What are the advantages/disadvantages of your job as an MCP?

A: I enjoy running a small business. It's fun performing a variety of tasks and meeting interesting business leaders and technologists. The MCP is a designation that carries some weight with potential clients. And the MCSD certification that I now hold is even more valuable because there are so few who have been successful in passing the necessary exams. I really haven't found any disadvantage to this designation other than I now get called by so many head hunters it's ridiculous.

WHAT YOU CAN EXPECT TO EARN

While the MCSD is commanding ever-higher salaries, which is due largely to the popularity of Microsoft technology, all MCSDs are not necessarily enjoying increases in pay. Salaries vary widely by region of the U.S., as denoted in Table 6-1. Salary bases also vary among employers, so it all depends on whom you are working for and where your employer is located, as well as years of experience. Tables 6-1 and 6-2 show salary ranges.

TABLE 6-1 MCSD SALARY RANGES BY REGION	
REGION	*SALARY RANGE*
Northeast	$65K–$125K
Midatlantic	$75K–$95K
South	$45K–$85K
West	$65K–$98K
Midwest	$60K–$85K

TABLE 6-2 MCSD SALARY RANGE BY EMPLOYER TYPES	
EMPLOYER TYPE	*SALARY RANGE*
Private company	$45K–$125K
Government	$25K–$65K
MSPs	$60K–$98K

IT Recruiters, Inc. (http://www.itrecruitersinc.com) conducted the salary survey informally and at random. As indicated in Tables 6-1 and 6-2, the MCSD salaries can vary widely by region, country, and employer, and of course years of experience.

WHERE TO FIND A JOB

Although there are many jobs for MCSDs in the U.S. and abroad, many of them are not so easily found. Compiled here are some of the major sources for jobs on the Internet that reside in job and resume banks. Their names and Web addresses (URLs) are listed for your convenience:

- Yahoo! Job Guide—www.yahoo.com./business/employment
- IT Specialist.com—www.itspecialist.com
- Monster Board—www.monsterboard.com
- Career Path—www.careerpath.com
- Career Magazine — www.careermag.com/index.text.html
- Online Career Center—www.occ.com/occ/
- Career Web—www.cWeb.com
- Job Web—www.jobWeb.com
- Career Net—www.careers.org
- The Riley Guide—www.jobtrak.com/jobguide/
- Job Bank USA—www.jobbankusa.com
- FedWorld—www.fedworld.gov

The job and resume banks listed constitute an ever-growing presence on the Web for opportunities in IT. However, the Web is not by any means the only source for jobs in the IT industry. Listed here are some of the more traditional sources for job information and opportunities.

Newspapers, Periodicals

While not the best method for job hunting, many individuals prefer this method of searching for employment to any other. Note: Many of the trade magazines and newspapers are online now and offer a much faster and more sophisticated way of hunting for jobs through the use of search engines on their Web sites.

Networking

Socialize with your peers as often as you can. Friends and associates in your field can often be the best source for a good-paying job. Also, don't forget about trade fairs; they are an excellent way to meet new people in your field.

Informational Interviewing

Ask for an interview with some of the biggest companies in the IT industry and you would be surprised by the response you get—usually positive. This method of interviewing can sometimes lead to an immediate job offer.

Although there are many methods of job hunting available to IT professionals, none beats the often free and easy access to jobs on the World Wide Web. Many employment Web sites are now becoming specialized and are catering to niche job markets, the way IT Specialist does. The IT Specialist Web site focuses entirely on MCPs. Newly certified network engineers, software specialists, trainers, and developers can post their resumes on the Web site, as can seasoned veterans of the MCP program.

KEY POINT SUMMARY

In summary, this chapter covered in detail the benefits and responsibilities of the MCSD. In this chapter you also learned of the various job titles that an MCSD can expect to hold in the IT industry. In addition, MCSD salaries were shown based on geographic areas of the U.S. This chapter also included interviews with MCSDs who are actively working in the IT field. Finally, the chapter discussed ways that a Solution Developer can keep his career on track and stay abreast with the latest developments in his profession.

- As an MCSD you can expect high wages, recognition as an IT professional, and considerable autonomy in the workplace.
- Being an MCSD requires excellent analytical skills and good math skills and be creative.

- As an MCSD you'll typically code applications in Microsoft Visual C++, Visual Basic, SQL Server, and Access.

- Most MCSDs are employed as programmer/analysts, Webmasters and technical leads, and program managers.

Opportunities for Microsoft Certified Professionals

While opportunities abound for those Microsoft Certified Professionals (MCPs) seeking full-time employment, even greater fortune awaits those individuals striking it out on their own. Be it the role of independent contractor or the entrepreneur, more and more high tech professionals are going it alone, and for good reasons.

With the corporate downsizing in the early '90s, many information technology (IT) professionals were furloughed or laid off. That set the stage for what is now one of the greatest surges of entrepreneurism seen in this century. Many of those workers who experienced the unsettling world of unemployment were determined not to let it happen again.

With the economy out of the doldrums, many IT professionals still opt for being their own bosses. These high tech professionals are choosing to set their own destinies as career professionals, largely because of the relative security of the booming business worldwide. Never has the IT sector provided such opportunity for IT professionals. There are many sources for subcontracting work and there are many effective methods for finding that work provided you have the skills and ambition to see the work through completion.

This section of *MCSE Career Microsoft®!* provides valuable information on how to find work as an independent consultant. This section also discusses the many opportunities open to MSP value added resellers (VARs) who are either just starting out as a small business or to those contemplating such a venture in the IT business.

MCPS Career Track Revealed

About Chapter 7

I n this chapter you will discover how a Microsoft Certified Product Specialist (MCPS) works as a professional in the world of information technology (IT). You will also learn through interviews with real MCPSs the responsibilities and issues one can expect to encounter working as a software specialist. In addition, this chapter discusses the expected salary ranges for MCPSs throughout the U.S., as well as where and how to find a job as a software specialist.

BECOMING A MICROSOFT CERTIFIED PRODUCT SPECIALIST: RECOGNITION AND REWARDS

Opportunities for MCPSs are wide open. Never before has the MCPS enjoyed such a wealth of job openings from employers in the U.S. and Canada. The MCPS can expect to find ample work well into the next century. On the other hand, MCPSs can also expect to be challenged with duties by their employers in keeping up with IT. As a software specialist you will have to keep pace with the extraordinary growth of Internet and intranet systems technology. When you're working as an MCPS, your employer will expect above-average performance on the job and with your career overall. You will be expected to maintain your career by attending trade shows, technical seminars and hands-on training, all while doing your job.

However, the financial rewards for becoming an MCPS are well worth it, especially if you are on the path to becoming an MCSE or MCSD. Average salaries for MCPSs range anywhere from $45K to $125K, depending on the capacity in which you are employed as an MCPS, where you live in the U.S. or abroad, and years of experience. Every aspect of the MCPS career track is discussed in detail to give you a better understanding of the opportunities and responsibilities of the MCPS.

One important distinction about the MCPS track as opposed to the Solution Developer or Systems Engineer path must be understood by prospective Microsoft Certified Specialists (MCPs). The MCPS track is actually an entry-level designation or title for the MCPs. Anyone who wants to become an MCT, MCSE, and/or MCSD must first become an MCPS by passing one of the core exams required by the MCP program. So while the average product specialist is usually on his or her way to becoming a certified instructor, systems engineer, or software developer, this is not always the case. Some individuals may elect to stay an MCPS and specialize in Exchange and/or the Internet by becoming an Exchange Server and Internet Product Specialist.

THE BENEFITS OF BECOMING A MICROSOFT CERTIFIED PRODUCT SPECIALIST

As you can determine from the previous introduction, the benefits of becoming an MCPS can be both tangible and intangible. The benefits are obvious: good pay, a certificate with Bill Gates' signature, and cash bonuses for signing on with a top-notch outfit. However, it's the intangible benefits that many IT professionals look for in a job as opposed to just pay and bonuses. Software or product specialists in particular look for challenging IT environments where can they get their hands on the latest applications software, such as Microsoft BackOffice and Office. They also look for many other hidden benefits that may or may not be so obvious to the novice who is just entering the field of software support or help desk management.

Some of the major benefits awaiting the MCPS are listed here.

Challenging Work Environment

Anyone who follows today's headlines is aware of the enormous pace that IT is currently undergoing, especially with respect to the software applications and the World Wide Web. Microsoft Certified Product Specialists are expected to keep pace with emerging general office automation and peripheral technologies, and in doing so they reap the rewards both professionally and financially.

Autonomous Working Environment

Software specialists by the very nature of their jobs are typically required to work under their own direction. Local- and wide-area networks, as well as individual workstations, are typically distributed throughout an organization. Therefore, software specialists can easily find themselves working alone in many instances. For some individuals this is an added bonus of the job—not having someone looking over your shoulder all the time.

Travel

Depending on whether you like to travel or not, software specialists are typically required to do some light travel, especially if they are working for one of the larger Microsoft Solution Providers (MSPs) or a Fortune 500 company. Today's MCPSs can easily find themselves all over the globe performing a variety of IT support tasks. Help desk support professionals often support as many as 500 individuals in one particular organization or branch office with the aid of help desk tools and support mechanisms.

Work with Cutting-Edge Technology

Software specialists who work for MSPs in particular can expect to work with most of Microsoft's latest systems technology. All MSPs are participants in Microsoft's beta evaluation program. A systems professional working for an MSP will naturally get advanced exposure to the latest systems from Microsoft. Some of the Fortune 500 companies are also members of Microsoft's software beta program, so software specialists at those organizations have the opportunity to gain advance knowledge of the software applications and operating systems coming out of Microsoft.

Skills in High Demand

With the immense growth in the demand for MCPs, specifically MCPSs, many software specialists can expect rewarding careers, both financially and professionally. Salaries for MCPSs are above average throughout the U.S. and abroad. Also, with the MCPSs skills in high demand, MCPSs maintain a high level of job security.

Management Opportunities

Microsoft Certified Product Specialists who are serious about their careers and continue with their professional development by staying abreast with IT can expect a promotion into the ranks of management. Some of the management positions that an MCPS can aspire to are help desk manager, MIS operations manager, and training manager.

HOW TO KEEP YOUR CAREER IN FOCUS

Setting career goals and keeping them in focus can be very difficult to do in addition to raising a child and keeping your finances in good shape. However, career planning isn't as difficult as you may think, provided you go about it earnestly and stick to it. Listed here are just a few of the steps you can take to enhance your career opportunities, both professionally and financially.

Read Trade Journals

Magazines that focus on professional development, such as *Windows NT*, *BackOffice*, and *Microsoft Certified Professional*, offer readers the latest news and information on a wide variety of topics concerning software specialists. Many of the trade journals are now online and offer viewers up-to-date information on technological developments, in addition to interactive forums such as chats and mailing lists.

Attend Technical Seminars

Some of the best technical seminars are held annually by Microsoft. Developer Days and TechEd are two of the largest conferences held in the U.S. for developers and engineers, respectively. You can find more information on these two conferences in subsequent chapters.

Continue Your Education

Microsoft Authorized Technical Education Centers (ATECs) and Authorized Academic Training Partners (AATPs) are excellent sources for hands-on technical training. They are located throughout the world and on the Internet's World Wide Web. In fact, Microsoft Certified Trainers versed in the latest systems and applications from Microsoft teach Microsoft Official Curriculum sessions in classroom settings as well as online via the Internet through ATECs and AATPs.

 concept link **For more information on ATECs and AATPs, see Chapter 3.**

Network with Peers

Interact with people, not machines! One of the best tried-and-true methods of staying abreast in your field is through friends and acquaintances. Professional associates can often provide valuable tips on where to find information critical to your success as an IT expert. Timing is everything, and tips can be the best source of leads to professional development. It is difficult at best to try to master the field of software, so build a network of people in your field—you would be surprised how much you can learn from them.

Join User Groups

No amount of training can replace the value of becoming a member of a user group or special interest group (SIG). These associations offer individuals the best help and guidance in the IT field anywhere on the planet. Two of the largest IT associations and user groups in the nation are Rocky Mountain Windows NT User Group in Denver, Colorado, and LANTUG (Los Angeles NT Users Group).out of Santa Monica, California. There are also SIGs within these groups such as the Exchange Specialist Special Interest Group and Internet Systems Special Interest Group. More information on user groups and SIGs can be found in Chapter 12.

Set Career Goals

If a manager or superior has the time or inclination, he or she should be helping you attain your career goals by providing you with the proper training and guidance. Unfortunately, managers often don't have the time and energy to look after a subordinate's career. Often it is up to the individual to set his goals for a successful career. Anyone who is serious about his career development should set realistic goals from time to time and stick to them.

Find a Mentor

This is one person often overlooked by IT professionals. With the busy, hectic lives that a typical software or computer specialist leads, it's often difficult to pair with one particular individual for help and guidance with one's career. Software specialists often report to many different superiors because of downsizing and flatter management structures in organizations. As a result, they need to actively pursue and find mentors to help them grow professionally. Start with the nearest manager or supervisor who you see eye to eye with.

ASSIGNMENTS THAT A MICROSOFT CERTIFIED PRODUCT SPECIALIST CAN EXPECT TO WORK ON

Most software specialists work on what are termed assignments. Assignments often entail anything from desktop operating system support for a user workstation to individualized training for an end user of Microsoft Office. However, as noted in the previous section, an MCPS can potentially work on a myriad of projects in IT depending on the goals of the individual. For practical reasons, however, the focus of this chapter is on the individual who wishes to remain an MCPS.

The MCPS can also work on traditional systems integration projects within IT departments as well. The typical MCPS can find himself in either context, especially if he is working for a large systems integrator or an MSP In either case, the software specialist is expected to perform well in either environment and do so professionally.

The MCPS is typically called on to perform a multitude of tasks, which may or may not involve pure software technical support. In fact, the MCPS can rightfully expect to be asked by his employer to do hands-on manual labor in addition to his normal software support duties. Unlike in programming, where you have well-defined curriculum, in software support services there are many gray areas with regard to duties and responsibilities.

Microsoft Certified Product Specialists also work on traditional systems integration projects within IT departments as well. The typical MCPS can find himself in either context, especially if he is working for a large systems integrator or an MSP. In either case, the developer is expected to perform well in either environment and do so professionally.

Listed here are just some of the projects and/or components of a project a dedicated MCPS can be expected to work on.

Local Area Network Installation and Configuration

Installing network operating system (NOS) software and configuring the server. This also includes loading desktop operating systems software such as Windows 95 and Windows NT Workstation. Additional duties may include configuring printers, faxes, and scanners.

Wide Area Network Installation and Support

Installing and configuring specialized computers known as routers for internetworking, intranets, and the Internet. Other duties may include configuring CSU/DSUs and ISDN equipment for specialized telecommunications services.

Internet/Intranet Server Installation and Configuration

The installation of Internet and intranet Web servers for hypertext transfer protocol (HTTP) for Web hosting, as well as internal intranets and/or extranets. For the client side, installation of a Web browser such as Microsoft Internet Explorer or Netscape Navigator.

Help Desk Support

Microsoft Certified Product Specialists help support Microsoft's full line of Office and BackOffice applications for Windows 95 and NT. Typical support duties include end user support of Windows printer, fax, and e-mail problems that occur on occasion. The MCPS may also support end users with computer cabling, fax, and modem hardware-related problems. Additionally, they may assist end users with macro development for Microsoft Word and Excel (and other applications like Lotus 1-2-3, Quattro Pro, etc.), system configuration, and software upgrades as a help desk technician.

Messaging Systems Support

Microsoft Certified Product Specialists such as Microsoft Exchange Server Specialists help support Microsoft's advanced messaging platform at both the user level and server systems level. They help set up and configure the mail system client on desktop systems such as Windows 95 and Windows NT Workstation. On the server side they maintain and configure distribution lists, public folders, and message queues for the entire network.

Network Maintenance (Upgrades, Patches and Fixes)

Upgrading NOS software and workstation clients on the network by applying version upgrades and patches or fixes for bugs in the software.

Telecommunications

Installing and configuring fax/modem cards or modem banks for remote access services. Additional duties may include installing network hubs and computer-telephony equipment such as a phone system PBX interface for network servers.

Backups

Performing crucial backups to all mission-critical applications and data on a regular and prescribed basis.

Training

Many MCPSs are employed as software specialists/trainers. Since they are certified experts in a particular operating systems and/or application, they are usually called upon to perform training. As trainers or instructors, they can train an individual one-on-one, in-house or off-site, as well as teach courses in a traditional classroom setting.

This list is by no means comprehensive, but it does include a majority of the types of jobs and functions that an MCPS is capable of performing. Many smaller companies may require an MCPS or software specialist to perform all of the jobs mentioned, while larger organizations may have many different software specialists on staff tending to each of the areas outlined.

INTERVIEWS WITH MICROSOFT CERTIFIED PROFESSIONALS IN THE FIELD

Given the diversity of jobs for MCPs in the field, this author has taken the liberty of interviewing a few MCPSs to find out just what they are up to in their profession. These are candid interviews with some of the more experienced software specialists who are actively working on IT assignments throughout the world.

INTERVIEW: GREG BROWN, NETWORK SYSTEMS ENGINEER

We begin our first interview with Greg Brown. Greg specializes in large-scale BackOffice projects for mid- to large-size companies. He is presently working on a development project using SQL Server and Visual Basic. He is currently an MCPS and is pursuing the Microsoft Certified Systems Engineer certificate.

Q: What is the nature of your work, duties, and responsibilities? What do you do during an average work day?

A: I am presently working on a software development project that is the first of its type for one of the Big Six accounting firms. We are using a Microsoft Visual Basic front-end with Microsoft SQL Server as the back-end database running on Windows NT Server 4.0. My role is to coordinate the database design and implementation, develop specifications for network requirements, and manage the implementation of the system into the network environment.

Q: Why did you decide to become an MCP?

A: I was working as a help desk coordinator and desperately wanted to move on to a more challenging position. I saw the MCP program as a way to prove my qualifications to an employer who might otherwise not give my resume a second look. I have been very satisfied

continued

continued

with the industry recognition of Microsoft certification as it has developed over the past few years and plan to continue my pursuit of the Microsoft Certified Systems Engineer and Microsoft Certified Solution Developer certifications.

Q: What is your working environment like? Deadlines, stress, workflow, hours, etc.

A: The current project I am working on has some strict deadlines that cause some stress but the challenge is a welcome change compared to other positions I have held. The hours have been fairly fixed at around 40 to 45 per week, with little or no weekend work.

Q: What do you like about this field?

A: I like the challenge posed by the variety of projects that Microsoft certification allows me to work on. If I want to learn about a new type of technology, the market for certified professionals has allowed me the option to do just that.

Q: What kind of person do you feel would do well in this job?

A: I feel that in order to excel in this type of work a person has to have the desire to continually enhance skills and have an intense desire to learn. I spend at least 10 hours a week reading industry magazines, newsletters, and books, in addition to study hours for whatever certification exam I am pursuing so that I can keep in tune with the current technology.

Q: What are the advantages/disadvantages of your job as an MCP?

A: The most obvious advantages are the industry recognition and the pay rates that go along with it. A disadvantage is that trends in technology move so fast that you have to make a sizable commitment in personal time in order to keep up. It is difficult to strike a good balance between the career and personal life, but I am finding that it can be done.

Q: What knowledge, skills (for success), and abilities are required for this type of work?

A: I believe that a background in business, whether it is from prior work experience or formal education, can be a great advantage in this type of work. If you are able to identify opportunities where a business might apply technology to make a process more streamlined or make workers more efficient, you will advance much further and faster than if you only know how to program using the latest language and don't like working with people.

Q: What are the advancement opportunities and outlook for this field?

A: I know from my own experience that the advancement opportunities for this field are excellent. With the projected movement to Microsoft solutions over the next three to five years there will be a huge market for those with the desire and commitment to excel.

INTERVIEW: DAVID FITZPATRICK, PRESIDENT OF CLIENT/SERVER SYSTEMS, INC.

Our next interview is with David Fitzpatrick. David is President of Client/Server Systems, Inc., located in Tyson Corner, Virginia. David specializes in Microsoft BackOffice and Windows 95. He has extensive experience in integrating legacy systems, whether those systems are mainframe, UNIX, or NetWare, using the latest technologies in the form of Microsoft Windows NT, Microsoft BackOffice, and Microsoft Windows 95.

Q: What is the nature of your work, duties, and responsibilities? What do you do during an average work day?

A: I am president and owner of an independent computer consulting firm specializing in Windows NT and the BackOffice. I am certified in Windows NT (both Server and Workstation), Exchange and Windows 95. My average engagement lasts from three to eight months and is always targeted to Windows NT and the enterprise.

My current contract is with a very large U.S. government institution. I am in charge of rolling out NT 4.0 Servers with SMS and Exchange 5.0. We are in the architecture and planning stages, so a lot of my day-to-day activities deal with high-level network design, etc.

Q: Why did you decide to become an MCP?

A: I bet my business on the promise of NT back in mid-1993, after spending 10 or so years in the IBM mainframe environment. NT has come a long way since the NT 3.1 days, and based on my inside view of how Microsoft operates, I see no end to the NT progress. If you tell a client you know something (i.e., NT), you should know it cold! Certification coupled with years of both NT and Enterprise experience is the only way I know of to virtually guarantee a client that he is getting the most bang for the buck.

Q: What is your working environment like? Deadlines, stress, workflow, hours, etc.

A: There are deadlines to meet in all professions, and being an independent consultant is no different. First and foremost there are project deadlines. Typically when a customer or client signs off on a contract for system installation he wants it implemented *yesterday*. This puts an immediate and sometimes immense burden on the company and/or individuals responsible for the implementation. Second, once a project begins there is no stopping until you're finished. This may seem obvious, but under a typical network operating system upgrade or migration, the client will not tolerate any downtime whatsoever. In other words, you often end up working long hours (including weekends) until the project is successfully completed.

Q: What do you like about this field?

A: The field of IT is always changing and *especially* for NT/BackOffice professionals. Microsoft is a virtual powerhouse of software development. It is continuously adding new features and subsystems to the Window NT Server platform, especially with regard to the Internet. As most IT professionals are aware, Microsoft is playing catch-up with the Internet. As a result, it is releasing upgrades, enhancements, and new applications for the Windows NT almost monthly. Keeping up with the stream of new products and enhancements from Microsoft is very exciting, albeit exhausting at times.

Q: What kind of person do you feel would do well in this job?

A: A self-starter. Someone who is capable of taking the initiative and seeing a task or job to completion. So much of the work that an MCPS does is done autonomously. You have to

continued

continued

be able to take the bull by horns and go with it. There is little room for slackers in this business. The person must also be a good listener and be able to pay close attention to details. Finally, an MCPS should also be very methodical and carefully plan all aspects of engagement. A haphazard approach to systems engineering and implementation will inevitably cause immense problems down the line. The MCPS must be thorough and methodical in his approach to any engagement.

Q: What are the advantages/disadvantages of your job as an MCP?

A: Some of the advantages of being an MCP are esteem and earning potential. MCPs are becoming more and more recognized as experts in the field of Microsoft technology. Consequently, MCPs are able to command higher salaries than their Novell counterparts, which is due in part to Microsoft's prodigious hold on the networking and desktop operating system market.

Some of the disadvantages of being a computer professional and self-employed are the long work hours and sporadic income respectively. As an MCPS I often work long hours, 50-60 hours per week. As a self-employed businessman I enjoy a higher-than-average hourly income as an MCPS, but there can be periods of unemployment. However, given the immense demand for Microsoft BackOffice products at this time, slack times are few and far between.

Q: What knowledge, skills (for success), and abilities are required for this type of work?

A: Experience, experience, and experience! Also, a little formal training never hurt. It cannot be emphasized enough that in order to be a successful MCPS you must gain as much experience as possible. All the classroom instruction in the world will *not* prepare you for the myriad of tasks and issues that pop up on a typical engagement. Get experience whenever and wherever you can. Experience is so essential to becoming a successful MCPS that without it you're doomed to failure as a computer professional.

A good place to begin getting experience is a training course that offers hands-on computer labs in addition to traditional instruction. Another excellent means of getting experience is to set up your own lab at home and start with the basics. Build the system from scratch and then break it down again, repeating the process until you have it down pat.

Q: What are the advancement opportunities and outlook for this field?

A: Mind-boggling! It's true. The opportunities available to MCPs are innumerable. Again, the demand for Microsoft products is so high throughout the world that MCPs are being sought after in every conceivable industry and organization. As a result, MCPs can pick and choose their employers!

The MCP program is fairly nascent when compared to Novell's CNE and CNA programs. As with any new and emerging field there is usually a wealth of opportunities. The opportunities open to an MCP's growth are both financial and professional. As an MCP, professional opportunities exist for individuals who are interested in management and entrepreneurship. From a financial perspective, MCP wages or income is rising rapidly due to a shortage of qualified and experienced MCPs throughout the IT industry.

WHAT YOU CAN EXPECT TO EARN

While the MCPS is commanding ever-higher salaries, which is due largely to the popularity of Microsoft technology, all MCPS's are not necessarily enjoying increases in pay. Salaries vary widely by region of the U.S., as shown in Table 7-1. Salary bases also vary among employers, so it all depends on whom you are working for and where your employer is located, as well as years of experience. Tables 7-1 and 7-2 show salary ranges.

TABLE 7-1 MCPS SALARY RANGES BY REGION	
REGION	*SALARY RANGE*
Northeast	$65K – $125K
Midatlantic	$75K – $95K
South	$45K – $85K
West	$65K – $98K
Midwest	$60K – $85K

TABLE 7-2 MCPS SALARY RANGE BY EMPLOYER TYPES	
EMPLOYER TYPE	*SALARY RANGE*
Private company	$45K – $125K
Government	$25K – $65K
MSPs	$60K – $98K

IT Recruiters, Inc. (`http://www.itrecruitersinc.com`)conducted the salary survey informally and at random. As indicated in the tables, MCPS salaries can vary widely by region, country and employer and, of course, years of experience.

WHERE TO FIND A JOB

Although there are many jobs for MCPSs in the U.S. and abroad, many of them are not so easily found. Compiled here are some of the major sources for jobs on the Internet that reside in job and resume banks. Their names and Web addresses are listed for your convenience.

- Yahoo! Job Guide—`www.yahoo.com./business/employment`
- IT Specialist.com—`www.itspecialist.com`
- Monster Board—`www.monsterboard.com`
- Career Path—`www.careerpath.com`
- Career Magazine—`www.careermag.com/index.text.html`
- Online Career Center—`www.occ.com/occ/`
- Career Web—`www.cWeb.com`
- Job Web—`www.jobWeb.com`
- Career Net—`www.careers.org`
- The Riley Guide—`www.jobtrak.com/jobguide/`
- Job Bank USA—`www.jobbankusa.com`
- FedWorld—`www.fedworld.gov`

The job and resume banks listed constitute an ever-growing presence on the Web for opportunities in IT. However, the Web is not by any means the only source for jobs in the IT industry. Listed here are some of the more traditional sources for job information and opportunities.

Newspapers, Periodicals

While not the best method for job hunting, many individuals prefer this method of searching for employment to any other. Note: Many of the trade magazines and newspapers are online now and offer a much faster and more sophisticated way of hunting for jobs through the use of search engines on their Web sites.

Networking

Socialize with your peers as often as you can. Friends and associates in your field can often be the best source for a good-paying job. Also, don't forget about trade fairs; they are an excellent way to meet new people in your field.

Informational Interviewing

Ask for an interview with some of the biggest companies in the IT industry and you would be surprised by the response you get—usually positive. This method of interviewing can sometimes lead to an immediate job offer.

Although there are many methods of job hunting available to IT professionals, none beats the often free and easy access to jobs on the World Wide Web. Many employment Web sites are now becoming specialized and are catering to niche job markets the way IT Specialist does. The IT Specialist Web site focuses entirely on MCPs. Newly certified network engineers, software specialists, trainers, and developers can post their resumes on the Web site, as can seasoned veterans of the MCP program.

KEY POINT SUMMARY

In summary, this chapter covered the benefits of becoming an MCPS, such as good pay, travel, and a challenging work environment. In addition, the chapter enlightened you on the types and kinds of roles an MCPS can expect to play within organizations and IT shops the world over. The chapter also discussed how to keep your professional career in focus by networking with peers and reading trade journals relating to the IT industry. Finally, the chapter discussed methods of searching for jobs as an MCPS and what you can expect to earn as an MCP.

○ The MCPS jobs provide good salaries, challenging workplaces, and a great deal of autonomy as information technology professionals.

○ As an MCPS you must keep your career in focus by reading industry trade journals, networking with their peers, and joining user groups and trade associations.

○ As an MCPS you can work as a help desk specialist, LAN technician, messaging systems specialist, computer specialist, or many other specialist titles.

○ Most MCPSs can find work through a multitude of sources both online and in the print media, such as newspapers and Web sites, as well as through informational interviewing.

MCT Career Track Revealed

About Chapter 8

In this chapter you will discover how a Microsoft Certified Trainer (MCT) works as a professional in the world of information technology (IT). You will also learn through interviews with real MCTs the responsibilities and issues one can expect to encounter working as an instructor. In addition, this chapter discusses the expected salary ranges for MCTs throughout the U.S., as well as where and how to find a job as an instructor.

INTRODUCTION

Opportunities for MCTs are wide open. Never before has the MCT enjoyed such a wealth of job openings from employers the world over. The MCT can expect to find ample professional opportunities well into the next century. On the other hand, MCTs can also expect to be challenged with duties imposed by their employers or clients in keeping up with IT. As an instructor you will have to keep pace with the extraordinary growth of Internet and intranet systems technology. When you're working as an MCT, your employer will expect above-average performance on the job and with your career overall. You will be expected to maintain your career by attending trade shows, technical seminars, and hands-on training, all while keeping up with your job.

However, the financial rewards for becoming an MCT are well worth it. Average income for an MCT ranges anywhere from $38K to $138K, depending on the capacity in which you are employed, where you live in the U.S. or abroad, and years of experience. Every aspect of the MCT career track is discussed in detail to give you a better understanding of the opportunities and responsibilities of the MCT.

One important distinction about the MCT track as opposed to the Microsoft Certified Solution Developer (MCSD) or Microsoft Certified Systems Engineer (MCSE) path must be understood by prospective MCTs. While the MCSE, software specialist, and programmer typically enjoy full-time steady employment, in most cases the MCT does not. At least half of all certified instructors work as independent contractors and are subject to fluctuating incomes. The other half work as salaried employees of Microsoft Authorized Technical Education Centers (ATECs) or Authorized Academic Training Partners (AATPs) throughout the U.S. and abroad. However, the average independent contractor makes nearly twice as much in income as the salaried MCT.

THE BENEFITS OF BECOMING A MICROSOFT CERTIFIED TRAINER

The benefits of becoming an MCT can be both tangible and intangible depending on how successful you are as an MCT. The benefits are obvious — above-average income and a certificate with Bill Gates' signature, to name a few. However, it's the intangible benefits that many IT professionals look for in a job as opposed to just money and prestige. Instructors in particular look for challenging work environments where they feel they can really make a difference when it comes to educating the public about Microsoft technology. Educators in general derive a great deal of pleasure interacting with others, and MCTs are no exception. Microsoft Certified Trainers also look for other hidden benefits that may or may not be so obvious to the novice who is just entering the field of education and classroom instruction.

Some of the major benefits of obtaining a certification in training with Microsoft are outlined in detail to help you better understand how MCTs really enjoy what they do as IT professionals.

Challenging Work Environment

Anyone who follows today's headlines is aware of the enormous pace that IT is currently undergoing, especially with respect to computer systems and software. MCTs are expected to keep pace with emerging Internet technologies and office automation software in order to properly convey concepts and procedures to students of the technology. MCTs are regularly challenged by students with difficult and often complex questions relating to information systems technology or, more specifically, Microsoft technology. MCTs must be prepared to properly handle such questioning in order to instill confidence in the students about the technology and themselves.

Autonomous Working Environment

Instructors by the very nature of their job are typically required to work under their own direction. Many trainers work as independent contractors and are very much their own bosses. They decide how to teach a particular class and are often allowed a great deal of freedom as to when and where classes are taught within the confines of the training center or academic institution.

Travel

Microsoft Certified Trainers are typically required to travel, especially if they are working as independent contractors for more than one ATEC or AATP. Today's MCT can easily find themselves all over the globe if they are working for a large organization or one of the larger Microsoft Solution Providers (MSPs).

Work with Cutting-Edge Technology

Instructors who work for MSPs can expect to teach classes in the latest Microsoft application and systems technology. All MSPs are participants in Microsoft's beta program. Any MCT working for an MSP will naturally get advanced exposure to the latest technology from Microsoft. Some of the Fortune 500 companies are also members of the Microsoft beta evaluation program, so instructors at those organizations have the opportunity to gain advance exposure to the operating systems and software applications being produced by Microsoft.

Skills in High Demand

With the tremendous growth in demand for Microsoft Certified Professionals (MCPs), in particular MCTs, many MCTs can look forward to a rewarding career in the technology training field, from both financial and professional perspective. As noted earlier, salaries for MCTs are well above average throughout the U.S. and abroad due to a shortage of skilled, professional instructors. In addition, with the MCT's skills in high demand, a trainer can expect a high level of job security as an MCT.

Entrepreneurial Opportunities

Microsoft Certified Trainers who work as independent contractors have a wealth of opportunity available to them as self-employed individuals. Not only is their income potentially unlimited, but so are their prospects for doing business. MCTs can team up with other ATECs on special projects, contract with more than one ATEC or AATP, and start their own ATEC, provided they have sufficient capital and other resources.

How to Keep Your Career in Focus

Setting career goals and keeping them in focus can be very difficult in today's business environment, much less focusing on the tasks at hand. However, it isn't an impossible task, provided you take the time to do a little planning and zero in on specific professional goals. Listed here are just a few of the steps you can take to enhance your career, both professionally and financially.

Read Trade Journals

Magazines that focus on professional development, such as *Microsoft Certified Professional* and *IT Specialist*, offer readers the latest news and information on a wide variety of topics concerning trainers or instructors. There are many other trade magazines on the market that can also help the MCT become a more effective and successful technical instructor. Look for such trade journals on the Internet using Yahoo!, and check with the various teacher's associations throughout the U.S. for trade publications.

Attend Technical Seminars

Some of the best technical seminars are held annually by Microsoft. TechEd and Developer Days are two of the largest conferences held in the U.S. for instructors interested in the development languages and Microsoft systems, such as C++, Visual Basic, and Back Office. Although TechEd and DevDays are focused more on the software developers and systems engineers, trainers are also encouraged to attend these and other events held by Microsoft.

Continue Your Education

Authorized Technical Education Centers and Authorized Academic Training Partners are excellent sources for hands-on technical training. They are located throughout the world and on the World Wide Web. In fact, MCTs versed in the latest systems and applications from Microsoft teach Microsoft Official Curriculum (MOC) courses, both in a classroom setting, as well as online via the Internet.

Network with Peers

Network or interact with people, not machines! One the best methods of staying abreast in your field is through friends and acquaintances in the business. Although born in the boom of the '80s, the term networking really seemed to take hold in the '90s. Next to joining an association or user group, nothing beats building a network of professional contacts and associates who can help you springboard to the top of your profession.

Join User Groups

No amount of training can replace the value of becoming a member of a user group or special interest group (SIG). These associations offer individuals the best help and guidance found anywhere. Some of the largest IT user groups in the nation are Rocky Mountain Windows NT User Group in Denver, Colorado, and LANTUG, the Los Angeles NT Users Group located in Santa Monica, California. These user groups also have SIGs within each group, such as the Exchange Specialist User Group and Internet Systems User Group. More information on user groups and SIGs can be found in Chapter 12.

Set Career Goals

If a manager or superior has the time or inclination, he should be helping you attain your career goals by providing you with the proper training and guidance. Unfortunately, many managers don't have the time or energy to look after a subordinate's career. Often it is up to the individual to set his own goals for a successful career. Anyone who is serious about his career development should set realistic goals from time to time and stick to them.

Find a Mentor

This is one person often overlooked by IT professionals. With the busy, hectic life that a typical trainer leads, it's often difficult to find an individual for help and guidance with your career in the form of mentoring.

SUBJECTS THAT A MICROSOFT CERTIFIED TRAINER CAN EXPECT TO TEACH

Most MCTs teach MOC courses in a variety of subjects. The subjects that MCTs teach can include anything from desktop operating systems to advanced topics like Microsoft BackOffice. However, as noted in the previous section, an MCT can teach classes on a myriad of subjects not necessarily limited to Microsoft technology. For practical reasons, however, this chapter focuses on the individual MCTs who concentrate on classroom instruction and teach mostly MOC.

Certified Instructors teach MOC courses in classrooms located in just about every type of organization found today. They can also teach classes remotely through distance learning facilities, such as the Microsoft Online Institute (MOLI).

The Microsoft Certified Trainer is typically called on to perform a multitude of tasks that may or may not involve teaching in the traditional sense. In fact, the MCT can rightfully expect to be asked by his employer or client to do hands-on manual labor in addition to normal software support duties. Unlike in programming, where you have well-defined curriculum, in the education services there are many gray areas with regard to duties and responsibilities.

Some MCTs also work on traditional systems integration projects within IT departments as well. The typical MCT can find himself in either context, especially if he is working for a large systems integrator or an MSP. In either case, the trainer is expected to perform well in either environment and do so professionally.

Listed here are just some of the subject matters MCTs teach, as well as duties an MCT can be expected to perform.

Desktop Operating Systems

MCTs often teach courses in Microsoft desktop operating systems such as Windows 95 and Windows NT Workstation. In a course such as Windows 95 Administration, MCTs will teach the students such topics as installation, configuration, administration, troubleshooting, messaging, and other support issues.

Network Operating Systems

MCTs can instruct students in the Windows NT network server operating system, as well as integration and migration issues with other network operating systems, such as Novell and UNIX. The MCT also teaches students how to plan and implement a multiserver network. Additionally, MCTs instruct students how to determine the appropriate hardware, software, and licensing needs for a Microsoft Windows NT Server-based environment.

Office Automation Software

Many MCTs instruct students on the ever-popular Microsoft Office suite of applications such as Excel and Access. Microsoft Certified Trainers generally teach classes that focus on the implementation, support, and troubleshooting of Microsoft Office, not end user training.

Enterprise Applications Software

The MCT can teach students in advanced enterprise applications systems such as SQL Server and Systems Management Server (SMS). Topics that are taught include administration and configuration of a Microsoft SQL database, including troubleshooting and maintenance. Microsoft Certified Trainers also instruct students how to install, configure, administer, and troubleshoot Back Office applications, such as Exchange Server and Proxy Server.

Programming Languages

MCTs can specialize in teaching Microsoft's Visual programming languages such as Visual C/C++, Visual Basic, and Visual J++.

Internet/Intranet Technology

MCTs versed in Microsoft systems technology train students in the latest networking and applications development technology for the Internet and intranets. They teach students how to implement Internet Information Server or Active Server, explain internetworking protocols such as TCP/IP, and cover scripting languages such as ActiveX.

Teach Students in a Classroom Setting

The majority of MCTs teach classes in Microsoft operating systems and applications in a classroom environment. Most MOC courses that are required must be taught in a traditional classroom, and only at ATECs or AATPs.

Train End Users On-Site

Microsoft Certified Trainers can also train end users in a classroom setting or individually at the customer's or client's site. Although this is not the preferred method (Microsoft requires MCTs hold MOC courses only at ATECs and AATPs), MCTs can teach other non-MOC courses less formally, on site in one to one settings and/or client training facilities.

Coordinate and Plan Training Classes

Microsoft Certified Trainers must carefully plan and prepare for all classes held at ATEC or AATP centers. Prior to holding an MOC course, MCTs are expected to practice delivering the course by rehearsing with other trainers and having mock questions posed to them by senior instructors.

Prepare a Computer Lab

This step goes hand in hand with planning and preparation for an MOC course. The MCT should go through all the steps involved in the student labs so that he or she can fully anticipate any problems or questions during a live training session.

Research Topical Questions

Microsoft Certified Trainers can expect a multitude of questions from students concerning the subject matters that they teach. Therefore, MCTs are expected to answer questions quickly and completely. A well-prepared instructor can answer most questions, but not all. Research will be required on at least 15% of all questions posed by students.

Distribute and Collect Course Evaluations

Microsoft Certified Trainers are expected to administer, collect, and forward course evaluations for Microsoft as part of the MOC course requirements. Improper use and/or neglecting this duty can jeopardize an MCT's certification and authorization to hold MOC courses at an ATEC or AATP.

Assist Information Technology Departments with System Integration Projects

Most system integration projects involve end user training as part of the turnkey process. For non-MOC-related classroom instruction, MCTs often find themselves assisting IT departments and other organizations with training materials production, class planning, and instruction.

This list is by no means comprehensive, but it does include a majority of the types of jobs and functions that an MCT is capable of performing. Many smaller companies may require a training specialist or instructor to perform all of the tasks mentioned, while larger organizations may have many different instructors on staff tending to each of the areas outlined.

INTERVIEWS WITH MICROSOFT CERTIFIED TRAINERS IN THE FIELD

Given the diversity of jobs for MCPs in the field, this author has taken the liberty of interviewing a few MCTs to find out just what they are up to in their profession. These are candid interviews with some of the more experienced instructors who are actively working on IT assignments throughout the world.

INTERVIEW: DEBBIE BANIK, VICE PRESIDENT AND CO-OWNER OF TRAINING COMPANY

We begin with Debbie Banik. She and two other business partners started SS Innovations to provide training services to their corporate clients on application software. Their training center is located in South Bend, Indiana. Debbie has been an MCT since October 1995 and is currently studying for the MCSE certification. Prior to becoming an MCT, Debbie was an IBMer for 10 years training end users in PROFS.

Q: What is the nature of your work, duties, and responsibilities? What do you do during an average work day?

A: As the co-owner of a training company as well as being an MCT, my days encompass many different challenges. If I am in town at my office, I am working with my business partner making business decisions (accounting, real estate, personnel), training decisions (which classes to hold, class fees), planning for future classes, maintaining equipment, and making contacts with ATECs to arrange teaching assignments for myself. In addition to the business side, I am also always studying and working on NT 4.0 and Windows 95. I am in a constant state of studying and fine-tuning the classes I teach.

If I am teaching a Microsoft-certified class, my day is spent training students and researching answers to their questions. Since our company is not an ATEC, all the classes I teach are out of town, so part of my Sunday is spent traveling.

Q: Why did you decide to become an MCP?

A: It was both a business and a personal decision. As far as a business decision, teaching certified classes would generate more income for the company. Personally and professionally I wanted to further my skills. I wanted to move out of application training and into working with more technical products and people. I saw

the potential for continued job opportunities and advancement in my career. Certifications are very hot right now. I wanted to continue to be on the front edge of the industry. I also feel being an MCP and eventually an MSCE will keep me in demand and give me job security.

Q: What is your working environment like? Deadlines, stress, workflow, hours, etc.

A: My daughter asked me recently if I ever stop working. I am constantly studying, reading trade journals, talking to potential clients, talking to potential instructors for my company, and thinking about how to make the company successful and profitable. As far as deadlines, I sometimes need to establish them for myself. If I am preparing for the first teaching of a class, I need to schedule the class and have that deadline to meet. That way I have to make sure I am prepared to teach the class. If I have no class scheduled, I will get involved with other things and put off studying and preparing for the class.

So I guess my hours are continual. However, they are flexible. I try to spend as much time as I can with my children when I am in town. I will bring them to the office with me, go to their school and extracurricular functions, and arrange my hours so that I can get my personal life in order. I will then put in quite a few hours working in the evenings.

Q: What do you like about this field?

A: The best part of my job is the people I have the opportunity to meet. I have had the opportunity to train in all parts of the country and meet people from all different companies and backgrounds. Learning about what they do and how they are implementing Windows 95 and Windows NT as well as other products is very exciting. It gives me the opportunity to experience more than just my environment. It allows me to see more of the big picture. I think sometimes we can get all wrapped up in our own little world that we lose sight of what else might be going on in the world. I also love the opportunity to keep learning new products. It's been a very long time since I have said that I am bored with my job. I am always learning new products, meeting new people, and traveling to different parts of the country. I also enjoy contracting to ATECs. This gives me the opportunity to see how different training companies organize their training rooms, equipment, etc.

Q: What kind of person do you feel would do well in this job?

A: Someone who loves technology and wants to pass that excitement on to others. Someone who wants constant change. The products are constantly being enhanced, new releases are coming out faster and faster, which means there is more to learn. Also, as far as training, a person has to be able to express himself well, be able to explain a concept in two or three different ways, be an excellent listener, and be able to ask questions effectively. I think a very good trainer is one who does more listening than talking.

Q: What are the advantages/disadvantages of your job as an MCP?

A: Advantages: Career advancement, resources available (MSN, MOLI, TechNet, books, support staff), job opportunities, travel, meeting new people, challenges.

Disadvantages: Too much travel at times, not enough time in a day to get everything done.

Q: What knowledge, skills (for success), and abilities are required for this type of work?

A: To be an MCT you need to have a good foundation—networking, DOS, hardware, applications. If you don't, you have to spend a lot of time getting the foundation and then moving on to the more technical products. Good presentation skills, good interactive people skills, good listening skills, and good questioning skills are musts for an MCT. You also need an intense desire to keep striving to know more. As an MCT you need the ability to find the information and answers you need to get your job done. You may not always have another person to ask, so you need to know how to use the tools at your disposal such as resource kits, documentation, TechNet and online forums. I have found MSN to be a valuable tool for me. The MCSE forums have given me the opportunity to ask questions and get many different answers. This allows me to look at the problem from different angles and different viewpoints.

Q: What are the advancement opportunities and outlook for this field?

A: Advance opportunities in this field are unlimited. There is a very high demand for good-quality MCTs. You can have the security of working for an ATEC, or there are plenty of opportunities for independent trainers who like to travel and work for themselves. With new products always under development, I think the field will be very lucrative for some time to come.

INTERVIEW: JENIFER WALD MORGAN, SENIOR TECHNICAL INSTRUCTOR

Our next interview is with Jenifer Wald Morgan. Jenifer does everything from teaching MOC to general computer consulting. She has a degree in Computer Science and has an extensive and varied career in IT. Jenifer is also studying to become an MCSE.

Q: What is the nature of your work, duties and responsibilities? What do you do during an average work day?

A: There is no average work day. As an MCT, I constantly strive to become a better teacher. This includes improving my teaching skills, increasing my product knowledge, and staying current on the industry and trends. I also do consulting in order to gain a thorough knowledge of the Microsoft software and operating systems and their interaction with a multitude of different types of applications, operating systems, and hardware.

This requires attendance at seminars, classes, technical association, and user group meetings, and I am also involved in the development of new projects and companies.

Q: Why did you decide to become an MCP?

A: After I was laid off from my job as an MIS Training Coordinator and Senior Instructor, I took a multitude of exams with the city's JTPA (Job Training Partnership Act) office. I scored the highest of any previous applicant and was immediately offered my choice of any type of training I wanted. There was a new type of certification available, the MCSE

This sounded like a challenging and an exciting field that matched my skills. But everyone else wanted me to become a full-time teacher. The school I had chosen to attend wanted to hire me at the end of the program to teach for them. But the very next day I was offered a full-time job by Ingram Micro

Corporation to become an MCT. They would pay for everything: my classes and instructor kits, my time attending classes and studying, exams, benefits, and a generous salary that would be raised each time I passed an exam. I started my new career as an MCT.

Q: What is your working environment like? Deadlines, stress, workflow, hours, etc.

A: What makes this career exciting is that it is never the same. The opportunities for an independent MCT are boundless. For those who like to travel, there are jobs available all around the world. For an independent consultant, the pay and benefits (travel, hotel, and food) are fantastic, but the hours are long.

For me, the stress is not there because I choose not to be stressed. All of my peers are more interested in helping me rather than in competing with me. There is a good underground network of MCTs. I do not travel out of town since that would cause me stress if I was away from my family. It is perfectly normal for people to feel stress when they take an exam or get up to speak in front of others. But not for me. I *love* to take exams. I am always prepared and I always pass. I *love* to teach.

Q: What do you like about this field?

A: I *love* to teach and help people learn. I am a bit of a ham. There is a similarity between being a technical instructor and being an actor. You prepare for the role, you perform, you find ways to teach in an entertaining manner, and you get reviewed.

Again, for an independent consultant the pay is excellent. But don't be fooled by our high rates ($800 to $1,400 per day plus expenses when traveling). When you take into consideration the total cost of being a consultant, which includes running a business, marketing, and updating the product (you), the before-tax pay on $120 per hour is less than $50. And you have to pay extra taxes for being self-employed. Plus there is no guarantee of steady work.

Other choices are using a broker to find you jobs or working as an employee for an ATEC or an AATP. This means you give up money (at a salary of $60,000 per year, the hourly rate is $28.85) but gain many other benefits. This is the best option if you do not want to constantly be looking for work. But it is not by any means a more stable life style because you still may have to travel, teach up to 12 hours a day, and switch between teaching evenings and teaching days. And you give up control of your life to the school.

Q: What kind of person do you feel would do well in this job?

A: Someone could come to this profession from one of two directions: have a technical background and have a natural talent for teaching, or be an excellent instructor and have the ability to learn *everything* about the topic you teach.

If you are the first kind of person (a "techno-geek"), you may not know until you try if you have the ability to get information across to people or how to reinforce it so that the information is retained. One instructor is a quiet, reflective gentleman in his private life. In front of a class he is transformed. He pulls out his bag of tricks and sight gags all ingeniously chosen to get across certain points. He uses the Groucho glasses, nose and mustache mask when describing TCP/IP and subnet masking.

If a problem occurs with the software, the bugs in his computer are usually followed by a giant plastic cockroach popping up. Being a teacher means caring if your students learn and being able to patiently describe in yet another way what something means.

As an experienced teacher you may find the technical information easy to learn. But don't be fooled into thinking that because you can learn any application software and teach it, learning and certifying to teach a Microsoft course is a piece of cake. Be prepared to study long and hard.

Follow up your classroom work with some real-life experiences. One of the worst complaints is having a teacher who knows nothing beyond the book. The courseware only covers a small part of what you really have to know about the subject. Microsoft expects someone to take a course and use the software for at least six months before taking the exam. Then you have to prepare for how you will teach each day of the course. What will you draw on the white board? What examples will emphasize a point? What does a certain acronym stand for? One very bad instructor reads out of the book and has even had his more knowledgeable students get up and teach the class for him.

Q: What are the advantages/disadvantages of your job as an MCT?

A: The advantages/disadvantages differ if you are a full-time employee or an independent contractor.

For more information about the process of becoming an MCT, refer to the Microsoft Certified Trainer Guide. You can download MCTGUIDE.DOC (117K) from http://www.microsoft.com/train_cert/download/cert/ mctguide.doc. Request a Microsoft Certified Trainer Information Kit by calling Microsoft at 800-688-0496. After you have reviewed the Microsoft Certified Trainer Guide and Information Kit, complete the MCT application included in the kit and send it in with the required documentation.

WHAT YOU CAN EXPECT TO EARN

While the MCT is commanding ever-higher salaries, which is due largely to the popularity of Microsoft technology, all MCTs are not necessarily enjoying increases in pay. Salaries vary widely by region of the U.S., as shown in Table 8-1. Salary bases also vary among employers, as shown in Table 8-2, so it all depends on whom you are working for and where your employer is located, as well as years of experience.

TABLE 8-1 MCT SALARY RANGES BY REGION

REGION	SALARY RANGE
Northeast	$75K–$114K
Midatlantic	$55K–$138K
South	$38K–$72K
West	$59K–$106K
Midwest	$45K–$78K

TABLE 8-2 MCT SALARY RANGE BY EMPLOYER TYPES

EMPLOYER TYPE	SALARY RANGE
Private company	$38K–$138K
Government	N/A
MSPs	$45K–105K

IT Recruiters, Inc. (http://www.itrecruitersinc.com) conducted the salary survey informally and at random. As indicated in Tables 8-1 and 8-2, the MCT salaries can vary widely by region, country, and employer, and, of course, years of experience.

WHERE TO FIND A JOB

Although there are many jobs for MCTs in the U.S. and abroad, many of them are not so easily found. Compiled here are some of the major sources for jobs on the Internet that reside in job and resume banks. Their names and Web addresses are listed for your convenience.

- Yahoo! Job Guide—www.yahoo.com./business/employment
- IT Specialist.com—www.itspecialist.com
- Monster Board—www.monsterboard.com
- Career Path—www.careerpath.com
- *Career*—www.careermag.com/index.text.html
- Online Career Center—www.occ.com/occ/
- Career Web—www.cWeb.com
- Job Web—www.jobWeb.com
- Career Net—www.careers.org
- The Riley Guide—www.jobtrak.com/jobguide/
- Job Bank USA—www.jobbankusa.com
- FedWorld—www.fedworld.gov
- Microsoft's MCT Forum—www.microsoft.com/partnering/atec
- *Microsoft Certified Professional*—www.mcpmag.com

The job and resume banks listed constitute an ever-growing presence on the Web for opportunities in IT. However, the Web is not by any means the only source for jobs in the IT industry. Listed here are some of the more traditional sources for job information and opportunities.

Newspapers, Periodicals

While not the best method for job hunting, many individuals prefer this method of searching for employment to any other. Note: Many of the trade magazines and newspapers are online now and offer a much faster and more sophisticated way of hunting for jobs through the use of search engines on their Web sites.

Networking

Socialize with your peers as often as you can. Friends and associates in your field can often be the best source for a good-paying job. Also, don't forget about trade fairs; they are an excellent way to meet new people in your field.

Informational Interviewing

Ask for an interview with some of the biggest companies in the IT industry and you would be surprised by the response you get—usually positive. This method of interviewing can sometimes lead to an immediate job offer.

Although there are many methods of job hunting available to IT professionals, none beats the often free and easy access to jobs on the World Wide Web. Many employment Web sites are now becoming specialized and are catering to niche job markets, as IT Specialist does. The IT Specialist Web site focuses entirely on Microsoft Certified Professionals. Newly certified network engineers, instructors, trainers, and developers can post their resumes on the Web site, as can seasoned veterans of the MCP program.

KEY POINT SUMMARY

In summary, this chapter focused on some of the significant benefits of obtaining a certificate as an MCT, such as travel, challenging and varied assignments, as well as the prestige of being an instructor of IT. In addition, the topic of career planning and development was covered to give you insight on how to help guide your career as a technical instructor. Also, this chapter focused on the various subjects that a Trainer can teach, such as network operating systems, network protocols, programming languages, and a bevy of other topics in Microsoft technology. Finally, the subject of job searches was covered to help the MCT find his or her way in the job market.

- The MCT job commands a level of respect both as instructors individuals and IT professionals.

- As an MCT you'll be one of the highest-paid IT professionals in the industry.

- The career track for MCTs is a challenging and very responsible position in the MCP program.
- As an MCT you'll teach a wide variety of topics at ATECs and AATPs.

Microsoft Certified Professional Contracting Opportunities

About Chapter 9

While most Microsoft Certified Professionals (MCPs) prefer to work in a steady full-time job, many MCPs are now choosing self-employment as a means of earning a living. Working as an independent contractor offers individuals the freedom to work and live according to their *own* goals. This chapter focuses on the many contracting opportunities open to MCPs in the world of information technology (IT).

This chapter also discusses the various methods of advertising one's services in the traditional sense as well as on the Internet. Finally, this chapter covers a critical aspect of determining the status of independent contractors per the IRS's guidelines. While these guidelines are currently under review by the IRS, they should be followed to the letter in order to avoid audits and/or severe financial penalties, which can occur if the guidelines are followed incorrectly.

Join Information Technology Industry and Trade Associations (Including Web Sites)

One of the smartest methods of networking and building your consulting business as an independent contractor is joining some of the industry and trade associations relating to IT. Most of the trade groups run local chapters for the benefit of members who are located throughout the U.S. and abroad, so access to them is easy. In fact, nearly all of them now have Web sites on the Internet. This section of the chapter focuses on the Web sites owned and operated by the major IT trade associations, as well as some of the referral services for independent contractors.

There are many benefits to becoming a member of a trade association. Chief among them are:

- Recognition as an IT professional
- Opportunities in leadership
- Referral network
- Access to the latest information in the IT industry

As with any opportunity, it's what you do with it that counts. Networking skills become all important when joining an association. You must "work the crowd" by attending the meetings and functions of the group in order to achieve your goals of growing your business. If you are looking for someone else to do your networking, you may want to seek the assistance of a consulting referral service.

There are many, many consulting referral services available to independent consultants. Finding the right one for you can be a matter of trial and error, but a few do exist that specialize in computer consulting. Just a few of the computer consulting services found on the Internet are listed here.

Finally, there are a number of very specialized industry trade sites appearing on the Internet that are of interest to independent contractors. They offer access to important and timely information, including contracting opportunities. A few of these Web sites are listed and should be bookmarked or saved as "favorite" in your Web browser.

tip One popular method of networking with other business people or consultants is joining a breakfast club, which usually meets between the hours of 7:30 a.m. and 8:30 a.m., before normal business hours. So you've got to be an early bird in order to take advantage of those networking breakfasts and you can't be late, either! Another networking opportunity is "Business after Business," usually held by the local chamber of commerce at member sites.

Network Professionals Association

The Network Professionals Association (NPA), shown in Figure 9-1, is a nonprofit association of network computing professionals that sets standards of technical expertise and professionalism. The group's mission is to advance the network computing profession. Its objectives are to unite network computing professionals in a worldwide association; determine member needs and interests; deliver programs and services to meet those needs and interests. Members number at least 8,000 network professionals worldwide who design, integrate, manage, and maintain networked computing environments. Full membership is limited to the following industry certifications: CNE, MCNE, CBE, CBS, MCSE, ASE, CLSE, CNX, CNP, PSE, and CCIE. Associate members must be in the process of attaining any of the previously mentioned certifications or hold any of the following certifications: CNA, MCPS, or CLP.

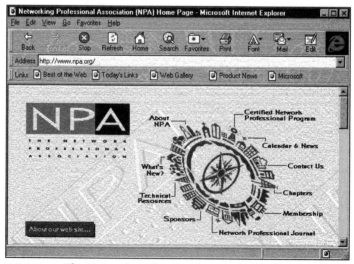

FIGURE 9-1   The Network Professionals Association home page.
The Web site is located at `http://www.npa.org`.

For more information on the NPA, call 888-379-0910.

Independent Computer Consultants Association

The Independent Computer Consultants Association (ICCA), shown in Figure 9-2, is a national nonprofit organization based in St. Louis that provides professional development opportunities and business support programs for independent computer consultants. Its members are computer and software experts who have practical experience with the industry's rapidly changing technology. They use, recommend, and install the latest products, and help corporations and individuals utilize the capabilities of the technology they own.

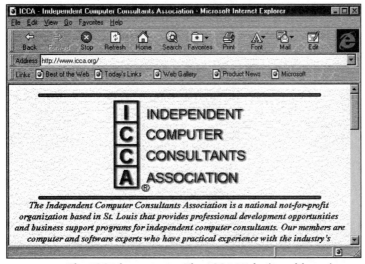

FIGURE 9-2   The ICCA home page. The ICCA Web site address is
`http://www.icca.org`.

For more information the ICCA, call 800-774-4222.

Association of Information Technology Professionals

The Association of Information Technology Professionals (AITP), shown in Figure 9-3, offers its members endless opportunities for professional and personal growth, helping them successfully achieve career objectives and meet the challenges of the information systems profession. It is the mission of AITP to provide superior leadership and education in IT. The AITP is dedicated to using the synergy of IT partnerships to provide education and benefits to its members, and to working with the industry to assist in the overall promotion and direction of information technology. The AITP is dedicated to providing industry leadership and professional development to members of the IT profession.

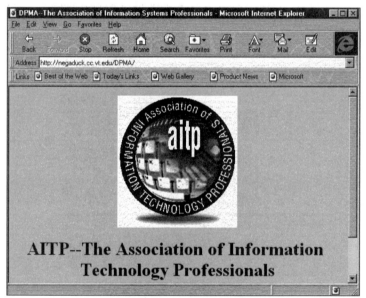

FIGURE 9-3   The AITP home page. The AITP Web site is located at www.aitp.org.

For more information on AITP's professional development programs, call 800-224-9371.

Association of Computing Machinery

The Association of Computing Machinery (ACM), shown in Figure 9-4, was founded in 1947. It is an international scientific and educational organization dedicated to advancing the art, science, engineering, and application of IT, serving both professional and public interests by fostering the open interchange of information and by promoting the highest professional and ethical standards.

There are currently more than 125 ACM professional chapters and local SIGs worldwide, 20% of which are outside the United States. The chapters host lectures by internationally known computer professionals through the ACM Lectureship Program, sponsor state-of-the-art seminars on the most pressing issues in IT, conduct volunteer training workshops, and publish informal newsletters.

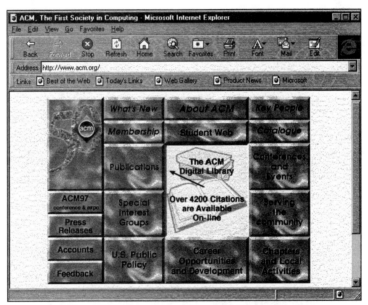

FIGURE 9-4   **The ACM home page. The ACM Web site address**
`http://www.acm.org`.

For more information on ACM's publications, e-mail `catalog@acm.org`.

The Software Contractors Guild

The Software Contractors Guild (SCG), shown in Figure 9-5, contains over 400 active independent software contractors for hire. The guild charges a small fee for contractors in return for being listed on the SCG Web site. The site is not a contracting agency and does not provide screening for organizations looking to hire software developers. For software developers looking to market their services, the SCG offers an inexpensive alternative to traditional advertising methods.

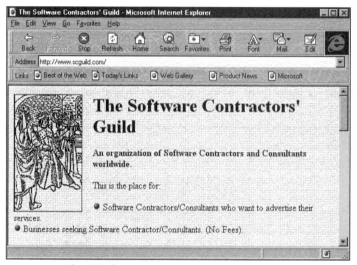

FIGURE 9-5   **The SCG home page located at** `http://www.` `scguild.com.`

For more information on the SCG, e-mail `admin@scguild.com`.

National Consultant Referrals Service

Founded in 1979, National Consultant Referrals, Inc. (NCRI) shown in Figure 9-6, came into existence to fill a perceived need for consultants with verified and validated experience to serve a clientele that is now international. Associate members of NCRI are experts in business, technical, scientific, marketing, international trade, and many other fields. Its clients include Fortune 100 companies, government agencies, startup firms, growing companies, and attorneys with case preparation needs. National Consultant Referrals, Inc. is a unique talent agency that markets the skills and expertise of highly qualified professional members. Its service to the clients is its ability to link them with the best-qualified experts for their project requirements.

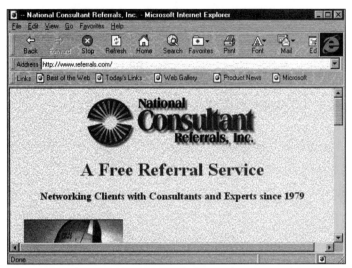

FIGURE 9-6   **The NCRI home page is located at** `http://www.`
`referrals.com.`

For more information on NCRI, call 800-221-3104.

Computer Enhancement Systems — Consultants Corner

The Consultants Corner's missions are to provide an effective avenue for consultants around the world to promote their services and establish themselves as experts in their fields; to offer a comprehensive listing of consultants that individuals and companies can refer to as a one-stop source for consulting services; to educate and inform consultants by providing valuable resources that help them market wisely, manage their businesses more effectively, and provide better service to their clients.

The four main areas of the Consultants Corner Web site (located at `http://www.pwgroup.com/ccorner`) are:

- **Find a Consultant:** You can choose from a list of categories of consultants such as computer consultants, trainers, programmers, management consultants, organizational consultants, and more!

- **Consultant's Resources & Training Materials:** If you have a product or service that helps consultants with their businesses or provide training materials, you would definitely want a listing here!

- **$ales & Marketing Resources:** This is not only a great place to find sales ideas, but it is also the perfect place for marketing consultants, PR professionals, and advertising agencies to promote their services!

- **Small Business Survival Guides:** If you have a product or service that helps small business owners, this is the place to promote your company. Accountants, business consultants, computer dealers, and more!

For information on the Consultants Corner, contact Computer Enhancement Systems at 800-524-2307.

Janet Ruhl's Computer Consultants Resource Page

Janet Ruhl's Computer Consultants Resource Page, shown in Figure 9-7, offers viewers a wealth of information on becoming a successful independent computer consultant. She has written two books on the subject of computer consulting and has extended her expertise on the Web to her new Web site. Any computer consultant worth his salt should visit Janet's site, especially if he is running a consulting practice in IT.

For more information on Janet Ruhl's Computer Consultants Resource Page, e-mail her at `102354.250@compuserve.com`.

The Association for Women in Computing

The Association for Women in Computing, shown in Figure 9-8, is a national, non-profit, professional organization for individuals with an interest in IT. The Association for Women in Computing is dedicated to the advancement of women in the computing fields in business, industry, science, education, and government.

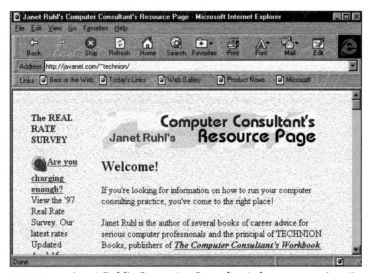

FIGURE 9-7   Janet Ruhl's Computer Consultants home page. Janet's Web site offers computer consultants a wealth of information on running a consulting practice in IT. Her Web site is located at `http://www.javanet.com/~technion`.

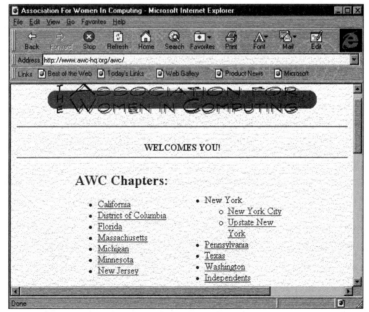

FIGURE 9-8   The AWC home page is located at `http://www.awc-hq.org/awc`.

The AWC's purpose is to provide opportunities for professional growth through networking and through programs on technical and career-oriented topics. It encourages high standards of competence and promotes a professional attitude among its members.

The three main goals of the association are:

o Promoting awareness of issues affecting women in the computing industry.

o Furthering the professional development and advancement of women in computing.

o Establishing and promoting growth of local AWC chapters.

For more information on becoming a member of the AWC, call 415-905-4663.

The Microsoft Site Builder Network

The Microsoft Site Builder Network (SBN), shown in Figure 9-9, offers independent software developers or consultants a unique way to leverage Microsoft's clout in the Internet content development and Internet/intranet systems markets. The SBN Level 3 is an exclusive membership designed especially to help professional Web consultants build their businesses.

Microsoft Site Builder Network Level 3 provides a wide range of benefits to help Level 3 member Web sites go above and beyond their competition:

o **Development information:** The latest development information and tools to create distinctive sites, plus Microsoft technical support and training opportunities.

o **Marketing support:** The power of Microsoft's marketing resources helps expand each member's customer base and bring visibility to the sites they build.

o **Relationship benefits:** By establishing a relationship, SBN Level 3 members and Microsoft work together to take member Web sites and businesses into the future.

For more information on becoming a Level 3 member of the Microsoft SBN, visit the SBN Level 3 Web page at `http://www.microsoft.com/sbnmember/levels/level3.asp`.

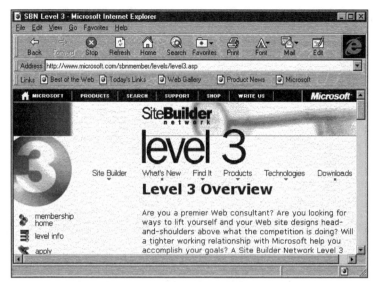

FIGURE 9-9   The Microsoft SBN Level 3 Membership information is located at `http://www.microsoft.com/sitebuilder`.

Microsoft's Smallbiz

The Microsoft Small Business Resource Center, or Smallbiz, shown in Figure 9-10, is dedicated to the small business operator/owner. It contains a wealth of information on starting, operating, and marketing a small business. The site is of particular interest to business owners, consultants, and entrepreneurs. The Partner Forum within the Smallbiz site offers valuable links to external resources from business planning to taxation. Any independent contractor interested in starting, running, and marketing a small business should pay a visit to this very important small business resource on Microsoft's Web site.

Microsoft's Sidewalk

Microsoft's latest online venture, called Sidewalk, shown in Figure 9-11, is in the business of providing local online entertainment content to communities throughout the U.S. Sidewalk is currently seeking freelance consultants and companies to assist its clients in the design and implementation of Web-based services and products for these community-based businesses.

FIGURE 9-10   The Microsoft Smallbiz resource center Web site is
located at `http://www.microsoft.com/smallbiz`.

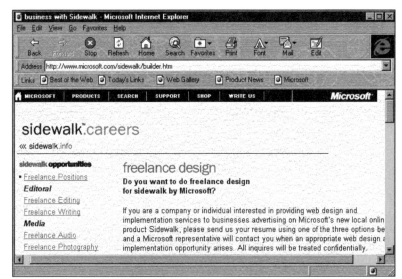

FIGURE 9-11   The Sidewalk home page for freelance contractors at
Microsoft is located at `http://www.microsoft.com/`
`sidewalk/builder.htm`.

If you own a company or are an individual interested in providing Web design and implementation services to businesses advertising on Microsoft's new local online product Sidewalk, Microsoft is looking for you! Some of the major cities that Sidewalk will be debuting in are Washington, D.C., Seattle, Los Angeles, New York, New Orleans, and Chicago. If you're an independent Webmaster or Internet software developer, this is your chance to work with the big guys!

For more information on freelance opportunities with Microsoft Sidewalk, contact:

Microsoft Corporation
Sidewalk Business Inquiries
Attention: Freelance Program
One Microsoft Way
Redmond, WA 98052

Independent Contractors Exchange

Independent Contractors Exchange (ICE), shown in Figure 9-12, is a member alliance of individual contract professionals and client companies brought together for the purpose of doing contract staffing business. Through Internet

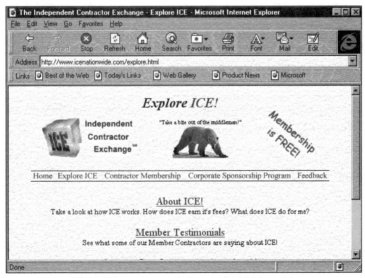

FIGURE 9-12   **The ICE home page is located at** `http://www.`
`icenationwide.com/explore.html`.

technology, ICE provides three basic services: 1) ICEmatch, an automated recruiting/matching system that notifies only qualified member contractors of contract opportunities; 2) POSTmatch, an automated "work in progress" system that supports the hiring process; and 3) a nationwide "employer of record" service that, when required by a client company, can assume third-party employer status. This service performs client billing and collection, processes payroll, and provides necessary professional insurance to the client.

 web links

Microsoft has recently added a new Web site specifically for consultants called Direct Access. The site is located at http://www.microsoft.com/directaccess.

NETWORK AT MICROSOFT SEMINARS

Microsoft holds hundreds of free and open IT seminars on its products and services almost daily in the U.S. and abroad. Any interested party can attend, provided you receive an invitation first. It's easy to get invited: Just visit Microsoft's Web site to find the latest information on a seminar near you.

The seminars usually cover topics such as Microsoft Exchange, MS SQL Server, the Internet, and intranets. Often at these and other open house events, Microsoft follows up each seminar with a Q & A session. During the Q & A attendees are often encouraged to network with other information technology professionals.

If you own a small consulting firm or if you're an independent contractor as well as a Microsoft Solution Provider (MSP), you are automatically invited to most of Microsoft's seminars. Also, at least once a year Microsoft invites MSPs to join in open house events to help market their products and services. The open house and technical seminars are excellent sources for new clients or customers. For the most part, Microsoft welcomes any individual, contractor, or organization that openly endorses or promotes its products for use with other computers. Finally, the technical seminars and open houses are often fun and exciting; as Microsoft touts its latest and greatest software, there is no shortage of hype and enthusiasm!

SUBCONTRACTING OPPORTUNITIES WITH MICROSOFT SOLUTION PROVIDERS

 tip

Find a suitable MSP in your area that may perform services closely related to your specialty (i.e., local-area networks, intranets, Internet, etc.). You may want to propose a deal whereby in the event that the MSP is in a pinch for, say, a network engineer, they can count on you to be there. They may pay a higher rate than normal for your service, but they are able to meet the demands of their customers. Also, contract with as many MSPs as possible. If the subject of proprietary systems or services comes up, be willing to sign a non-disclosure and/or non-compete agreements as long as it does not prohibit your activities as a consultant elsewhere.

As an independent consultant there are hundreds if not thousands of opportunities across the U.S. and abroad for contracting with MSPs. Many MSPs are willing to subcontract with consultants who specialize in training, custom application development, and system engineering projects. Often MSPs prefer working with MCPs because of their familiarity and expertise with Microsoft technology.

A large percentage of MSPs are actually small businesses with 10-25 employees. Therefore, it is often difficult for them to cover all the bases when it comes to Microsoft's ever-expanding base of computer software products. In fact, Microsoft Authorized Technical Education Centers (ATECs) and Authorized Academic Training Partners (AATPs), in particular, prefer to contract with Microsoft Certified Trainers, as opposed to hiring them full-time.

Microsoft Solution Providers themselves are encouraged by Microsoft to network with each other to help deliver mission-critical systems and applications to customers. Therefore, if you're a small independent contractor (MSP), look to make new relationships with other non-competing MSPs in your vicinity.

Some of the MSPs contracting opportunities are outlined here:

o **Custom application development.** Many MSPs are in dire need of application developers who specialize in C/C++ and MS SQL Server.

o **Training.** Many ATECs and AATPs prefer a contractual arrangement as a basis of employment.

- Web design and development. Many MSPs have short-term contracts for Internet/intranet design and implementation.
- Systems engineering. Many federal contractors are also MSPs. Most of their contracts are limited in time, so they are always on the lookout for trained and competent MCSEs for temporary employment or contract fulfillment.

Microsoft offers a free CD that contains the entire list of MSPs worldwide called the InfoSource. The CD is available by contacting Microsoft at 800-SOLPROV.

SUBCONTRACTING OPPORTUNITIES WITH TECHNOLOGY CONSULTING FIRMS

 tip **When contracting with any organization to perform services, make sure that both you and the party with whom you are contracting understand the risks involved with the implementation and the timeline necessary to complete the project successfully, as well as all deliverables. In other words, nail down all of the specifics of the project that you can possibly think of in the contract. That way, if any misunderstandings arise during the course of the engagement, both parties can refer to the agreement to resolve the issue.**

While MSPs are a good source for contract work, the majority of contracting opportunities can be found with the high-tech consulting firms that service the multitude of large- to medium-sized businesses and organizations throughout the U.S. and abroad. Some of the larger IT consulting firms are actually divisions of the top recruiting firms, such as Robert Half and Don Richard Associates. They are on a constant lookout for highly skilled and experienced computer specialists who are willing to work on a contract basis. Nonetheless, many Fortune 500 companies as well as mid-sized corporations find it hard to justify hiring a full-time IT professional for a short-lived project and instead opt to hire a computer consultant on a contract basis. Consequently, there will always be a need for independent computer consultants so long as computers are in use by society and the fees charged by consultants remain relatively high.

One important caveat for the independent contractor: Always sign an agreement *before* beginning work. Make sure that you and the customer fully understand the task at hand (i.e., requirements, timelines and costs) before proceeding with the project. Even if the client is your family, friend, or associate, a solid contract is a good foundation for the relationship. If things do go wrong, or if responsibilities somehow become muddled during the course of the engagement, both parties have the agreement to fall back on from both technical and legal standpoints.

SAMPLE INDEPENDENT CONSULTANT CONTRACT

As an example, a sample computer-consulting contract is shown here. The agreement stipulates clearly the parties to the contract, the type of services to be performed, the rate at which the contractor will bill the client, and, most important, signature lines for the contracts approval.

CONSULTING AGREEMENT

This Agreement is made effective as of April 24, 1997, by and between NT Independent Consulting Services of 123 Main St., Suite 1001, Anywhere, Maryland 20814, and Let's Do Business, Inc., 1101 Leesburg Pike, Suite 520, Tysons Corner, Virginia 20234.

In this Agreement, the party who is contracting to receive services shall be referred to as "Client," and the party who will be providing the services shall be referred to as "Consultant."

Consultant has a background in Windows NT Networking and Internet/intranet planning and design, and is willing to provide services to Client based on this background.

Client desires to have services provided by Consultant.

Therefore, the parties agree as follows:

1. DESCRIPTION OF SERVICES. Beginning on January 1, 1998, Consultant will provide the following services (collectively the "Services"): Install and configure Windows NT Servers, Workstations (Windows 95 and Windows NT), Internet Information Server, Microsoft FrontPage Web Management System, telecommunications/ISP interconnects.

2. PERFORMANCE OF SERVICES. The manner in which the services are to be performed and the specific hours to be worked by Consultant shall be determined by Consultant. Client will rely on Consultant to work as many hours as may be reasonably necessary to fulfill Consultant's obligations under this Agreement.

continued

continued

3. PAYMENT. Client will pay a fee to Consultant based on $125 per hour for services provided by Consultant. This fee shall be payable monthly, no later than the 28th day of the month following the period during which the services were performed. Upon termination of this Agreement, payments under this paragraph shall cease, provided, however, that Consultant shall be entitled to payments for periods or partial periods that occurred prior to the date of termination and for which Consultant has not yet been paid.

4. SUPPORT SERVICES. Client will provide the following support services for the benefit of Consultant:

   - office space

5. NEW PROJECT APPROVAL. Consultant and Client recognize that Consultant's Services will include working on various projects for Client. Consultant shall obtain the approval of Client prior to the commencement of a new project.

6. TERM/TERMINATION. This Agreement shall automatically terminate upon completion by Consultant of the services required by this Agreement.

7. RELATIONSHIP OF PARTIES. It is understood by the parties that Consultant is an independent contractor with respect to Client, and not an employee of Client. Client will not provide fringe benefits, including health insurance benefits, paid vacation, or any other employee benefit, for the benefit of Consultant.

8. DISCLOSURE. Consultant is required to disclose any outside activities or interests, including ownership or participation in the development of prior inventions, that conflict or may conflict with the best interests of Client. Prompt disclosure is required under this paragraph if the activity or interest is related, directly or indirectly, to:

   - a product or product line of Client
   - a manufacturing process of Client
   - any activity that Consultant may be involved with on behalf of Client

9. EMPLOYEES. Consultant's employees, if any, who perform services for Client under this Agreement shall also be bound by the provisions of this Agreement. At the request of Client, Consultant shall provide adequate evidence that such persons are Consultant's employees.

10. INJURIES. Consultant acknowledges Consultant's obligation to obtain appropriate insurance coverage for the benefit of Consultant (and Consultant's employees, if any). Consultant waives any rights to recovery from Client for any injuries that Consultant (and/or Consultant's employees) may sustain while performing services under this Agreement and that are a result of the negligence of Consultant or Consultant's employees.

11. INDEMNIFICATION. Consultant agrees to indemnify and hold Client harmless from all claims, losses, expenses, fees including attorney fees, costs, and judgments that may be asserted against Client that result from the acts or omissions of Consultant, Consultant's employees, if any, and Consultant's agents.

12. ASSIGNMENT. Consultant's obligations under this Agreement may not be assigned or transferred to any other person, firm, or corporation without the prior written consent of Client.

13. INTELLECTUAL PROPERTY. The following provisions shall apply with respect to copyrightable works, ideas, discoveries, inventions, applications for patents, and patents (collectively, "Intellectual Property"):

   a. CONSULTANT'S INTELLECTUAL PROPERTY. Consultant does not personally hold any interest in any Intellectual Property.

   b. DEVELOPMENT OF INTELLECTUAL PROPERTY. Any improvements to Intellectual Property items listed on Exhibit A, further inventions or improvements, and any new items of Intellectual Property discovered or developed by Consultant (or Consultant's employees, if any) during the term of this Agreement shall be the property of Consultant, subject to the irrevocable right and license of Client to make, use, and/or sell products and services derived from any such Intellectual Property without payment of royalties. Such rights and license will be exclusive for the term of this Agreement and any extensions or renewals of this Agreement. After termination of this Agreement, such rights and license shall be nonexclusive but shall remain royalty-free. Each party shall execute such documents as may be necessary to perfect and preserve the rights of either party with respect to any such Intellectual Property.

continued

continued

14. RETURN OF RECORDS. Upon termination of this Agreement, Consultant shall deliver all records, notes, data, memorandum, models, and equipment of any nature that are in Consultant's possession or under Consultant's control and that are Client's property or relate to Client's business.

15. NOTICES. All notices required or permitted under this Agreement shall be in writing and shall be deemed delivered when delivered in person or deposited in the United States mail, postage prepaid, addressed as follows:

> Consultant:
> NT Independent Consulting Services
> Joe Bloe, Senior Consultant, 123 Main St., Suite 1001, Anywhere, Maryland 20814
> Company:
> Let's Do Business, Inc., Sam Easy, President, 1101 Leesburg Pike, Suite 520, Tysons Corner, Virginia 20234

Such address may be changed from time to time by either party by providing written notice to the other in the manner set forth above.

16. ENTIRE AGREEMENT. This Agreement contains the entire agreement of the parties and there are no other promises or conditions in any other agreement whether oral or written. This Agreement supersedes any prior written or oral agreements between the parties.

17. AMENDMENT. This Agreement may be modified or amended if the amendment is made in writing and is signed by both parties.

18. SEVERABILITY. If any provision of this Agreement shall be held to be invalid or unenforceable for any reason, the remaining provisions shall continue to be valid and enforceable. If a court finds that any provision of this Agreement is invalid or unenforceable but that by limiting such provision it would become valid and enforceable, then such provision shall be deemed to be written, construed, and enforced as so limited.

19. WAIVER OF CONTRACTUAL RIGHT. The failure of either party to enforce any provision of this Agreement shall not be construed as a waiver or limitation of that party's right to subsequently enforce and compel strict compliance with every provision of this Agreement.

```
20. APPLICABLE LAW. This          NT Independent Consulting
    Agreement shall be governed    Services (Joe Bloe)
    by the laws of the State of
    Maryland.                      Let's Do Business, Inc.
                                   By:
    NT Independent Consulting      _____
    Services
    By:                            Let's Do Business, Inc. (Sam
    _____    Easy)
```

ADVERTISING ON THE INTERNET AND IN THE MEDIA

Marketing your services as an independent contractor is fairly easy and straight-forward.

To begin with, the most affordable and easiest method of advertising is the Internet or World Wide Web. Start by designing and building a Web site that carefully explains your qualifications, skills, and accomplishments. The cost for hosting a Web site varies widely, so it pays to shop around, but most entry-level prices for Web hosting start around $20 per month with a one-time setup fee of roughly $100. This is the most effective advertising considering the coverage (worldwide) and the $24 \times 7 \times 365$ round-the-clock publishing of your Web site! The only downside to advertising on the Web is that you can easily get lost in the crowd of a millions! Pick up a good Web book on getting noticed on the Internet; they're a dime a dozen.

Advertising in traditional print media, such as newspapers, is usually prohibitively expensive for a small business or independent consultant. With luck the Internet will eventually neutralize the exorbitant fees that newspaper publishers charge for advertising nowadays! If you feel compelled to advertise in a local newspaper, don't be shy about haggling, especially if the ad size is a fourth-page or more. Most will give in to pressure for a discount on fees.

One of the best all-time places to advertise is in the Yellow Pages. However, it can be very expensive to place an ad, especially if you're just starting out as a consultant. Unfortunately, most Yellow Page advertising is not open to negotiation, but there are various discounts for advertising in more than one place in the book.

Also, the Yellow Pages is a good place to start with advertising with startups because the phone company is willing to finance your ad copy by adding it to your monthly phone bill.

 note **It is the wise individual who requests a "special number" for advertising in the Yellow Pages. The reasons are many, but the most important is tracking incoming calls based on the ad.**

The only downside to Yellow Pages advertising is that you tend to get a large proportion of "shoppers," who happen to base their purchase decisions on price rather than quality of service. So if you want the business, be prepared to haggle!

 tip **Beware of being duped into advertising. Always initiate advertising from within your company, never the other way around. Once you begin to advertise for the first time, you will invariably be hit upon by every major local newspaper, telephone book, and telemarketer in your vicinity. It's easy to get in over your head quickly with ad fees — you're ripe for the pickin', so watch out! Also, it's okay to experiment with various methods of advertising; that's what you have to do in the beginning, at least, until you find your niche market.**

QUALIFYING AS AN INDEPENDENT CONTRACTOR PER THE IRS'S GUIDELINES

The IRS has established guidelines to determine whether a worker is an independent contractor or an employee. Simply stating in an agreement that a worker is a contractor is not sufficient. If an employer incorrectly pays a worker as a contractor rather than an employee, there could be adverse tax consequences for both parties concerned. The employer could be liable for payroll taxes on the compensation and for the withholding taxes that would have been withheld had the worker been treated as an employee. In addition, if a retirement plan is in place, it could be jeopardized if not all employees' wages are considered.

The IRS guidelines consist of 20 factors. These factors are applied based on the facts and circumstances of each case. A worker does not have to meet all of these factors to be considered an employee. Nor does any one factor carry more weight than another. They are designed to determine how much control and direction the employer has over the worker. The more control an employer has, the more likely the worker is an employee. Again, the IRS has established 20 guidelines to help employers determine whether a worker should be treated as an employee or an independent contractor for tax purposes. Those 20 guidelines are:

1. **Instructions.** Employees comply with their employer's instructions about when, where, and how to work, or the employer has the right to control how a worker's work results are achieved. independent contractors have more flexibility.

2. **Training.** Employees may receive training from their employers to perform services in a particular manner. Independent contractors usually use their own work methods and receive no training from those purchasing their services.

3. **Integration.** Employees' services are usually integrated into the business's operations because they are key to the success or the continuation of the business. Independent contractors are independent of the business' operation.

4. **Services rendered personally.** Employees render services personally. Independent contractors render services as contractors.

5. **Hiring assistants.** Employees work for an employer. Independent contractors can hire, supervise, and pay assistants under a contract that requires them to provide materials and labor and to be responsible for the results.

6. **Continuing relationship.** Employees generally have ongoing relationships with their employers. Independent contractors' relationships will usually be more sporadic.

7. **Set hours of work.** Employers usually set their employees' work hours. Independent contractors usually set their own hours.

8. **Full-time required.** Employees may be required to work or to be available full-time. Independent contractors may work when and for whom they choose.

9. **Work done on premises.** Employees usually work on their employers' premises or on a route or at a location approved by their employers.

10. **Order or sequence set.** Employees may be required to perform services in the order or sequence set by their employers. Independent contractors can establish their own sequence.

11. **Reports.** Employees may be required to submit reports to their employers. Independent contractors are not required to submit reports to their clients.

12. **Payments.** Employees are paid by the hour, week, or month. Independent contractors are usually paid by the job or through a commission.

13. **Expenses.** The business and travel expenses of employees are generally paid by their employers. Independent contractors are responsible for paying their own expenses.

14. **Tools and materials.** Employers normally furnish their employees with the key tools and other materials they need to do their jobs. Independent contractors normally furnish their own tools and materials.

15. **Investment.** Employees normally do not invest in the facilities. Independent contractors have a significant investment in the facilities they use to perform services for someone else.

16. **Profit and loss.** Employees do not experience a profit or loss; independent contractors can.

17. **Works for more than one person or firm.** Employees usually work for one firm at a time. Independent contractors may work for multiple persons or firms at the same time.

18. **Offer services to the general public.** Employees usually work for one employer. Independent contractors make their services available to whomever they want.

19. **Right to fire.** Employees can be fired by their employers. Independent contractors cannot be fired as long as they produce results that meets the specifications of their contracts.

20. **Right to quit.** Employees have the right to quit a job at any time without incurring liability. Independent contractors usually agree to carry out specific tasks or series of tasks and are responsible for completing those tasks satisfactorily, or else they are legally obligated to make good for failing to do so.

The emphasis on this test by the IRS cannot and should not be overlooked by the independent consultant. Failure to qualify as an independent contractor with the IRS can be a costly and terrible mistake. Until such time that the IRS eases the restrictions for qualifying as an independent contractor, in particular an independent computer consultant, it would be wise for any individual to consult both an attorney and an accountant *before* proceeding to work as one.

KEY POINT SUMMARY

In summary, this chapter discussed the many ways that an independent consultant and MCP can offer services to the general public. The chapter also discussed the many subcontracting opportunities open to the MCP, such as MSPs and high-tech computer consulting firms. Additional topics covered in this chapter included advertising in the print media as well as on the World Wide Web. Finally, the subject of contracting as an independent contractor was covered, as well as IRS guidelines that a freelance consultant must adhere to in order to qualify for tax breaks as a sole proprietor.

- Microsoft Certified Professionals acting as independent contractors or consultants need to network with business leaders at functions like breakfast clubs and chamber of commerce events.
- Consultants should attend at a minimum of Microsoft seminars to stay abreast with the technology and network with local Microsoft district office staff.
- There are many opportunities to contract with MSPs, provided you have the experience, training, and a good track record.
- There are hundreds, if not thousands, of high-tech computer consulting firms around the world in search of competent IT professionals who are willing to work on a contract basis.
- Advertising is a good bet provided you choose your niche carefully and don't overspend your advertising budget!
- There are approximately 20 "tests" or questions you must adhere to in order to qualify as a bona fide computer consultant under the watchful eye of the IRS—know them!

Tools and Information for Microsoft Certified Professionals

This section discusses many valuable resources available for Microsoft Certified Professionals (MCPs). You also learn how to use those resources to your maximum advantage as information technology (IT) professionals. Microsoft's TechNet and Developer Network CDs are prime examples of such resources. They offer quick and reliable access to a plethora of information on Microsoft operating systems, applications software, and development languages, to name a few.

NT user groups located throughout the U.S. and abroad offer MCPs a wealth of opportunities for learning, networking, and leadership in the IT industry. NT user groups are typically based in large U.S. cities, although some are based in the suburbs.

Trade associations also offer many benefits for MCPs. Association for Windows NT Professionals (NT*Pro) is the first trade association for Windows NT professionals. NT*Pro has more than six special interest groups (SIGs) offering seminars and other technical meetings on systems ranging from Microsoft C++ to SQL Server.

Finally, a fast emerging resource for MCPs are study groups that focus on the Microsoft Certification program. Study groups can help prospective MCPs prepare for such exams as Windows NT, Exchange Server, and Networking Essentials—some of the more technically daunting system exams developed by Microsoft.

Starting Your Own Microsoft Solution Provider VAR

About Chapter 10

In this chapter the Microsoft Solution Provider (MSP) program is covered to provide would be entrepreneurs or businessmen with the information necessary to start such a value added reseller (VAR) business. From the application process to start-up costs, these and other details are discussed in order to educate the reader with requirements necessary to enter the MCP program. The subject of niche markets is also discussed to help the reader understand the various information technology markets open to MSPs, both in the United States and abroad. Finally, the subject of industry associations is discussed, such as the Association of Microsoft Solution Providers (AMSP), which can help MSPs develop their business through seminars and other networking opportunities held throughout the United States and abroad.

BECOMING A MICROSOFT SOLUTION PROVIDER

Only a few short years ago, becoming an MSP was as easy as submitting a two-page application form and a check for $195 in addition to listing yourself as the owner and sole employee. Back in 1992 it was called the Solutions Channel Program and very few people had even heard of the Value Added Reseller (VAR) program from Microsoft. It's interesting to note that during the initial stages of Microsoft's VAR program, Windows NT was but a gleam in Bill Gates' eye, and Windows for Workgroups was Microsoft's answer to workgroup computing!

The MSP program has come a long way, and so has Microsoft. The MSP program now offers two levels of membership under the VAR program, as well two special programs that authorize an MSP to operate as an authorized education center with classes in Microsoft Official Curriculum (MOC). The fees and requirements for the MSP program have gone up considerably since its early days. However, the basic VAR program is entirely within the reach of even the smallest of IT companies (two- or three-man shops) and should be seriously considered by any IT company worth its salt.

According to Microsoft, the definition of the MSP program is: "Microsoft and Microsoft Solution Providers team together and make mutual investments to capitalize on the potential of the computer solutions market. As part of its commitment to this partnership, Microsoft will build awareness of and equity for MSPs in the marketplace" reads the MSP program Statement of Goals and Objectives.

Microsoft defines the MSP further in saying: "Microsoft Solution Providers are independent companies that team with Microsoft to solve business challenges for organizations of all sizes in many industries. The MSPs use Microsoft products as the building blocks for various value-added services, such as integration, consulting, software customization, application development, technical training and support."

Although the MSP isn't intended for every type of IT organization, it can benefit most information technology shops, especially if their focus is on Microsoft technology.

Finally, this chapter focuses on the application process in becoming an MSP, start-up costs for both member levels, program requirements dictated by Microsoft, and finding a niche in the MSP information technology market. The AMSP is also covered in this chapter.

THE APPLICATION PROCESS

 tip

Be sure to complete the application profile carefully and be honest about your firm's capabilities. Microsoft refers customers to you through its automated referral tool known as ART, which in turn uses your profile information in conjunction with the type of Microsoft Certified Professionals (MCSE, MCSD, etc.) that you have on staff to determine the best MSP for the job or lead within a given geographic area.

To begin the process of becoming a member in the MSP program, shown in Figure 10-1, you must first request an application kit from Microsoft. To do so, call 800-SOLPROV and ask that a member application kit be sent to you. It takes approximately ten days to two weeks to receive the kit once ordered. Once you receive the kit, make sure to take the time to read it over carefully. It is very important that you fully understand the relationship that you are about to enter into, as with any business contract or agreement. Microsoft has invested a great deal of time and money in the program and expects its members to do the same.

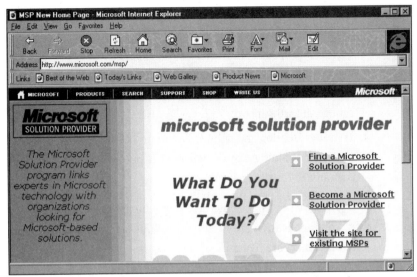

FIGURE 10-1   The Microsoft Solution Provider home page shown here
is located at `http://www.microsoft.com/msp`.
(Screen shot reprinted with permission from Microsoft Corporation.)

The first step in the application process is to complete the corporate profile
for your organization. This includes properly identifying your organization's products and/or services so that Microsoft can help market your organization through
its own marketing efforts worldwide. The profile helps Microsoft refer and match
your organization's expertise to customers in need of similar products or services.

The five major types of services that MSPs typically offer are listed below:

- **Solution Development (ISV):** Develop and ship packaged applications
  directly or through resellers or agents. These may include client/server,
  line-of-business or other shrink-wrapped applications. Solution
  development may involve customizing the application to meet customer
  needs.

- **Custom Application Development:** Develop custom, client-specific software
  solutions that meet unique customer needs. Custom application
  development can involve consulting and design services as they relate to
  the development and deployment of the custom application.

- **Infrastructure Installation and Integration:** Design, install, configure,
  support and maintain networking, file and print, systems management,
  messaging projects, and intranets including system architecture and
  design (LAN, WAN, database, messaging, computer/telephony and

Internet/intranets); installation setup and configuration services; integration services and migration services.

○ **Technical Support:** Deliver technical support and/or maintenance services for software or hardware products. Technical support may be delivered for the company's or other vendor's products in the form of direct end user or contract-based support.

○ **Training:** Develop and deliver classroom training and/or self-study training materials. Training may be delivered as publicly offered training courses or customized on-site training.

The services listed above are comprehensive of information technology business. Your application profile should include one or more of the specialties to give Microsoft an accurate picture of your business.

As an overview of the actual profile form itself, some of the information that you will need to supply is listed below:

○ Organization name or "Trading As" name

○ Federal tax I.D. number

○ Actual street address (no P.O. boxes are allowed) of your business of organization

○ Organization/business president and/or owner

○ Primary contacts (sales, marketing, technical, etc.)

○ Microsoft Certified Professionals (MCPs) on staff (including MCP I.D. numbers) Note: At least two MCPs must be on staff to qualify a business as an MSP.

○ Sales and service metrics (gross sales information, product/service sales breakdown, etc.)

○ References (three business customers)

Once the profile is completed, a corporate or organization officer must sign and date the profile form. The profile, along with a check for the application, is submitted to Microsoft Corporation for approval. Approval usually takes anywhere from four to six weeks. Microsoft prorates the annual fee depending on the time of the year that you apply for membership into the MSP program.

For example, if you are an organization based in the U.S. and you enroll in the MSP program during the period November 1 through March 30 (1996-97), you would pay an annual fee of $1,995. If you joined the following quarter your MSP fee would be prorated to $1,745. If you decided to join mid-year your pro-rated fee would be $1,495. Finally, if you decided to become a member of the MSP in the fall, the cost would be $1,245. The MSP program is an annual or calendar year program. All MSPs are required to renew their applications once a year and pay the annual fee.

To become a Microsoft Authorized Technical Education Center (ATEC), special requirements must be met in addition to becoming an MSP. In the effort to ensure that Microsoft has the resources necessary to meet its training goals, that is, to provide high-quality service to organizations wherever it is needed and to maintain a loyal and profitable education channel, only a small percentage of applicants are admitted into the Microsoft ATEC program, shown in Figure 10-2. Admission is based on a number of factors, including the strength of each applicant's current technical training business, a demonstrated ability to market training and certification effectively, the ability to fulfill a business need as determined by the local Microsoft Education and Certification Manager, a demonstrated understanding of the technical training business, a history of successful education center management, and professional reputation.

Based on the strict requirements for qualifying as an ATEC, as noted above, most startup MSPs are precluded from being ATECs, at least initially. For practical purposes related to this chapter (i.e., MSP startups) the basic ATEC requirements are listed below. You must:

- Be an MSP
- Complete the ATEC application and submit it to Microsoft ATEC program
- Submit a technical-training business plan
- Submit photographs of your training facilities
- Submit copies of current advertising and promotion materials
- Submit a current public training schedule or course catalog or your Internet Web site address

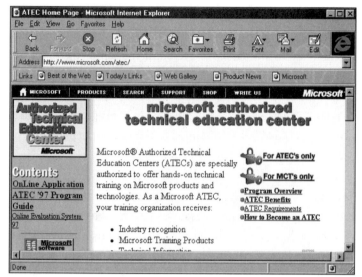

FIGURE 10-2   **The Microsoft ATEC home page shown here is
located at** `http://www.microsoft.com/atec`.
(Screen shot reprinted with permission from Microsoft Corporation.)

After submitting all of the materials listed above, the final step is to apply for
a Site Application Review. Each prospective training site is evaluated independently by the Microsoft Education and Certification Manager. Acceptance into the
ATEC program is at the sole discretion of Microsoft. So even though you meet all
the requirements for qualification as an ATEC, Microsoft can reject your application if it deems your education center is unsuitable and does not meet its standards as an ATEC.

It is advisable that any training service organization or information technology startup that is contemplating becoming an ATEC do so only after operating an
MSP VAR for at least a year. This way you can become familiar with the myriad of
programs, events and products that Microsoft has to offer within the MSP program before attempting to augment your organization's repertoire with training
services for the general public. Besides, in order to maintain your status as an
ATEC, 15 percent of your gross sales must be derived from the sales, support and
integration of the Microsoft core product line.

For more information on the ATEC MSP program call 800-688-0496.

STARTUP COSTS OF A SOLUTION PROVIDER

While the cost of becoming a basic MSP VAR (member level, see next section) may seem small, there are many hidden pitfalls or costs that can cripple a startup MSP if it is unprepared to deal with them appropriately. Typical problems with small business startups are:

- Inadequate business plan or *no* business plan
- Poor cash flow or *no* customer base
- Inadequate offices or training facilities
- Moderately trained technical employees
- Lack of marketing plan and/or inadequate sales force

While these factors relating to business startups are true for any business, they are of particular importance to newly formed MSP VARs. The requirements for becoming an MSP at the "member" level are minimal when compared to the partner and ATEC/AATP programs with Microsoft. However, if you want to be a successful MSP you should have a business plan and proper capitalization before attempting to graduate into the higher-level VAR programs at Microsoft.

For example, if you start out as a startup specializing in network installation and support services but plan to offer training classes later on (i.e., become an ATEC), then you should plan for expansion of your office space with dedicated facilities for classrooms. The plan should also include the costs of all workstations required for lab sections of MOC or courses that you plan to offer. This is just one prime example of the unanticipated costs or hidden expenditures that can dampen your growth as a startup MSP.

MEMBER LEVEL

The MSP program has two levels, member and partner, each with its own requirements and benefits. Microsoft Solution Provider members provide Microsoft solutions for various value-added services to solve business issues for organizations of all sizes in many industries. MSP members receive technical, marketing and sales information as well as Microsoft products and technical support.

MSP Member Benefits Overview

The following summarizes the member benefits of the MSP program. Note: Microsoft may expand, change the scope of contents of, or delete any features under the program at any time. The information is based on 1997 program benefits.

Product licenses

Microsoft Solution Provider members receive internal-use licenses for a comprehensive set of products, including Microsoft Office, Microsoft Windows operating systems, development languages, and Microsoft BackOffice client and server products. Microsoft Solution Providers receive a copy of the most recent version of each product in a monthly mailing and a license to reproduce the product within their organizations to encourage evangelism and product recommendations.

Not-for-Resale Products Purchase program

The Not-for-Resale Products Purchase program makes "Not for Resale" (NFR) products available to MSPs at a discounted price. Not for Resale products include full packaging and documentation and may include variations on products that are not included in the monthly mailing (like DEC Alpha and Macintosh versions). MSPs are entitled to order *one* copy of each product.

Product betas

Microsoft Solution Provider members are automatically enrolled in the beta evaluation program. This program issues up to twelve beta evaluation CDs annually so members can evaluate and familiarize themselves with the latest Microsoft products. The beta evaluation CDs are included in the MSP monthly mailings.

TechNet

Microsoft TechNet is the official source of technical information for those who support or educate end users, administer networks or databases, and recommend or evaluate information technology solutions that use Microsoft products. Microsoft Solution Provider members receive a monthly TechNet CD that includes the full Microsoft Knowledge Base, resource kits and other technical information. Members also receive monthly a CD that contains current drivers and patches for most Microsoft products.

Microsoft Developer Network Universal

The Microsoft Developer Network (MSDN) is the definitive source of software development kits, device driver kits, operating systems, and programming information on developing applications for Microsoft Windows, Windows NT and Microsoft BackOffice. Microsoft Solution Providers receive an annual membership in the MSDN Universal subscription. The MSDN Universal subscription includes product CDs for BackOffice, Office, and Developer Studio.

Customer service program assistance

Microsoft Solution Provider members can call the MSP telephone hotline (800-SOLPROV) to order collateral, discuss certification requirements, and get answers to questions about the MSP program.

Microsoft Solution Provider Information Network

The Microsoft Solution Provider Information Network (SPIN) provides MSP members with up-to-date information about Microsoft products and programs. The members can use SPIN to answer MSP-related questions, access sales and training tools, and retrieve product information that supplements the general information found in MSN and on the Internet. The Solution Provider Information Network also provides the contents listing for the current monthly mailing.

Technical support

Microsoft Solution Provider members receive a Microsoft Priority Comprehensive account with tensupport incidents. Microsoft Priority Comprehensive provides technical assistance for the Microsoft Windows NT operating system, Microsoft SQL Server, Microsoft messaging systems, and other business system products. Microsoft Priority Comprehensive also covers all other Microsoft products. Note: Microsoft Priority Comprehensive support incidents vary among the various Microsoft products (i.e., some count as an incident and some do not).

Additional support options

If additional backup support for Microsoft products is necessary, MSPs can also consider using one of Microsoft's Authorized Support Centers (ASCs). Authorized Support Centers are among the most highly qualified support services providers in the industry. Each ASC must meet stringent criteria prior to approval and offer a full range of IT life cycle services to include systems integration, multi-vendor consulting, network installation and configuration, help desk outsourcing, multi-vendor support, on-site support and more.

Referrals/leads

An Internet-based worldwide referrals and leads system is available for MSPs. The tool contains a directory functionality to enable customers to look up local MSPs and generate leads with a customer's permission. Leads are qualified on the data submitted in the MSP's profile application, including geography, product specialty, services, MCPs on staff and desired opportunity size.

Solution News

The Solution News is an index to the MSP monthly mailings and a pointer to important information and resources found on the Internet and elsewhere. The Solution News newsletter is included in the monthly mailing box.

Microsoft Solution Provider CD

The Microsoft Solution Provider CD is a suite of tools that helps MSP members navigate through Microsoft's product marketing, sales and pricing information as they assemble their market strategies. It is an excellent reference tool that MSP members can use to easily build custom sales presentations and business plans.

Microsoft Solution Provider identity kit (logo)

There is a single MSP brand identity worldwide. Microsoft widely markets this identity in its advertising, public relations, events, promotions, marketing collateral and MSP program materials. Members can use this identity in advertising, on business cards, and for other communications.

Microsoft Corporate Solutions pilot program

The Microsoft Corporate Solutions pilot program provides an easy and cost-effective way to administer hardware and software evaluations. It is a structured 120-day evaluation program intended to help organizations conduct thorough evaluations of Microsoft BackOffice and related applications.

Marketing/public relations tool kits

Marketing/PR tool kits provide you with information and materials needed to make the most of and build your business. These tools include customizable materials for hosting a seminar, writing an effective business plan and establishing a public relations plan.

Locally delivered sales and technical seminars

The local Microsoft sales offices provide sales and technical seminars to MSP members on a one-to-many basis. These seminars are based on key product initiatives and are intended to provide product sales and technical knowledge to MSPs so they can effectively sell and service Microsoft products.

Microsoft InfoSource directory listing

The CD-based electronic directory provides customers with a comprehensive listing of your organization's products and services. It is distributed to organizations worldwide for no charge, upon request.

Microsoft also holds a number of other co-marketing events for MSPs, including open houses and trade fair shows annually.

PARTNER LEVEL

An MSP member can earn a nomination into the MSP partner program through demonstrated expertise with Microsoft products, a significant commitment to Microsoft, established sales and marketing skills, and proven contributions to the success and sale of Microsoft products. Only Microsoft field representatives can nominate members for consideration as MSP partners. Microsoft Solution Provider partners provide Microsoft-based solutions for a variety of organizations ranging from small to large companies in many industries. The MSP partners have a one-to-one account management relationship with Microsoft to deliver value-added services to solve a variety of business issues.

note ▜ **Microsoft Solution Provider partners must have a minimum of $200,000 in sales service MCP-derived business) per annum and be subject to on-demand sales reporting by Microsoft.**

MICROSOFT CERTIFIED PROFESSIONAL REQUIREMENTS

The MCP program qualifies technical professionals who are skilled in building, implementing and supporting solutions with Microsoft products. Certifications provide a benchmark for organizations to use when hiring technical staff, determining training needs, or outsourcing technical services. Microsoft Certified Professionals at the member level must have at least two MCPs on staff, or 100 percent of technical staff qualified as MCPs. Technical staff is defined as those employees involved in consulting, application development and testing, system installation, integration and/or migration, technical training or technical support.

Certification also plays an important role in referrals. Microsoft will refer prioritized leads your way from its ART based on the Microsoft products for which your MCPs are certified.

Finding a Niche in the MSP Market

tip **One of the hottest horizontal markets that an MSP can target is intranets, which according to the latest estimates, will be a $6 billion dollar industry by the year 2000. Another potentially lucrative niche is electronic commerce for the Internet or World Wide Web. The significant savings incurred by implementing e-commerce on the Internet, as opposed to traditional EDI applications, will drive this niche market into the billions as well.**

Although this chapter focuses on entrepreneurial startups who are contemplating becoming MSPs, established independent consultants who are freelance trainers or software developers may want to pay close attention to these niche markets for employment opportunities.

Some of the best prospective market niches for any MSP are carefully outlined here. While some opportunities are obvious, most of the vertical markets offer viable business opportunities well into the next century. Following Microsoft's lead in the information technology business is always a good bet, especially during the 1990s, and many MSPs are actively pursuing the list of business opportunities or market niches as outlined here.

Internet/Intranet Services

This market niche is one of the most promising areas of opportunity for an MSP. Microsoft has recently released a bevy of new subsystems for Windows NT, including Internet Proxy Server, Merchant Server and Internet Information Server. This entire suite of applications designed for Windows NT Server is also bundled as a suite of applications named Microsoft Site Server. Microsoft Solution Providers can take full advantage of Microsoft's inroads into the Internet and intranet market by offering implementation and support services for these products.

Custom Application Development/Software Customization Services

Microsoft Solution Providers who specialize in software development can put their expertise to work by offering the latest in programming technology for the Internet and intranets. The demand for ActiveX and Java programming expertise for today's interactive Web sites is creating a wealth of opportunities for information technologists who specialize in these scripting languages.

Systems Integration

Information technology firms specializing in migration, integration and multi-vendor environments are in huge demand in both public and private industry. The need to integrate legacy systems (mainframes and minis) with local area networks and the Internet is becoming increasingly important. Microsoft Solution Providers have the tools and expertise to take on such projects with Microsoft systems such as SNA Server, SQL Server and Novell NetWare support and migration services that are built in to Windows NT.

Local/Wide Area Networking Services

Microsoft Solution Providers can offer network design, implementation and support services to small, medium and large businesses. This is by far one of the more popular services offered by smaller MSPs. With the incredible growth of local area networks in general and the trend in migration from Novell to Windows networking, the small IT company can tap into this growing market niche.

Retail

Microsoft is readying its merchant server system in preparation for the potentially explosive growth of electronic commerce on the Net. Microsoft Solution Providers can sell integration services utilizing Merchant System Server and Site Server to provide customers with the ability to transact business securely and efficiently from their Web sites.

Consulting

Microsoft Solution Providers can offer computer consulting services in the form of systems analysis and design, business process re-engineering, network planning, project management and Internet/intranet design. Computer consulting has always been a lucrative field, with average billings per hour anywhere from $150 to $250. Microsoft Solution Providers also get an assist from Microsoft through their MSP marketing programs and technical support services such as Microsoft Comprehensive Priority support.

Hardware Sales and Service

Computer hardware sales and service has been a low-margin business for quite some time. However, if done well it can be potentially lucrative, especially if you join Microsoft's Reseller program, shown in Figure 10-3. The Reseller program is targeted at computer manufacturers (large or small) for purposes of a marketing channel. Original equipment manufacturers (clone makers, too) can benefit from the Microsoft Reseller program by getting volume discounts through distributors like Merisel and Ingram Micro. Resellers pre-load Microsoft operating systems and applications for resale to the general public.

While there are many more areas of specialty within the major market niches for information technology services, the areas listed here are the most viable for an MSP.

One last note on the MSP program. While most companies join the MSP program with the intention of selling and supporting Microsoft products and services, some do not. Instead they join for the purposes of obtaining the $20,000 in software and technical support they receive as a member of the MSP program, and have no real intention of either selling or supporting Microsoft products and services over the long run.

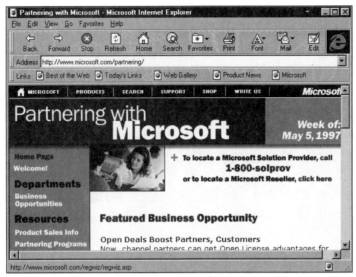

FIGURE 10-3   The Microsoft Partnering home page shown here is located at `http://www.microsoft.com/partnering.`
(Screen shot reprinted with permission from Microsoft Corporation.)

Unaware that Microsoft offers the same software and technical support through its MSDN, these companies unwittingly apply to become MSPs. Not only do these bogus MSPs cause confusion in the marketplace, they belittle the MSP program by not living up to the program's terms and conditions as stipulated by Microsoft.

 concept link **For more information on the Microsoft Developer Network, see Chapter 11.**

For more information on the Microsoft reseller program call 800-426-9400.

ASSOCIATION OF MICROSOFT SOLUTION PROVIDERS

The Association of Microsoft Solution Providers, formerly the National Association of Solution Providers, was incorporated in 1994 as a Texas nonprofit corporation. The AMSP, shown in Figure 10-4, is a professional association with geographic chapters designed to give MSPs the opportunity to develop alliances with each other and effectively form "virtual" corporations to expand their capabilities, thereby making each more valuable in today's marketplace.

The AMSP mission is to advance MSP members through MSP partnering, open communications with Microsoft, information exchange, and professional educational forums for building strong, ethically sound and profitable working relationships.

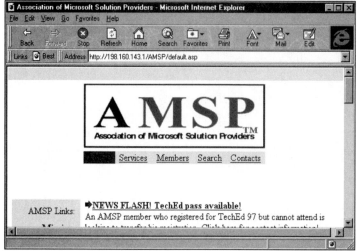

FIGURE 10-4   **The AMSP home page shown here is located at**
`http://www.amsp.org`.
(Screen shot reprinted with permission from Microsoft Corporation.)

For more information on joining the AMSP call 713-580-4966.

KEY POINT SUMMARY

In summary, this chapter covered in detailed the steps necessary to become an MSP. The chapter also discussed the start-up costs associated with starting an MSP VAR business. In addition, the subject of niche target markets were covered to help the reader understand some of the traditional information technology markets open to the MSP. Finally, the subject of trade associations was discussed with a focus on the AMSP.

- The entry fee to the MSP program is relatively low, but there are also a few hidden costs in becoming a VAR with Microsoft.

- Microsoft requires at least two MCPs or Microsoft Certified Product Specialists on board for their Member Level MCP program.

- Some of the niche markets wide open to MSPs are Intranets and electronic commerce on the Net.

- As an MSP it's always a good idea to join a trade association.

MCP Technical Resources

About Chapter 11

Two very important, if not overlooked, resources available to Microsoft Certified Professionals (MCPs) are Microsoft TechNet and the Microsoft Developer Network (MSDN). These technical resources available on compact disc and the Internet offer MCPs a wealth of information and tools such as Product Knowledge Bases, white papers, resource kits, software documentation, sample code, newsletters, magazines, and a plethora of articles on every conceivable product and service of Microsoft.

Other technical resources available from Microsoft come in the form of seminars and conferences held annually and semiannually each year. These technical conferences and seminars offer MCPs a chance to meet and learn with their peers in locations around the globe. Most are held in the within U.S. borders for strategic reasons and because they offer the very best accommodations for the large crowds that Microsoft events draw.

This chapter focuses on each of these technical resources in detail in order to better describe the benefits and opportunities for education that each has to offer. For example, the TechNet CD is portable and can prove to be a very important asset for Microsoft Certified Systems Engineers (MCSE) working in the field. On the other hand, the TechNet Web site contains the very latest information on software patches and fixes for the technical professional supporting Microsoft operating systems and applications. Both versions of TechNet are excellent resources, and both have their advantages and disadvantages.

MICROSOFT TECHNET – SUBSCRIPTION SERVICE

The Microsoft TechNet CD program began back in 1992 as a small compendium of technical articles in a rudimentary Knowledge Base. Since then it has become a full-blown technical resource for Microsoft professionals with well over 100,000 pages of valuable information.

Microsoft touts that TechNet can reduce the total cost of ownership of Microsoft products by providing fast, easy access to almost any technical article on Microsoft products in the CD's Knowledge Base and technical directories. Microsoft also claims that the product can actually help train technical support personnel via the myriad of technical articles on everything from Excel to Windows NT Server and more. It's true to some extent — check it out for yourself.

A subscription to the TechNet CD, shown in Figure 11-1, which is updated and mailed out monthly, costs anywhere from $299 to $1,029 depending on your needs. For individuals, the subscription rate is $299 a year in the U.S., $399 in Canada, and $429 for an international version that includes a supplemental driver CD for those who need it. For companies or organizations the cost starts at $699 and goes up to $1,029 depending on how many users access the CD over the network or LAN.

FIGURE 11-1   The Microsoft Subscriber Services home page
(Screen shot reprinted with permission from Microsoft Corporation.)

If you are a computer consultant, computer reseller, or systems integration firm the subscription is well worth it. TechNet can be a godsend when it comes to supporting end users and diagnosing operating system problems. It is also an excellent resource for training on Microsoft products.

 As an added bonus Microsoft now offers any new Microsoft Certified Product Specialist (MCPS) or Trainer (MCT) a free one month subscription to the TechNet CD for passing the MCPS or MCT exams. For Microsoft Certified Systems Engineers (MCSE) and Microsoft Certified Solution Developers (MCSD), Microsoft offers a free one-year subscription to the TechNet CD as a reward for becoming certified in their advanced track certification programs.

For more information on TechNet, call Microsoft at 800-344-2121.

Who Needs TechNet and Why

TechNet is an essential tool for MCPSs and MCSEs. The CD-based tool can be carried into the field to help diagnose critical problems with Microsoft technology. With most of today's systems engineers and products specialist toting laptops with CDs, TechNet makes an excellent arsenal for tackling hardware- and software-related problems with microcomputers.

Microsoft Certified Systems Engineers in particular face daunting challenges with some of Microsoft's more advanced systems such as Windows NT and Microsoft Exchange Server. It's nearly impossible to master the myriad of problems that can potentially crop up on Microsoft's advanced BackOffice line of applications software. With TechNet's Knowledge Base, which, by the way, is the same one used by Microsoft's own in-house technical support personnel, an engineer can rapidly query the database of technical articles on known issues of Microsoft products. Ditto for MCPSs who often support end users with applications such as Word and Excel.

TechNet CD: How to Use It to Your Advantage

Many new subscribers to the TechNet subscription program often overlook or forget to use the CD to their advantage. They are used to resolving hardware and software problems through trial and error, via technical support phone calls, or by looking up information on a problem in a service manual. It always takes a while to change old habits, but an information source like the TechNet CD can save you a lot of time, aggravation and expense if used properly.

The first thing any subscriber to TechNet, shown in Figure 11-2, should do each month after receiving the CD is open it and peruse the latest additions to it. The new pages and directories are typically marked with a red dot to let you know what new information has been added since the last month's issue. Second, keep the CD accessible at all times. Don't lock it up, pass it around or put it in a desk drawer. Keep it out in the open where you'll notice it and most likely use it, much like a dictionary. If you carry a laptop around with you on jobs, bring the TechNet CD with you in a special protective carrying case. Finally, if you own a server version of the product, make sure you share it out with the rest of the network so others can use it. Train others how to use it and you could reduce your burden of supporting your internal network and concentrate on better servicing your company's clients.

FIGURE 11-2   The Microsoft TechNet CD opening screen.
(Screen shot reprinted with permission from Microsoft Corporation.)

TechNet: Welcome

If you're using Windows 95 or Windows NT and you have the AutoPlay function turned on, starting TechNet can be a snap. Simply place the CD in the drive and watch TechNet load automatically—even return exactly where you left off on a specific subject! TechNet remembers where you were in the directories or Knowledge Base. TechNet also has a bookmark function for returning to favorite topics and information located in the database and information directories.

TechNet: What's New

This is one of the most important sections of the TechNet CD to refer to each month once you have received the CD. The What's New section, shown in Figure 11-3, contains some of the most important technical developments with Microsoft products and services. Overlook this section and you could be missing a lot. Actually, reading this section each month is one of the best methods of staying abreast with just about every development in Microsoft systems and applications, including product support and maintenance.

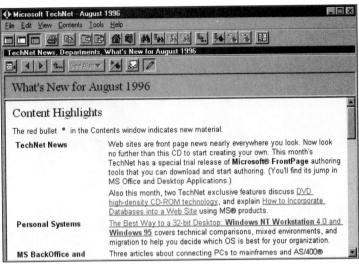

FIGURE 11-3   TechNet's What's New section.
(Screen shot reprinted with permission from Microsoft Corporation.)

TechNet: BackOffice

The BackOffice section of the TechNet CD, shown in Figure 11-4, contains information on the entire suite of BackOffice applications including SNA Server, Systems Management Server, Microsoft SQL Server, Internet Information Server and Microsoft Exchange Server, its enterprise messaging system.

TechNet: Personal Systems

For the MCPS and MCSE, the Personal Systems section, shown in Figure 11-5, of the TechNet CD contains vital information on desktop operating systems such as Windows 3.1, Windows 95 and Windows for Workgroups. Also included in this section is the Ultimate Printer, which contains detailed information on a multitude of printers and printing information.

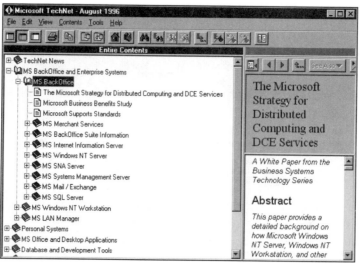

FIGURE 11-4   TechNet's BackOffice section.

(Screen shot reprinted with permission from Microsoft Corporation.)

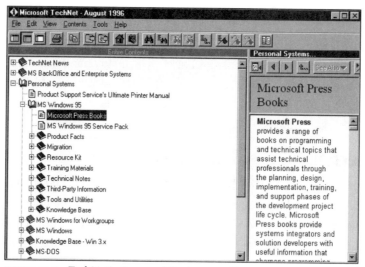

FIGURE 11-5   TechNet's Personal Systems section.

(Screen shot reprinted with permission from Microsoft Corporation.)

TechNet: Microsoft Office and Desktop Applications

In the Office and Desktop section, shown in Figure 11-6, you will find information on the complete suite of Microsoft Office applications, including Word, Excel, PowerPoint and Access. You will also find technical support articles on Microsoft FrontPage and Microsoft Project. Finally, look for the Microsoft Office resource kit, a valuable tool for supporting MS Office in an enterprise environment.

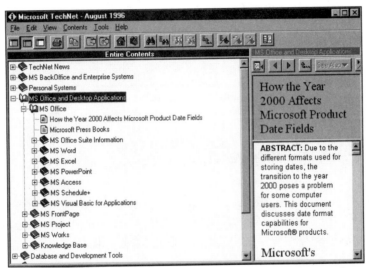

FIGURE 11-6   TechNet's MS Office and Desktop Applications section.
(Screen shot reprinted with permission from Microsoft Corporation.)

TechNet: Database and Development Tools

Developers who specialize in Microsoft FoxPro, Visual Basic and VB Script may want to bookmark this Database and Development Tools section, shown in Figure 11-7, of the TechNet CD. It offers documentation on using the new VB Script scripting language for Internet-based applications such as hooking databases to HTML front ends for a Web site. Also included in this section is information on Microsoft Source Safe, which can now be used to manage Web sites, and Microsoft Test, for thoroughly testing your apps.

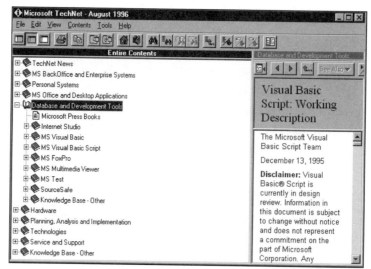

FIGURE 11-7   TechNet's Database and Development Tools section.
(Screen shot reprinted with permission from Microsoft Corporation.)

TechNet: Hardware

TechNet's Hardware section, shown in Figure 11-8, includes information on some of Microsoft's hardware products like the Natural Keyboard, Hardware Compatibility Lists for Windows NT (HCL) and Knowledge Base for hardware-related problems. The Ultimate Printer manual is also included in the section.

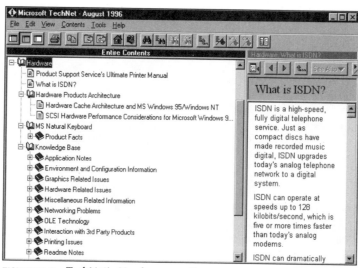

FIGURE 11-8   TechNet's Hardware section.
(Screen shot reprinted with permission from Microsoft Corporation.)

TechNet: Planning, Analysis, and Implementation

The Planning, Analysis and Implementation section, shown in Figure 11-9, is best suited for the MCSE. Here you will find information on how to plan, analyze and implement enterprise systems. A model system is also proposed for the ideal help desk solution. Also, articles on integrating a Windows NT Server domain with a Novell NetWare local area network are included in this section of the CD.

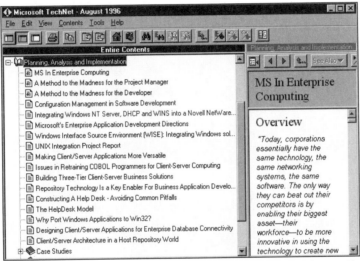

FIGURE 11-9   TechNet's Planning, Analysis and Implementation section.
(Screen shot reprinted with permission from Microsoft Corporation.)

TechNet: Technology

A comprehensive section on the Internet is included in the Technology section, shown in Figure 11-10, of TechNet. Everything from how an ISP operates to understanding how databases connect to HTML files is included in this directory. Also, all of your favorite acronyms are covered in detail, including TAPI, ODBC, WOSA and OLE for those of you bent on understanding and using these software APIs.

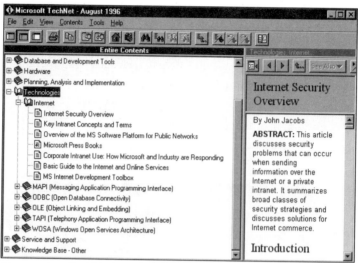

FIGURE 11-10   TechNet's Technology section.
(Screen shot reprinted with permission from Microsoft Corporation.)

TechNet: Service and Support

Under the Service and Support section shown in Figure 11-11, you will find information on Microsoft's channels partner programs like the Microsoft Solution Provider (MSP) VAR, including directories of every MSP in the world. Also included in this section of the CD is a copy of the Microsoft InfoSource CD, a directory of MSPs, and third-party ISVs. Finally, if you dig deep enough, you will find information on TechNet, MSDN, and Microsoft beta evaluation program.

TechNet: Knowledge Base

Every month, TechNet's Knowledge Base shown in Figure 11-12 delivers the most recent edition of basically the same library of technical support information developed and used by Microsoft support engineers, including over 55,000 topics, troubleshooting tips, work-arounds and much more.

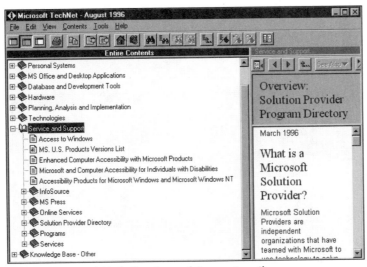

FIGURE 11-11 TechNet's Service and Support section.
(Screen shot reprinted with permission from Microsoft Corporation.)

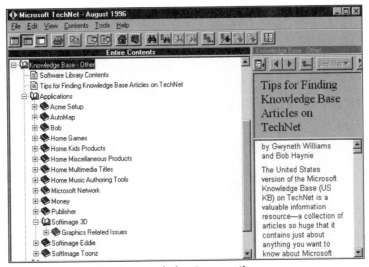

FIGURE 11-12 TechNet's Knowledge Base section.
(Screen shot reprinted with permission from Microsoft Corporation.)

TechNet: Query Tool

Without the powerful Query tool shown in Figure 11-13 and search engine, the TechNet CD would be about as useful as a yellow pages directory without phone numbers. With well over 100,000 pages of critical information on this CD, a quick, efficient search engine is essential. The query engine is capable of performing advanced searches rapidly, provided you construct the query properly. Full help and instructions are provided to assist novices with search engines functions.

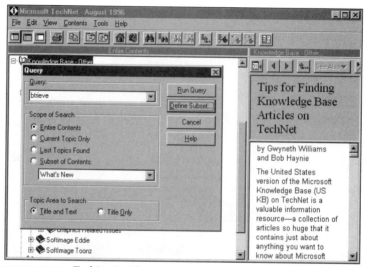

FIGURE 11-13   TechNet's Primary Query tool.

(Screen shot reprinted with permission from Microsoft Corporation.)

TechNet: Bookmark Tool

The Bookmark tool shown in Figure 11-14 in the TechNet CD is a very handy feature. You can mark your favorite sections of the CD quickly with just two clicks of the mouse. So the next time you enter the program, you can simply select from the drop-down menu, and bingo, you're there!

The TechNet Web Site at Microsoft

The TechNet home page shown in Figure 11-15 at Microsoft's Web site mostly relates to information about subscribing to the TechNet subscription program. However, Microsoft is now expanding some of the information and services on the TechNet Web site to include online technical support wizards. How far Microsoft takes this wizard technology is anybody's guess, but based on the overwhelming popularity with wizard technology there is no telling how much of TechNet may end up online vs. CD.

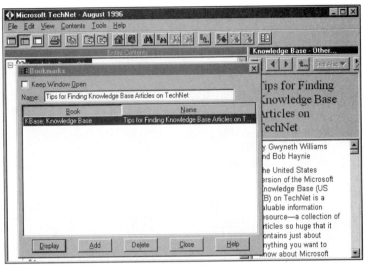

FIGURE 11-14   TechNet's Bookmark tool.
(Screen shot reprinted with permission from Microsoft Corporation.)

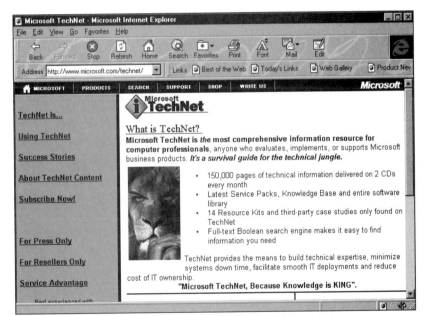

FIGURE 11-15   The Microsoft TechNet home page is located at
`http://www.microsoft.com/technet`.
(Screen shot reprinted with permission from Microsoft Corporation.)

For more information on subscribing to the TechNet CD program call
800-1426-9400.

MICROSOFT DEVELOPER NETWORK SUBSCRIPTION SERVICE

The Microsoft Developer Network CD subscription service is a library of technical articles, product documentation, royalty-free sample code and Knowledge Base. There are four different subscription levels available to subscribers.

- **Library Subscription (level 1)** delivers the quarterly MSDN Library CD-ROM, with royalty-free sample code, product documentation, technical articles, Microsoft Developer's Knowledge Base, and more. Cost for a one-year membership is $199 (U.S. only).

- **Professional Subscription (level 2)** includes the Library subscription plus the latest in Microsoft systems technology, providing API-level systems technology, including Windows client desktop operating systems (licensed for development testing) and Microsoft SDKs and DDKs. Cost for a one-year membership is $499 (U.S. only).

- **Enterprise Subscription (level 3)** includes both the Library and Professional subscriptions but also includes Microsoft BackOffice enterprise systems software like Windows NT Server, Systems Management Server, SNA Server and MS SQL Server. Cost for a one-year membership is $1,500 (U.S. only).

- **Universal Subscription (level 4)** includes the Library, Professional and Enterprise subscriptions, plus BackOffice Test Platform, Microsoft Office 97, Visual Studio and InterDev. Cost for a one-year membership is $2,499 (U.S. only).

Microsoft offers a new free online version of MSDN that contains over one gigabyte of sample source code.

web links **To sign up for this free service visit MSDN at** http://www. microsoft.com/msdn.

Who Needs Microsoft Developer Network and Why?

The Microsoft Developer Network is a comprehensive source for programming information and technologies from Microsoft. If you're an MCSD or an MCT specializing in development languages, then you should at least subscribe to level 1 or the Library version of MSDN to keep abreast in your field. Developers will naturally benefit most from the subscription service, but MCTs can also use it to brush up on specific issues concerning products like Visual Basic, Visual C++, and Web programming tools like Visual Studio and InterDev.

MSDN CD: How to Use It to Your Advantage

If you subscribe to the Universal MDSN CD subscription and you're a computer geek, well, you probably feel like it's Christmas every quarter. In the level 4 mailer you get the latest versions of all of Microsoft's operating systems and applications and Internet development tools. As an MCSD or MCT you should try to familiarize yourself with most Microsoft applications and systems in order to handle questions both from clients and students.

Like the TechNet CD, any new additions to the MSDN are flagged by a red dot on the directory trees or documents. You should check out any updated information because it could contain important release patches or fixes to code that your application depends on. As with the TechNet CD, you can bookmark favorite sections of the CD for quick access.

MSDN: Welcome

The Microsoft Developer Network main interface shown in Figure 11-16 resembles Microsoft Explorer for Windows 95 & NT. Navigation is simple and quick. To expand or contract directories, you simply click on the minus (-) sign or plus (+) sign depending on the latest setting in the directory tree (i.e., it toggles). On the toolbar you will find search icons in the form of binoculars and a flag, which represents the bookmark function. From time to time you may just want to browse the directories to see what's new (indicated by a red dot), but if you are in a hurry, remember to use the excellent search engine included with the CD.

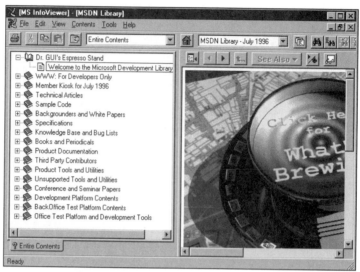

FIGURE 11-16   The MSDN CD's opening screen.
(Screen shot reprinted with permission from Microsoft Corporation.)

MSDN: Dr. Gui's Expresso Stand

One of your first stops on your quarterly perusal of the MSDN CD is Dr. Gui's Expresso Stand shown in Figure 11-17. Dr. Gui puts programming into a new light with his daft humor and wit. He covers the latest developments in the ActiveX and C++ worlds. If you're a hacker bent on having fun while you learn about new Microsoft technology, make sure to check him out each quarter.

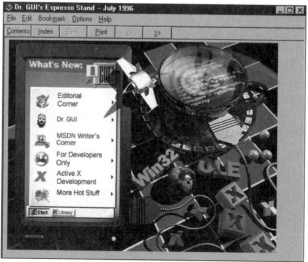

FIGURE 11-17   The MSDN CD's Dr. Gui's Expresso Stand.
(Screen shot reprinted with permission from Microsoft Corporation.)

MSDN: Member Kiosk

Everything you always wanted to know but were afraid to ask on the MSDN program is included in the Member Kiosk section shown in Figure 11-18 of the CD. It's basically an offline bulletin board (of the old fashioned kind) where posts from Microsoft, the Developer Network Team and Microsoft Certification Board can be found for reading.

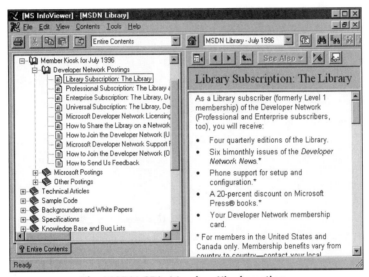

FIGURE 11-18   The MSDN CD's Member Kiosk section.
(Screen shot reprinted with permission from Microsoft Corporation.)

MSDN: Technical Articles

A complete archive of every question ever posed to Dr. Gui is included in the Technical Articles directory, shown in Figure 11-19, of the MSDN CD. Also included are articles on Visual C++, FoxPro, Microsoft Access and Microsoft SQL Server. If you are a WordBasic programmer you may want to check the articles on WordBasic and Office 95, which are also included in this section of the MSDN CD.

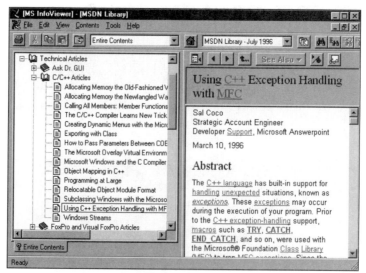

FIGURE 11-19   The MSDN CD's Technical Articles section.
(Screen shot reprinted with permission from Microsoft Corporation.)

MSDN: Sample Code

More than 1,500 royalty-free samples that demonstrate development techniques in the Visual Basic programming system, Visual C++ development system, Microsoft Foundation Classes, Visual FoxPro, database management system, Microsoft Office and more can be found in the Sample Code directory, shown in Figure 11-20, on the CD.

MSDN: Backgrounder and White Papers

If you are interested in the very latest Web technology from Microsoft you will definitely want to check out this Backgrounder and White Papers section, shown in Figure 11-21, of the MSDN CD for its white papers on ActiveX technology. Also included in this section are vital articles on case studies performed by Microsoft of successful implementations of Microsoft technology throughout the world. Developers will enjoy the information on Microsoft Foundation Classes (MFCs) for Windows programming.

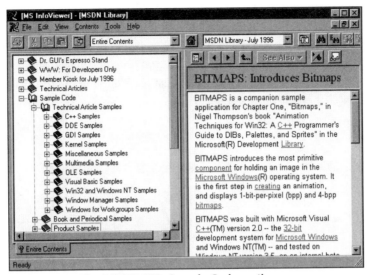

FIGURE 11-20   The MSDN CD's Sample Code section.

(Screen shot reprinted with permission from Microsoft Corporation.)

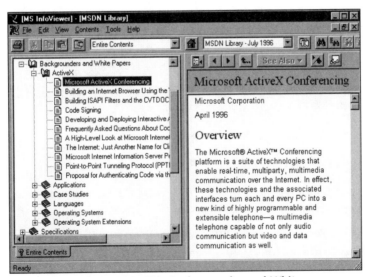

FIGURE 11-21   The MSDN CD's Backgrounder and White
Papers section.

(Screen shot reprinted with permission from Microsoft Corporation.)

MSDN: Specifications

The latest specifications, covering popular technologies such as Plug-and-Play, True Type and Sockets, are included in the Specification section of the CD, shown in Figure 11-22. The Telephony Application Programming Interface (TAPI) is also discussed, along with SPI and TSI specifications for hardware interfacing with telephony applications.

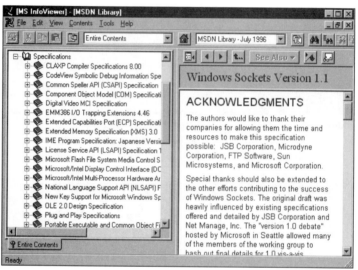

FIGURE 11-22   The MSDN CD's Specifications section.
(Screen shot reprinted with permission from Microsoft Corporation.)

MSDN: Knowledge Base and Bug List

The complete Microsoft Developer Knowledge Base and Bug List shown in Figure 11-23 includes more than 40,000 articles with bug reports and work-arounds on all Microsoft development products. You are bound to find the information in this treasure-trove of information. Remember to use the search engine; it's a complete waste of time browsing this baby!

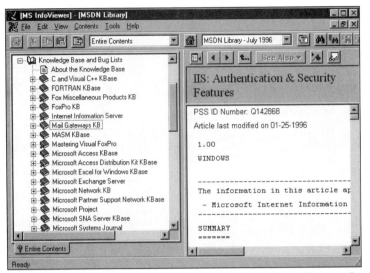

FIGURE 11-23   The MSDN CD's Knowledge Base and Bug Lists section.
(Screen shot reprinted with permission from Microsoft Corporation.)

MSDN: Books and Periodicals

Microsoft Press books, such as the full text of Cluts's Programming the Windows 95 User Interface and excerpts from Learn Java Now, Building Microsoft Exchange Applications and others can be found in the Books and Periodicals section of the MSDN CD, as shown in Figure 11-24. Complete issues of Microsoft Systems Journal, as well as selected articles from Inside Visual Basic, Visual C++ Developer, Inside Access, Fox Talk and more are included in this section of the MSDN CD-ROM.

MSDN: Product Documentation

All Product Documentation, as shown in Figure 11-25, for Microsoft development products and toolkits, including Visual Studio 97, Microsoft Office 97, Developer Edition and the Platform SDK, are included in the section of the CD.

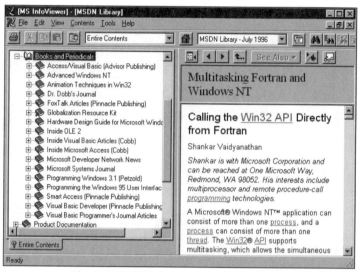

FIGURE 11-24   The MSDN CD's **Books & Periodicals section.**

(Screen shot reprinted with permission from Microsoft Corporation.)

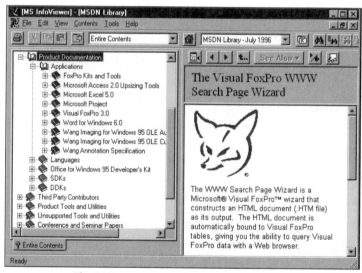

FIGURE 11-25   The MSDN CD's **Product Documentation section.**

(Screen shot reprinted with permission from Microsoft Corporation.)

MSDN: Product Tools and Utilities

In the Product and Tools section, shown in Figure 11-26, of the MSDN CD you will find lots of free goodies, like the Access Upsizing Tool for upgrading Access database to MS SQL Server, the latest version of Internet Explorer, all of the Microsoft Office viewer apps for viewing files offline from their applications, and OLE debugging tools for developers.

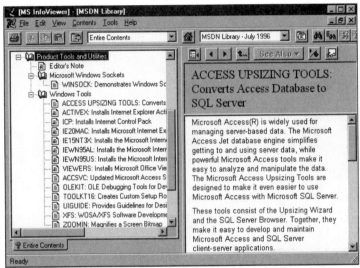

FIGURE 11-26   **The MSDN CD's Product Tools and Utilities section.**
(Screen shot reprinted with permission from Microsoft Corporation.)

MSDN: Conference and Seminars

In the Conference and Seminars section, shown in Figure 11-27, of the MSDN CD you will find information on Microsoft Tech Ed and Developer Days conferences, as well as information on all of the many seminars and functions held by Microsoft throughout the U.S. and abroad.

The Microsoft Developer Network Site at Microsoft

The Microsoft Developer Network Web site shown in Figure 11-28 is a low-cost alternative to the MSDN subscription service. Actually, it is the online version of the level 1 membership, which includes technical articles, sample code, and other developer goodies like Microsoft Systems Journal and Microsoft Interactive Developer magazines. The Web site version of MSDN also includes important links to other areas of Microsoft relating to developers, such as the Site Builder Network for Webmasters.

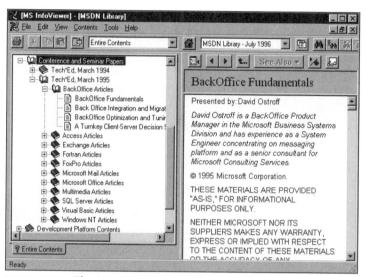

FIGURE 11-27   The MSDN CD's Conference and Seminars section.
(Screen shot reprinted with permission from Microsoft Corporation.)

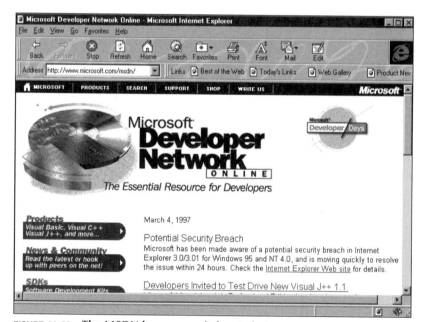

FIGURE 11-28   The MSDN home page is located at
`http://www.microsoft.com/technet.`
(Screen shot reprinted with permission from Microsoft Corporation.)

For more information on subscribing to the CD program call 800-426-9400.

Microsoft Developer Seminars and Conventions

Each year Microsoft holds numerous seminars and conventions, but two stand out above them all: Developer Days and Tech Ed. These two technical conferences run the gamut on Microsoft technology. The conferences are held in different parts of the U.S., with Tech Ed typically held in the South, Developer Days on the West Coast.

For the serious Microsoft professional, the conferences not only offer technical seminars on the latest Microsoft systems and applications, but give attendees a chance to network with their peers. In this day and age it is imperative that you build a network of individuals, and Tech Ed and Developer Days offer information technology professionals an excellent opportunity to meet and make new friends in the industry.

TechEd

Tech Ed is an annual conference that provides technical information on Microsoft products used to develop, integrate or support Windows-based solutions. The target audience for this conference is integrators, developers, support professionals and technical managers. Tech Ed, shown in Figure 11-29, provides hundreds of "how-to" technical sessions on Windows, Windows NT, Microsoft Excel, Windows 95, Word, Visual Basic, Visual Basic for Applications, Microsoft Access, FoxPro, SQL Server, Solutions Framework, Visual C++, Project, Multimedia, SNA Server, OLE, MAPI, Windows 95 and Exchange Server. The last Tech Ed was held in May 1997 in Orlando, Florida.

For registration information contact Microsoft at 800-426-9400.

Developer Days

Developer Days, or DevDays as the "Redmonians" refer to it, is a world-class conference for Microsoft professional developers. Held in more than 25 countries worldwide, Developer Days is by far the industry's largest information technology conference. The conference is designed to educate developers and enable them to share information and experiences on the latest Microsoft tools for integrating client/server, Internet and intranet development. The conference is also hosted on more than 95 Web sites throughout the world to help developers who cannot afford the time or money to attend and offer insight on the latest developments in Microsoft technology. Figure 11-30 shows the Developer Days Web site.

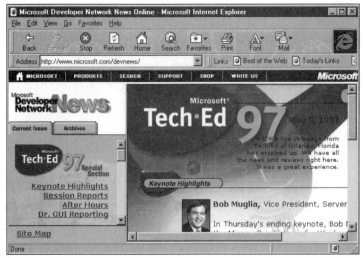

FIGURE 11-29   The Microsoft Tech Ed home page on the MSDN Web site.

(Screen shot reprinted with permission from Microsoft Corporation.)

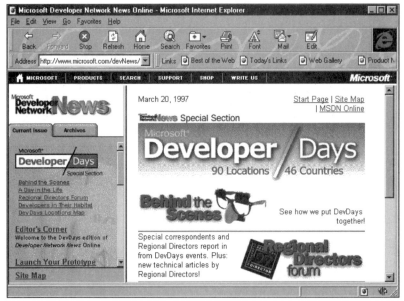

FIGURE 11-30   The Microsoft Developer Days home page on the MSDN Web site is located at `http://www.microsoft.com/msdn`.

(Screen shot reprinted with permission from Microsoft Corporation.)

Topics covered at the conferences include information on development languages and tools such as Visual Basic, Visual C++, FORTRAN, and others. The latest integrated tool packages such as InterDev and Visual Studio are discussed to help developers work smarter and more efficiently. Also, many software tools vendors are present at the conference to educate developers on the latest technological breakthroughs in programming tools and utilities for testing and augmenting code.

For registration information call Microsoft at 800-426-9400.

KEY POINT SUMMARY

In summary, this chapter covered in detail both the Microsoft TechNet CD and Developer Network CD, two very important tools for MCPs. The chapter also discussed the importance of each technical resource with respect to each MCP track. In addition, subscription rates for each program were covered to help the MCP differentiate from the various subscriber rates offered through Microsoft, especially with respect to the MSDN CD program. Finally, this chapter discussed two new companion sites on Microsoft's Web site for the TechNet and Developer Network CD subscription programs.

- Microsoft's Technet CD is a great technical resource and is geared more for the MCSE and MCPs, but all MCPs can benefit from its use.
- The MSDN CD is also a great technical resource for MCPs, but is designed more for the MCSD and MCT who concentrates in Microsoft development languages.
- Microsoft TechEd and Developer Days technical conferences are two excellent resources for training, networking with peers and having fun.

MCP Community Help

About Chapter 12

Microcomputer user groups first had their start in the early '80s, after the IBM personal computer (PC) made its debut. Their members tended to be hobbyists and end users who had a common interest in PCs and the software that ran them. Nowadays, user groups are much more sophisticated in their approach to helping individuals conquer their PCs. Many user groups found today mimic nonprofit organizations or associations in the size, depth and scope of the services they provide to members. Indeed, some user groups have now made the transformation to trade associations.

Study groups are another phenomenon beginning to emerge on the scene of information technology (IT), especially with microcomputers. While the traditional study groups found in most colleges and universities are cliquish at best, the study groups that are beginning to form for Windows NT professionals are open to anyone seriously interested in learning Microsoft technology.

In this chapter, the subjects of user groups, trade associations, and study groups are covered in detail so that you may better understand the value of these very important groups or associations. Interviews with some of the leaders of the first Windows NT user groups and NT study groups from across the nation are included to give you a close-up of what takes place at meetings and how you can benefit by joining them. Finally, instructions on how to form your own local user group or study group are included for those interested in taking on leadership positions in the IT industry.

USER GROUPS FOR PROFESSIONALS

Computer user groups have a lot to offer IT professionals. They provide a focal point for IT professionals to exchange information and ideas. A user group offers a friendly and often relaxed atmosphere for learning and exchanging ideas, obtaining assistance and services, and taking full advantage of computers and software for its members.

User groups take on various forms. Some are very large, with special interest groups (SIGs) organized within them. Others are small, nascent user groups that support only one specific area of interest. The average professional user group has anywhere from 50 to 100 members and is located within a specific geographic area such as a city or suburb.

A professional user group, regardless of its form or size, generally has:

- A constitution and/or bylaws
- Elected or appointed officers
- Monthly meetings
- Communication activities (newsletter, Web site)
- A library of public domain software

At monthly meetings, professional user group members often hear presentations and panel discussions, participate in question-and-answer sessions, and converse with people who share common interests.

To supplement the meetings, most professional user groups publish electronic newsletters via e-mail containing helpful hints and experiences. Most professional user groups now operate Web sites to disseminate information, tools and software to their constituent members.

Typically a group has several interests, and to address these interests the group establishes subgroups or special interest groups. Special interest groups concentrate on specific IT subjects such as Microsoft Exchange Server, Microsoft SQL Server or Visual C/C++.

If you are interested in forming your own local Microsoft user group, you may want to check out the Mindshare home page, shown in Figure 12-1.

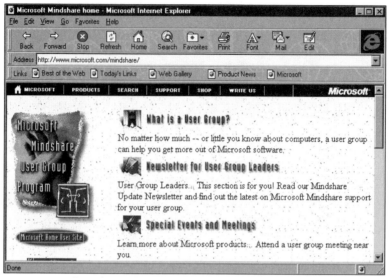

FIGURE 12-1   The Microsoft Mindshare home page is located at
www.microsoft.com/mindshare.

(Screen shot reprinted with permission from Microsoft Corporation.)

 web links   **One source for finding local NT users groups is** www.bhs.com. **This Web site has a directory of NT user groups.**

Los Angeles Windows NT User Group

One of the nations largest Windows NT user groups, Los Angeles Windows NT User Group (LANTUG), shown in Figure 12-2, offers Microsoft Certified Professionals (MCPs) a multitude of seminars and meetings that concentrate on the Windows NT Server platform. For Windows NT Professionals or specialists, the resources, training and networking opportunities can't be beat. As with many computer user groups, membership in LANTUG is free and attendance is optional. Many of the technical seminars held at LANTUG's monthly meetings in Santa Monica are led by independent software vendors and hardware manufacturers who build systems for the Windows NT platform. At a typical meeting each vendor will present a one-hour presentation covering their product's features, which is then followed by a Q&A session that runs roughly 15 minutes to a half an hour. All meetings begin with announcements of the group's activities and a lead-in for the guest speaker who will be presenting that session.

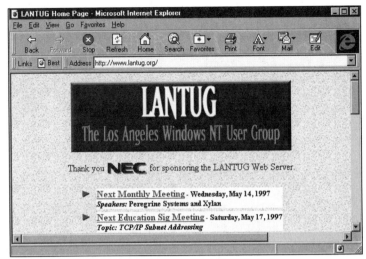

FIGURE 12-2   The LANTUG home page is located at
`www.lantug.org`.

For more information on joining LANTUG e-mail Mark Kapczynski at `markkap@microsoft.com`.

INTERVIEW: MARK KAPCZYNSKI, PRESIDENT OF THE LOS ANGELES WINDOWS NT USER GROUP (LANTUG)

Mark Kapczynski is the founder and president of the Los Angeles Windows NT User Group (LANTUG). His LANTUG meetings are held just outside Los Angeles in Santa Monica. LANTUG has many members that work in the movie industry who use Windows NT as a platform for running CGI programs and tools for computer software animation.

In an interview with Mark, the author discusses important issues with running a Windows NT user group.

Q: Can you briefly summarize how a typical NT user group can help MCPs with their careers?

A: It gives people the opportunity to come out and interact with other people from a specific community. In this particular case it is the NT community, and the associated technologies—other back office technologies, development technologies and so on. Basically, it brings together the people most interested in these areas—consulting firms, mission providers, training centers, headhunter-type companies, and corporations interested in recruiting and hiring new people. So you get one of the rare events that actually brings so many different types of parties together for one common thing. There are certain other events usually centered around, "Let's just sell you a product," or "Let's tell you about training or one thing". This is a gathering that is at the same time informative.

continued

continued

Q: As head of the Los Angeles Windows NT User Group, what sort of time requirements does that role impose on you?

A: It really depends on your personal strategy for what you would like to accomplish. My role timewise is only five or maybe ten hours a month total, and that includes actually attending meetings as well. What works out really well is having enough other people to help support it so that you are not doing it by yourself. It could turn into a full-time job because people like the concept of the user group and are going to want other resources that are tied to it, for example, a Web site, or this or that. The whole idea is to get as many people involved as possible and distribute the work.

Q: What are the typical duties of the president or director of a local user group?

A: I would say the typical duties are to ensure that the monthly meetings happen. Make sure you solidify a space to house your meeting, speakers to attend, if you will have food – the basic logistics of bringing people together, advertising that you are having the meeting and so on. Then you get into some of the unwritten things such as building a relationship with the local Microsoft office, local vendor representation, working with the system engineers and sales folks in the Microsoft local office, etc. This also includes working with vendors like Compaq, Seagate, etc., to get them on a local level to know that this is yet another local resource for them. Companies are aware of user groups. For example does Compaq know that their individual SEs are working with local user groups? They would probably say that they are slightly involved. But you talk to the local people and they say that is a great opportunity and they love doing it; they help drive their customers to the events. At the high national, corporate level of these companies there is probably very limited involvement. It really comes down to personal relationships with the local vendors and so on.

Q: If an MCP desires to take an active leadership role in a local Windows NT user group, what role can he or she expect to perform and how much personal time, on average, would be required to successfully fulfill that role?

A: Probably no more than five, maybe ten hours a month. To run one main meeting is not too hard. A couple of people do that and keep it going. What ends up happening is that you get more people active and involved and they want to take and create a SIG-type meeting. In Los Angeles, we have the NT User Group. It's really composed of four or five individual meetings each month. So I may be the leader of the whole group, but there are five front leaders who lead their own SIGs. For example, there is one on Exchange, one on 3-D Animation and Multimedia on NT, because that is big in LA and the Hollywood community. We have one that is focused on actually training and helping people get their MCSEs and MCSDs. We are also tied in with sequel server groups; you have all the different pockets being covered.

Q: How many members does the Los Angeles Windows NT User Group have at this time?

A: It has somewhere between 3,200 and 3,500 members. It is one of the few events that is non-product- or non-company-specific, and it ties in a lot of different types of individuals.

Q: Is membership growing or declining? And at what rate?

A: I would probably say that it is growing 15 or 20 percent a year. We are kind of unusual. I would say that most of the groups that have started up are less than a year old. Most of the user groups across the country are less than a year old. We have been around for over three years, so our numbers are really not growing as dramatically as other groups. It comes down to who are the local people running it. I know that I have been doing this for a few years, and it's tough to keep the challenge going and interest growing. So the important thing is to get new people and new faces helping lead it and drive it; my role becomes more of a facilitator for everyone else. I still have great contacts and relationships that they can leverage to keep the group going.

Q: Will local Windows NT user groups ever charge for membership?
A: That is really a local user group issue. Some people charge, some don't; most do not charge. The thing is that you have to show value. If you can't show value, why should someone pay a hundred dollars a year? What do you get for that hundred dollars? That's one of the things when you start to get into an issue of where does WANTUG play into this. The thing with WANTUG is to really provide an umbrella for all these local user groups like NT Pro. It is basically to provide some common tools and resources to the local user groups, but that may come at a price to the local user group. We are still trying to figure out if that is worthwhile.

Q: How active is your group? What percentage of members actually show up for the meetings, on average?
A: At the monthly meetings, we get about a hundred people, which is pretty significant. That would be about 12 percent. The percentage is quite small, but at the same time you get different people going to the SIG meetings. So that's 100 for the main meeting, but you get some different responses. You are going to get 60 people just going to the Exchange meeting each month. So that percentage is great. Sometimes

the numbers vary depending on the topic and so on, or giveaway. We did monthly user groups as part of the NT 4.0 Tour, and Microsoft put out information stating that we were going to be giving away a free copy of the software; everyone shows up. So I would say on average for the monthly meeting we have 100 people, and then depending on the SIG, between 40 and 60 people each, and that's been pretty consistent.

Q: What differentiates one user group from another?
A: Really, not much. User groups are trying to do the same thing whether they are in the United States, Japan, Europe. They all want the same thing, they want to know what's going on, they want to see how its done, they want to help get trained, they want new jobs, and so on. If I could get back to WANTUG - WANTUG and us see that there are these common goals - we all are trying to develop the same resources, and to manage those different tools and so on. Let's come up with a common set of tools and share them instead of every user group having to build a little database to track people who attend.

Q: What percentage of your local NT user group is made up of MCSEs ?
A: Actually, I think that number is growing. I would say at least 15 or 20 percent of the people inside the groups are MCSEs, or least have some type of MCP—probably even more.

Q: Do you see meetings taking place in the near future over the Internet using teleconferencing tools like NetMeeting as opposed to actual physical meetings at LANTUG?

continued

continued

A: No. People have tried doing that; chat and those kinds of things are horrible. What I see happening is a streaming video, the netshow-type thing. The interactive stuff is not there yet. The whole thing about the user groups and why I think that the Beverly Hills International user group thing has not gone anywhere is because the user group is interactive. People want to get out, meet each other, see what is going on, network with each other. You can't do that online. It's only a one-to-one thing online.

Q: Could this be a threat to local NT user groups if VTC took off?
A: No, I think it is one more way of reaching out. You would still have your normal meetings and just tie in an interactive part.

How to Start Your Own User Group

Starting your own user group can be fun, exciting and professionally rewarding, but steps must be taken to ensure its success. You may want to start out by visiting some of the more successful Windows NT user groups such as LANTUG or visiting Microsoft's Mindshare Web site illustrated earlier in this chapter. These organizations can help you get started with the process of forming the group as well as how to attract members from your local community.

Outlined below are some of the crucial areas that you will need to address when forming your group or association.

Finances

Most user groups assess nominal dues and participation fees from their members in order to cover expenses. The treasurer of the group normally collects these dues and fees at meetings or through other channels such as the mail.

Meeting location/fees

In general, new user groups start fairly small and are able to hold meetings in members' homes or offices. As the group grows, additional space may be required and the group may start meeting at local Microsoft offices (Microsoft permitting).

Most groups have demonstrations of personal computer software and hardware at meetings. A large-screen projection device makes the demonstration visible to many people at the same time and alleviates the need to demonstrate the product multiple times to small groups.

Meetings

A typical user group holds a general group meeting monthly to conduct user group business, hear presentations, see demonstrations, and exchange information or public domain software between members. Attendance is open generally to all members, prospective members and guests of the user group.

Special interest groups

Often, a user group establishes one or more SIGs to meet varied interests and needs of its members. Special interest groups normally function as subgroups of the sponsoring user group. They usually follow the same constitution and bylaws as the user group and enjoy the same benefits. A SIG is normally coordinated by a chairperson who reports to the user group officers. Special interest groups usually establish their own rules and activities, such as assessing participation fees, holding separate meetings, and submitting articles to the user group's newsletter.

Newsletters

One of the most important benefits a user group offers its members is a newsletter. A group's newsletter often starts out as a flyer or brochure about the group's activities. Many user group newsletters are now electronic and are distributed each month automatically through the group's e-mail distribution list maintained by its members.

Web site/software database

User groups generally provide members with access to their Web sites on the Internet. The user group Web site often contains archives of past newsletters and special announcements, freeware or shareware software, and links to other important sites like job and resume banks.

WINDOWS NT PROFESSIONAL ASSOCIATIONS

Some of the Windows NT professional associations found today have their roots in user groups. They started out as small user groups only to grow in size to become trade associations. These professional associations offer many of the same benefits as user groups but are more professional in their approach to member support.

Professional associations are typically more sophisticated than user groups and can draw larger talent such as dignitaries of industry because of their clout and budget. The officers and staff of nonprofit associations are often well-connected individuals who dedicate their professional lives to their respective industries. They are often experts in their particular industry and know how to plan and hold regional conferences, draw leaders of industry to special events, and educate members in topics in their field.

Association of Windows NT Systems Professionals

The very first Windows NT user group and now a professional association, the Association for Windows NT Systems Professionals or NT*Pro, shown in Figure 12-3, is the premiere technical resource for Windows NT Professionals. Located in Washington, D.C.'s outskirts, the group meets once a month, including all six of its related SIGs, to help not only Windows NT experts, but also Exchange

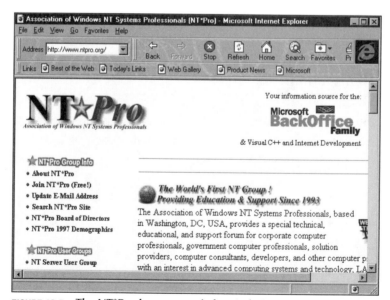

FIGURE 12-3   The NT*Pro home page is located at `www.ntpro.org`.

Specialists, Visual C++ programmers, Internet Webmasters, SQL Server Specialists and SNA engineers learn about the latest developments in their field. For those who can't make it to their monthly meetings and seminars, NT Pro boasts one the most comprehensive Web sites for Microsoft professionals in the world. Much of the information discussed at the meetings and/or seminars is available on their Web site in one form or another (such as PowerPoint presentations, minutes of the meetings, and other technical notes). Feel free to download any of this information from the NT*Pro Web site once its been posted.

For more information on becoming a member of NT*Pro e-mail Charles Kelly at `ckelly@msn.com`.

INTERVIEW: CHARLES KELLY, PRESIDENT NT PRO: ASSOCIATION OF WINDOWS NT PROFESSIONALS

*Charles Kelly is the president and founder of the NT*Pro in Washington, D.C. (`www.ntpro.org`). The world's first Windows NT-based group, NT*Pro was launched in October 1993 by Microsoft President and CEO Bill Gates. The group currently has over 9,000 members and covers all Microsoft BackOffice products and 32-bit development.*

As a regional director for the Microsoft Developer Days program, Charles Kelly has been associated with Microsoft's developer programs for several years on many different levels. He has been a key player at various summit meetings, has served on numerous Microsoft advisory councils, and has been and continues to be an integral part of the product-planning cycle for many Microsoft Internet and development tools. Charles was a member of the 1996 and 1997 Microsoft Tech Ed Advisory Committees.

Since 1990 he has worked as a computer systems analyst at the National Science Foundation (`www.nsf.gov`). In his spare time Charles writes a regular column titled "On The Job" for Government Computer News (`www.gcn.com`) and occasionally writes feature articles for Windows NT.

Q: What inspired you to start the very first Windows NT user group?

A: It seemed like the thing to do. By that I mean that my vision of where the computer industry was going seemed to be in synch with where I saw Windows NT going. To be honest, I'm not sure many other people, if any, shared that vision in 1993. Windows NT hadn't even been released at that time; it was still "vaporware." One person who did share my vision and even matched my enthusiasm was a friend named Bob Fulton, who worked as a Microsoft Certified Systems Engineer (MCSE) in the Washington, D.C., Microsoft office. "Wow!" I thought. "Here's someone else who believes in this wacky idea." All it took was one other person to validate the idea in my mind. I was determined that this NT user group would take off in a big way.

Our group started as the Advanced Systems User Group. I suppose this was our way of expressing our vision that Windows NT would finally meet the unfulfilled promises of the UNIX operating systems.

As the group grew and evolved, we decided to change our name to more accurately reflect

continued

continued

how we actually operated and how our members saw the group. We selected the Association of Windows NT Systems Professionals as our new name, and NT*Pro as our acronym.

Q: Was it difficult getting folks to attend the first few meetings, and if so, how did you manage to attract members initially?

A: It turned out to be amazingly easy to attract people. Simply, we lined up a blockbuster speaker, and we did a targeted invite mailing to computer professionals in the D.C. Metro area. The rest is history.

Bob and I were able to convince one more person who shared our vision and enthusiasm to speak at our first meeting in October 1993. We had much assistance from Alan Horowitz, who was the Microsoft Federal Marketing Manager, in arranging the speaker.

About 800 people showed up in Georgetown's Four Seasons Hotel on a rainy Sunday afternoon to hear Microsoft Chairman and CEO Bill Gates talk about Windows NT. Gates was really pumped up by the fact that we had such a large turnout and, in my opinion, gave one of the best talks I've seen him give.

The good news was that the end result of this meeting was almost 800 members on the first day/meeting. The bad news was that we had to follow in Bill Gates' huge shadow.

Being very competitive people, we rose to the challenge. We asked ourselves, "What do technical computer professionals want?" The answer we always came back to was that they wanted a technical resource, a place where they could share the latest technical advances (and the resulting opportunities) with their peer group. We found those people and we managed to give them what they were looking for.

Q: What is NT*Pro's mission?

A: We provide a special support, educational and technical forum for corporate computer professionals, government computer professionals, solution providers, computer consultants, developers and other computer professionals with an interest in advanced computing systems, advanced networking, a wide range of development issues, and advanced client/server computing.

Q: Are there specialty areas within NT*Pro?

A: Yes, those areas evolved as the group, and NT*Pro itself, evolved. We actually view these areas as separate user groups that function under the NT*Pro umbrella. We currently have seven such areas that happen to map across the Microsoft BackOffice and development tools product lines. We have the following eight groups:

- NT*Pro Windows NT Server User Group
- Capital Area SQL Server User Group
- Exchange User Group
- Systems Management Server User Group
- SNA Server User Group
- Advanced Internet Information Server User Group
- Mid-Atlantic Visual C++ User Group
- Internet Developers User Group

We also are starting another new group that will be focused on Enterprise Development and Microsoft Transaction Server.

Finally, and perhaps the one group that I'm most proud of, we have worked in conjunction with Dr. Roy Beasley of Howard University to build a very successful MCSE Certification Program.

Dr. B. worked with NT*Pro to start a Windows NT study group. The focus of this study group was to help get members ready to take the MCSE exams. From this humble beginning, Dr. B. has built a full-fledged Authorized Academic Training Partner with an ever-increasing number of fully certified alumni. In fact, the first MCSE to graduate from this program, Mark Wheatley, can now be seen online answering tech questions on Windows Sources Magazine's "Expert NT Answers Forum."

Roy's ultimate goal is to morph this particular program into a Distance Learning Lab, allowing interested people from around the world to gain certification skills via special educational programs across the Internet. We are very proud to be associated with the Howard University effort. We have provided promotion and encouragement. Dr. B. and his team have done all the work!

Q: How many members does your Association of Windows NT Systems Professionals now have?

A: As of mid–April 1997, when this interview is taking place, we have just passed the 9,000-member mark. Over the last 18 months we have averaged over 400 new members each month. We are not content to rest, though. We are currently planning several ambitious programs that we feel will bring many additional benefits to our new and existing members.

Q: What takes place at a typical NT*Pro User Group meeting?

A: Each of the eight individual groups holds its own monthly meeting. The structure of each of those monthly meetings is typically the same. Meetings generally open with a 15-minute session by the group leader reviewing new issues and products and beta news and information. This is followed by a 30- to 45-minute technical question-and-answer session. After everyone has had the opportunity to get their questions answered, a one-hour (or longer) presentation takes place. Our presentations are generally of a technical/educational nature rather than product demonstrations, though we occasionally have product demos. The typical monthly meetings will draw an audience of 50-150 people.

Every three months we have a quarterly general meeting. There is generally a theme for these quarterly meetings and a featured name speaker. The last quarterly meeting prior to this interview featured Microsoft Group Vice President Jeff Raikes. These meetings typically draw an audience of 750-1,400 and often feature an exhibition area with 15-20 vendor displays or a job fair with an equal number of companies exhibiting.

Q: How does a person join NT*Pro and what are the benefits of becoming a member of your group?

A: Joining is very easy. The only requirements are that you be a computer professional (no hobbyists, please!) and that you completely fill out the registration form. Regular membership is *free*! We do plan on starting a Members Plus program during 1997. There will be a nominal fee to join the Members Plus program, but there will be eight to ten specific benefits available only to those members. One of those benefits, planned as of this interview, will be automatic acceptance into the official Microsoft Beta Program, featuring monthly CDs with the latest MS betas.

Q: What role did you play in the creation of the Worldwide Association of NT User Groups?

A: The Worldwide Association of NT User Groups (WANTUG) was created by the leaders of NT-based user groups from around the world. In a sense, all of us together created WANTUG. The real impetus came when Mark Kapczynski, of the Los Angeles Windows NT User Group, distributed e-mail to all the existing leaders in April 1996. The result was that Mark arranged a face-to-face meeting for all group leaders interested in forming a national NT user group. Jeff Silha of SOFTBANK Forums (SOFTBANK Expos at the time) facilitated and funded the meeting in Chicago in June 1966 on the Sunday prior to

continued

continued

Spring Comdex. The on-site participants in that meeting were me, and Mark and Dan Hibbitts, of the Ann Arbor Computer Society. During the afternoon we were also joined via telephone conference call by Marjorie James, WiNTUG (Bellevue, Washington); Jason Perlow, Gotham Windows NT User Group (New York City); and John Luria, Gotham WNTUG.

That meeting in Chicago formed the basis for the association. Mark was chosen as the interim president and Marjorie and I were selected to fill out the interim officer positions. The three of us worked together for the next two and a half months gathering input from other group leaders and planning what WANTUG should be.

The creation process culminated in August 1996 with the initial election of officers. This took place during the Windows NT Intranet Solutions Conference in San Francisco. I was elected president. The other officers elected were Dennis Martin, Rocky Mountain NT UG (Denver), vice president, technology; Lisa Thomassie, Atlanta BackOffice UG, vice president, marketing; John McMains, Triangle NT UG (Raleigh, North Carolina), treasurer; and Dan Hibbitts, Ann Arbor Computer Society, secretary.

The real highlight of that initial election meeting for me was that I had the opportunity to meet privately with Steve Ballmer, Executive Vice President at Microsoft to discuss WANTUG and to solicit his support for our efforts. He not only agreed to support us in the endeavor, he also agreed to another meeting in December 1996 to discuss details of how Microsoft could best support the WANTUG user groups.

World-Wide Association of NT User Groups

The World-Wide Association of NT User Groups, shown in Figure 12-4, was established to help coordinate the activities of the various NT User Groups located throughout the world. Rather than continuously "reinventing the wheel" and creating redundant member services for Windows NT professionals, the group set out to synchronize all NT User group initiatives. User groups enabled greater efficiency of operations, as well as communications for members located around the globe. Only Windows NT User Groups are allowed membership in WANTUG. The association does not permit individual Windows NT professionals to become members at this time. Although WANTUG does not charge a fee for membership at this time, it will soon begin instituting fees to help cover the costs of administering the association in the near future.

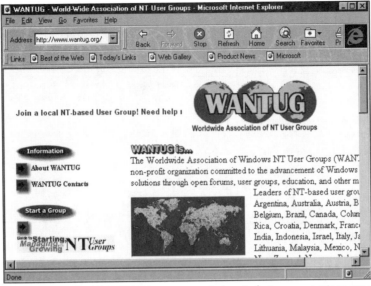

FIGURE 12-4   The WANTUG home page is located at `www.wantug.org`.

INTERVIEW: MARK KAPCZYNSKI, FOUNDER OF WANTUG: THE WORLDWIDE ASSOCIATION OF NT USER GROUPS

The World-Wide Association of NT User Groups was founded to help its constituent members (local NT user groups from around the world) focus their efforts to become a more cohesive force in the Windows NT information technology field.

Mark Kapczynski is one of the founders of the Worldwide Association of NT User Groups, along with Charles Kelly, Marjorie James and Dennis Martin. He agreed to be interviewed for this book regarding the groups activities.

Q: What is your exact role at WANTUG?
A: WANTUG was an idea that I had several years ago. The whole idea was that I was doing things in my local user group and people across the country were doing things, and we started chatting and discovered that we had the same kinds of common goals. The local user groups were all competing with each other for

resources from various companies, and none of the groups was big enough to approach Microsoft or Compaq. They couldn't say that they wanted to strike a deal with these companies for speakers, etc. The groups were being viewed separately, as 80 groups with 1,000 people, instead of as one whole entity. The idea was to form WANTUG to represent all the user groups and be able to go into Microsoft or Compaq corporate and say that we have a channel of user groups that think this is an issue. The other main idea was to basically have something that local user groups could feel that they were part of on a national or international level. So, for example, if we tied it to a convention like we did last year, the Windows NT Internet Show, they felt like they were part of a bigger thing. So they weren't just going to the

continued

continued

show; we had some WANTUG breakout meetings. And we plan to do that this year as well. When I attended the show, it turned out that I knew a lot of people from user groups across the country and other user group presidents. It was a way of bringing us together.

Q: Is WANTUG structured as a typical association?

A: We are trying to figure that out. We want to make sure that we develop a good relationship with Microsoft and Compaq. We are trying to figure out what the right model is. We are struggling with the dues issue. Do we want to charge local user groups for our services? This would force them to somehow raise the money locally. Part of the issue is that we don't want to just go ahead and spend all this time and effort and then just give everything away. There's no value. So we are still trying to figure that out. We are looking to leadership at Microsoft and some other groups to help us figure that out.

Q: How is WANTUG associated with Microsoft?

A: We have a great working relationship with Steve Ballmer, who is a great supporter. I contacted him last year and he was really excited. He met with our core executive group last year at the NT Internet Show and then invited us to come up to corporate and talk with

him. We were able to soundboard ideas off him. He committed to fund our organization and provide us with some sponsorship money. We are working with the folks in the SP channel at Microsoft as well as some of the product groups to help integrate user groups into their marketing strategy, e.g., NT 5 is coming out; let's start planning the user group tour.

Q: How much communication takes place between NT user groups throughout the world?

A: We do have online chats to support the international folks. We have found that most individuals read in English and can communicate that way. Speaking is a little more difficult. When we spoke with individuals in Japan we had to have translators. The Web site helps; getting those people involved, those will become issues that we will have to overcome. It also means that they will need to help us with translations.

Q: Does it charge its member local NT user groups a fee to join? If not, do you intend to charge member groups eventually?

A: I would say that there is going to be some charge to the local user groups for the services. The amount is still to be determined. As I said, there is a value question; by paying for it you expect something in return.

BackOffice Professionals Association

The BackOffice Professionals Association (BOPA), shown in Figure 12-5, serves as an Internet-based, nonprofit virtual community for education, technical support and communication among MCPs, analysts, developers, trainers, administrators, Webmasters, and other Microsoft Windows NT and BackOffice professionals.

Its members benefit through general group meetings and SIG meetings. In the future, BOPA will deliver meetings, chat sessions and other information through interactive multimedia broadcasts across the Internet, reaching all BOPA members across the globe.

The BackOffice Professional Association brings together MCPs with real-world experience and provides affordable peer-to-peer support, technical problem solving, and advance access to future technology.

FIGURE 12-5   The BOPA home page is located at `www.bopa.org`.

For more information on becoming a member of the BOPA, e-mail the association at `BackOffice@ariscorp.com`.

STUDY GROUPS

Today's IT study groups have a life of their own. While most of us are aware of how and why study groups are formed, the study groups found today are a lot different from the ones held at either grade school or college. Most traditional study groups are tenuous or short-lived and are extremely focused. Not so with today's seemingly professional study groups, which focus on IT; you get a lot more than expected.

In fact, one of the very first study groups for Windows NT has evolved into a full-blown Microsoft Authorized Academic Partner (AATP). In the next section, just such a study group is covered. You will be amazed at what it has to offer in the way of quality instruction and hands-on training.

Howard University's Windows NT Study Group

Howard University's Windows NT Study Group, shown in Figure 12-6, began as a small traditional study group in a corner of Howard University's sprawling campus. Founded and headed by Dr. Roy Beasley, Howard University's NT Study Group is now a full-blown AATP with Microsoft. While the group has expanded somewhat, Dr. Beasley hopes to return some of the original group's roots with hands-on, highly personalized training for prospective and existing MCPs. For anyone who is serious about Windows NT as a career and really wants to roll up their sleeves to participate in the act of learning, Dr. Beasley's study group is for you!

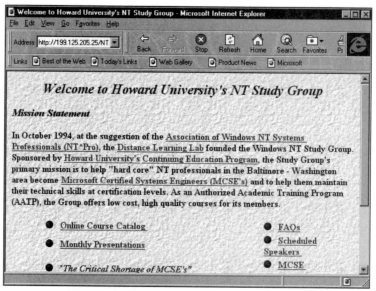

FIGURE 12-6   The Howard University Windows NT Study Group home page is located at `http://199.125.205.25/NTSTUDY`.

INTERVIEW: DR. ROY BEASLEY, LEADER OF HOWARD UNIVERSITY WINDOWS NT STUDY GROUP

Headed by Dr. Roy Beasley of Howard University, Washington, D.C., the Howard University Windows NT Study Group is a very unique study group, to say the least. It has all of the attributes of a traditional study group but takes on exam preparation in a whole new light. Dr. Beasley's approach to learning and studying is both comprehensive and demanding for his students.

He agreed to sit down for an interview in order to enlighten those who may be interested in joining his group.

Q: I understand that NT*Pro suggested that you form a study group back in 1994. Why did NT*Pro choose the Distance Learning Lab at Howard University for the very first NT Study Group?

A: Actually at one of his monthly meetings, Charles Kelly—the president of what is now called NT*Pro but was then called the Advanced Systems Users Group (ASUG)—asked if anyone wanted to form an NT study group. It sounded like a good idea, so we just took it from there.

Q: Why does your study group only focus just on MCSEs and not on any of the other certifications in the Microsoft Certification program? Do you have plans in the future to include their certifications?

A: It might help for me to explain how we got to where we are today. When we started the NT Study Group back in October 1994, we didn't set it up as a business venture or a teaching operation. It was just a bunch of computer professionals meeting together on a weekly basis to help each other learn about the new NT operating system. But as the months went by, the tenor of the group changed from mutual instruction to instructor-led teaching. I suppose this evolution was a natural one, given the fact that teaching is something I have done all my life.

We were initially interested in NT because in July 1994, my group—the Distance Learning Lab at Howard University—had received a substantial contract from DARPA to produce convincing demonstrations of the value of the Internet for education at various levels: high school, college, and adult education. When we had first proposed this project to DARPA in 1993, we made two technical bets—a bet on NT and a bet on the World Wide Web. Needless to say, we've come up as big winners on both bets.

In 1993, I was already aware that Microsoft was very serious about NT. By the spring of 1994, I began attending Kelly's monthly ASUG meetings. I also wanted all the members of my group to become certified. Although Novell's certified systems engineers had become a "drug on the market," I knew that this wouldn't happen with NT because NT was too complicated for most people to master—although its familiar GUI was dangerously deceptive. More than a few misguided twerps thought it was just "Big Windows."

We currently teach the most popular NT systems and Back Office applications. However we will expand our course offerings during our upcoming sessions in the fall of 1997 to include languages which can be used to develop Web sites on intranets. In particular, our new courses will cover Visual Basic, Visual Basic for Applications, and VB Script. I must confess to having some misgivings about the notion of certifying anyone's capabilities as a developer. I believe that an MCSE can manage a small- to medium-sized network

continued

continued

"by the book." But I'm skeptical that anyone can develop any significant computer applications "by the book." Good development is good design and good design requires creative designers. Microsoft can certify a developer's knowledge of the most significant features of Microsoft's application development tools, but Microsoft can't certify a developer's capacity to use these tools creatively.

Somewhere down the road, we would like to become the center of a community of creative computer professionals who are committed to a life-long continuation of their technical development within an academic context—a context which can provide them with a sound conceptual framework for their experience. Like Lord Keynes once said, there is nothing as practical as a good theory. Indeed, our experience to date strongly suggests that the students who pass the certification exams with minimal elevation of their blood pressure or distortion of their family lives do it the old fashioned way—by understanding concepts underlying the course materials. Unfortunately, we also have many students who are addicted to Transcender, Wave, Big Red, and other "exam prep" publications. I have come to regard these people as the MCSE world's equivalent of crack heads. They're always looking for short-cuts, or "quick fixes" which they never find. They don't spend much time on the course materials, and they never read the recommended reference materials. Ironically, they end up spending more time on their short cuts and get lower scores and higher exam failure rates than the students who focus on learning how NT works and why.

Our long term goal is to put Howard University on the map—as the Harvard, Yale, or Stanford of NT training.

Q: What does your study group offer MCP candidates?

A: Our most important feature is our academic context. If the subject matter were relatively trivial—like Novell 3.X—any moderately intelligent computer professional could learn it in a few two or three day workshops. But NT is as conceptually complex as UNIX, and is becoming even more so with each new version. So it's silly for anyone to think that they can master it in short workshops, about as silly as trying to lose 100 pounds by spending three days at a "fat farm".

As an academic institution, we deploy the full array of teaching tools which have been developed within academia over the last three thousand years—lectures, discussions, quizzes, exams, tutoring sessions, required reading, course evaluations, recommended reading, homework assignments, lab assignments, etc. We also make extensive use of newer teaching techniques, such as the Web and e-mail. All of our instructors are highly experienced professionals who invest a substantial amount of time keeping up with NT's latest developments and anticipating the next ones. We really enjoy this stuff, so teaching NT isn't just a job.

Q: I understand that Howard University is now an AATP with Microsoft, is that correct? Did Howard University's AATP program form as an outgrowth from the Howard University Windows NT Study Group?

A: Yes, we are an AATP. Our AATP program grew out of the Study Group, but we decided not to change the name. As I noted earlier, when we started the Study Group back in October 1994, it was just a bunch of computer professionals holding weekly meetings to teach each other about NT. Over the course of the next eighteen months the volunteer Group evolved into an AATP.

Q: How successful is your Windows NT Study Group?

A: We post an ever expanding list of our students who have passed the certification exams on our Web site. I challenge other NT training operations to do the same. Beyond this, we're making a lot of money on tuition, even though our rates are still well below the current market standards.

Q: For someone who is contemplating starting a Windows NT Study Group, what would you say are the essential ingredients for its success?

A: A supportive dean. We were very lucky that Dr. Eleanor Franklin was dean of Howard's Continuing Education program when we were getting started. She allowed us to use the classrooms, the computers, and other resources we needed—at no charge—while we were learning how to teach each other about NT.

I can't see how a Study Group can survive without access to classrooms and computers for presentations and hands-on demonstrations. An overhead LCD projector is also very useful, especially if you're using PowerPoint slides to present Microsoft's official course notes.

Q: Do you provide advice to others that would like to start a Windows NT Study Group?

A: Yes, but there aren't very many groups like ours. Starting one is a very difficult thing to do. I succeeded because of a combination of factors. For one thing, I'm still a very energetic guy. I had a research contract which funded some of the computers we needed. And I had a very supportive Dean.

State Department NT Study Group

The State Department NT Study Group is actually a more traditional study group in the sense that the group meets at specific times and is not affiliated with any sort of official training or study program. The group was started to help State Department employees as well as others outside of the department to prepare for the Microsoft certification exams. The group meets twice a week at the State Department in Washington, D.C. For more information on joining the group contact J.B. fields, MCP/MCT of CA/EX/CSD at `jbfields@msn.com`.

How to Start Your Own Study Group

This is one of the easier types of groups to form, as you might imagine. The first step in getting a group of Windows NT enthusiasts and/or professionals together is to put out the word that you are forming a group. You can do this in a multitude of ways, but one of the best methods now available is via the Web. If you do use the Web, it's important to put the announcement where it will be *noticed*! Try asking the Webmaster if he would mind running a scrolling marquee on your organizations Intranet or wherever appropriate, just so long as it is not buried. Another great place to announce the notice is a bulletin board at school, work or a community center.

Once you have the word out and a group formed, try to find a local facility like your neighborhood library or community center. Often, they will let you use a room at no charge if it's for a good cause. You will also want to get your hands on some sort of projection unit so that topics can be more efficiently conveyed to the group.

Finally, you want to assign at least a few team leaders in order to keep the study group together and properly motivated. Topics should be delegated to everyone for research and presentation. Try hard to keep everyone involved, and do not tolerate any slackers in the group. Get rid of any deadwood; if you don't, they will only make studying and preparation for the exams more difficult because you will have to take up their slack!

Key Point Summary

In summary, this chapter covered the various intellectual and professional resources available to MCPs, such as NT*Pro, the Association for Windows NT Systems Professionals and Howard University's NT Study Group. The chapter also described in depth interviews with some of the leading industry experts in Microsoft technology. Finally, the chapter disclosed in detail the procedures for starting your own local user group, as well as a study group in order to enhance your prospects for developing your career and help in passing Microsoft's rigorous certified professional examinations.

- Microsoft Certified Professionals can benefit professionally by joining a user group in their local community.
- Professional Associations offer IT professionals a wealth of programs and services for enhancing their careers.
- User Groups offer excellent leadership opportunities for those seeking to become experts in their industry.
- Study Groups are an excellent way to increase your chances of passing the Microsoft certification exams the first time around.

Resources

Study Tips

In addition to the basic skill sets and training that were covered in Chapters 1 and 2 of *MCSE Career Microsoft®!*, there are two skill sets that every professional should have in his repertoire. The first is study skills. As most knowledgeable people are aware, learning is a lifelong pursuit and does not end with graduation from high school or college, nor when you are hired for a job. Instead, learning takes place every waking day of our lives—at least for most of us.

Learning involves study for most technically skilled professionals. Unless you have an incredible attention span and/or photographic memory, studying is a must in order to master a new subject. For those who lack the former, a detailed map of study skills is outlined here to help you learn faster, retain more, and master a subject matter in preparation for exams or just for the sake of learning.

In addition, Appendix B covers the subject and skill of negotiation, specifically *salary* negotiation. For many of us, this is a particularly touchy subject and can lead to a great deal of consternation. However, salary negotiation does not have as painful or difficult as you might imagine, provided you take the time and care to deal with it appropriately.

For those folks who are just plain lousy at wheeling and dealing or lack the confidence to make counter-offers to prospective employers, the topics on negotiation should help erase your worst fears of "blowing" a job offer. In fact, just by understanding a few of the golden rules of negotiation, like "he who speaks first loses," (as discussed) should come away ahead of the game.

WHY ARE GRADES IMPORTANT?

Good grades are one key to your future. They can open many doors for you—to higher pay, to any future education, to a job that you want. You can control the grades you get and the amount of information you learn. Much of it depends on how hard you work; more depends upon your attitude. The more positive you are, the better you will do. It's completely up to you!

Remember that while you are in training, some of your goals should be:

- Learn as much as you possibly can.
- Earn good grades.
- Make the most of all of your talents.

GETTING BETTER SCORES ON EXAMS

People will often tell you that you need to study hard to get good grades. This advice is not really very useful. What does it mean to study hard? How do you study so that your hard work pays off in good grades? It is very important to learn good study skills and then *use them*.

Better study skills can lead to better grades. They can also improve your actual learning of the material you are studying. Of course, learning the material will help you throughout life. The information you learn now will be with you for many years and help you in many situations. In addition, the information you learn now will not have to be "relearned" later—for other classes, for real-life situations, maybe never.

Basic Things to Think About

Be ready to learn when you go to school. This means that you should do the following things:

- Have a positive attitude.
- Being positive will always help you do better in any situation.

- Be an active learner.

- Listen carefully. Think about what you are hearing and doing. Concentrate when the action is taking place; you will learn much more easily. Ask questions if you don't understand something. Participate in class. Don't be afraid to give a wrong answer or ask questions. Instructors need to know if their students understand what they are teaching. You will be helping them out and they, in turn, can help you out.

- Learn how to study for each subject

- Different subjects require different approaches and different mental skills. Once you find a method for learning a subject more easily, keep using that method.

- Get help from others when you need it.

- Study with friends or associates. Ask your superiors for help with a particular subject or problem; see your instructor. There may also be free tutoring available in your company or training center. Your instructor will be able to guide you to these services if they are available. Never be afraid to use help from all of these sources.

- If you do badly on a quiz or lab section, see your instructor immediately.

- Let your instructor know you care about your grades. *Find out exactly what you did wrong and how to improve. Learn from your mistakes*; make mistakes worthwhile! If you really don't understand something, learn it *now*; don't wait until it's time to take the exam. Ask for specific suggestions and advice on how to improve your learning for that class or session.

- Remember that much of what you learn is a building block for more of the subject matter. Therefore, if you learn the basics, you will learn the next part more easily. That is why it is important to learn and understand each new thing that is taught each day. You cannot cram real learning at the last minute.

Getting Ready to Study

Studying is more than just looking at an open book or some notes. The following tips can help you better absorb and remember what you study.

Have a place where you can study

Find a quiet place with few distractions. Keep your "tools" nearby so that you can find them when you need them. This will include paper, pencils, pens, etc. Make certain you have good lighting so that your eyes don't become strained. If music helps you study, make certain it is low and not distracting.

Schedule your study time when it's best for you

Will you study better before dinner? Or will you do a better job by taking a break when you get home from work? Try to study when you will be at your best. But you must also be flexible about your study time. Look at the amount of homework you have each day. Then plan enough time to do it. If you have a lot of homework and a work activity, you may have to forgo a favorite TV program or workout. Plan carefully!

Take a break now and then from your studying

A short break will refresh your mind. Take a walk, breathe deeply, and go outside for some fresh air and a change of scene. Your body will also be refreshed. Studies have shown that your physical well-being affects your mental well-being. This break will relax your mind and refresh you—to be ready to tackle your studying again.

Plan your study time

You may find it more rewarding to do the shorter or easier reading assignments first. With those done, you will feel rewarded or be able to concentrate better on longer or harder subject matter. You won't be worrying about the others.

However, some people like to do the harder or longer reading assignments first; they have more energy to tackle them. Others will work on the harder or longer ones for a while; they will then put them aside and concentrate on doing the others. After they take a "mental break" by completing the others, they are ready to go back to the first ones they started. Find out what works the best for you and plan on doing your studying that way.

Develop critical thinking skills

What do we mean by "critical thinking skills?" These skills allow you to listen to or read information and make good judgments about it. You will ask yourself questions such as:

- Does this make sense in relation to other information I have?

- Is this always true? Or, When is this true and when is it false?

- How will this be affected by changes? What will affect it?

- Is this just someone's opinion or is it backed up by facts? Are the "facts" being quoted really facts or are they words taken out of context and put together to appear as facts?

- Are these really facts or has the presenter used careful wording and statistics to make them look like facts?

- Is the presenter using emotional words to make me feel a certain way or are the facts really making me feel this way?

By learning to question, compare, contrast, and analyze information, you will be learning how to make decisions. You will be able to solve problems. These are all very important skills that you will need for your future.

Now that you have completed your studies for the next day, you can go to bed and get a good night's sleep. Being refreshed for the next day is important. Being tired cuts down on your learning ability. Your mind will be "fuzzy" if you are too tired. And you will not perform well in class.

If you have an quiz or lab the next morning, you might want to get up early to review before you go to school. A quick review with a fresh mind may make some information clearer or a fact stick in your mind—just for that quiz.

Read all of the study skills topics to learn more about how you can master information, and be prepared to reach your goals. You can learn how to get the most from school. Take the time now to learn the habit of using good study skills. New habits can be hard to learn, but this habit can pay you back in ways that will make you very glad that you learned it!

A Note on Nutrition

Studies have shown that the proper nutrition—food—can also help your learning. *Don't skip breakfast*! Your body has received no nutrients for eight or more hours when you wake up in the morning. It needs protein and carbohydrates to function properly. This is especially true for your mental functioning. So breakfast is an important aid in how well you will do in school. *Eat breakfast*!

IDENTIFYING STUDY PROBLEMS

Are you having problems with a particular subject or class in training? Does it give you a headache or an empty feeling in the pit of your stomach? Do you feel upset, angry, or afraid when you go to that class? Or do you feel helpless or frustrated? Maybe you work hard but you don't seem to be getting anywhere. You are not alone. Many students want to do better in certain subjects but feel stuck.

Why do you feel this way? Why does this only happen in certain courses? Your problems may be caused by:

- Interest level
- Anxiety level
- Approach

Interest Level

Let's say you're having problems in TCP/IP or Networking Essentials. You just don't want to pick up the textbook and do the suggested readings. You think, "Who cares about all that stuff? It's the things geeks thrive on. I just can't get into it." A person with this opinion of networking has a *low* interest level in the subject. Someone with a low interest level doesn't usually get good grades in that subject.

Anxiety Level

When you walk into an NT Server class, you get upset. You go to class to do the lab, and your mind goes completely blank. You just know you won't do well. Your feelings keep you from succeeding in the training class.

Approach

You know you're interested in computers, and you're not anxious about it, but you're still just not getting it. Why? Maybe you're not attacking the subject from the best direction. You might need help with your study skills. Maybe some ideas you have are getting in your way. Maybe your style of learning does not match how your instructor chooses to teach.

WHAT TO DO ABOUT STUDY PROBLEMS

Try these suggestions; you might be surprised at how well they help.

For Low Interest Level

The more interested you are in a subject, the more likely you are to succeed in that subject. It's always a challenge to do well in a class that you don't like. Here are some ideas that might help.

Motivate yourself

Try talking to yourself and saying positive things about the class, such as:

- "I am doing better in this training class every day."
- "I need this training class for that promotion (for example, pay raise). I will do the best I can."
- "The employers that interest me will be looking at my scores in this class; I need good grades to get the job."
- "I can do well in this training class even if my main interests are somewhere else."
- "If I learn it now, I won't have to relearn it later."
- "I may have to study this subject again, and it will be easier if I learn the basics now."

Keep positive thoughts flowing and you probably will do better.

Reward yourself

Take notice when you do well. Try bribing yourself. For every week that you study hard you could treat yourself to something special. Then, after accomplishing this goal, choose a higher goal for the class.

For instance, every day that you attend class and really learn something new, treat yourself to an even larger reward. The exact reward, of course, will depend on you. It could be a small food treat, a movie, or time with a friend. You might even try negotiating with your boss for rewards or favors for attending classes that are particularly challenging.

The way to overcome a low interest level in a class is up to you. But it can be done! Be creative. Think of ways to motivate yourself by focusing on the positive and treating yourself well. Then try out your ideas to see what really works best for you.

Anxiety

The best way to know whether you are afraid or anxious about a particular subject is to pay attention to yourself. How do you feel when you go into that class? Do you feel like you'd rather be almost anyplace else? Do you perspire, have a headache, have a stomach ache, or breathe differently? Also, you might be thinking negative things, such as:

o "I really hate this class."

o "I won't ever do well in this class."

o "I think it's ridiculous that I have to take this class."

o "I won't use this stuff—ever."

o "I just know I'm going to fail this class."

These are all signs of anxiety.

So what do you do if you think your problem is subject anxiety? One thing you can do is learn to be relaxed. It takes practice to learn how to do this. You will need to practice changing the way you feel and the way you think about the training class.

The first step is to picture a time or a place where you are really comfortable, when you are at your best. With practice, you can feel the same way in your problem class. Here's what you can try:

1. Breathe deeply and imagine yourself in a relaxing scene (such as at the beach or on vacation).

2. When you are really feeling good, picture yourself in a class that you really like and do well in. You should continue to feel relaxed.

3. Now, picture yourself in your problem class. Continue to breathe deeply and imagine the relaxing scene. Focus on staying relaxed. Your anxiety level should get lower and lower as you practice.

The point is that if you can do this in your imagination, you can do it for real. Whenever you think about being in that class, first breathe deeply and think of your peaceful scene.

Whenever you go to the class, do it again. Whenever you're in class and start feeling terrible (such as when you're doing a hands-on lab session), breathe deeply and picture your peaceful scene again.

Another way to relieve subject anxiety is to change the way you think about the class. You have to "reprogram" the way your mind works.

First of all, find something positive about the class. Do you have a good friend or fellow worker in there? Are there ever any enjoyable projects or movies or something that you enjoy? By looking for the positive, you will reduce the negative.

In addition, whenever you think negative thoughts about a class, think positive thoughts instead. For example:

- Replace "I really hate this class" with "I am learning to like this class."
- Replace "I think it's ridiculous that I have to take this class." with "This class can probably help me in the long run."

You can have control over how you think and feel. And you will find that having a positive attitude toward things, all things, will make you succeed at them much more easily.

Tips for Reading Effectively

Good reading skills can help you in all of your classes. If your reading skills are lacking in some way, you could find yourself in trouble very quickly. Generally, the better you understand what you read—and retain what you read—the better you will do in your classes. One way to improve your reading comprehension is called SQ3R (survey, question, read, recite, review). There are five steps to this method.

Step 1 — Survey
Briefly look over the material to become familiar with it. Get a feel for the main topics. One good way to survey a book is to read all chapter titles and summaries.

Step 2 — Question
From headings and subheadings in the reading material, make up (and write down) questions to yourself about the subject. Later, when you read the material, see if you can answer your questions. You can also ask yourself questions about the content, such as the writer's goals, how the material is related to what you

already know, and what experiences you may have had that relate to the material. These kinds of questions can help make the subject mean more to you.

Step 3 — Read

Now read the material slowly and carefully. Give special attention to answering the questions you asked in Step 2. Take care to connect what you are reading about the subject to what you already know.

Step 4 — Recite

Once you have read a section of the material, stop and answer the questions raised in Step 2. This helps you check on how well you understand what you have read, and helps the content mean more to you. It also helps you remember more of what you read.

Step 5 — Review

Focus on going over the material one more time. Pay special attention to the questions in Step 2 that were the most difficult for you to answer.

No matter how good your reading skills are, they can probably be improved by using this method. Give it a try! Help is always available for your problems. Mostly what it takes is learning what your problem areas are and then acting on getting some help. Sometimes it is hard to ask for help, but it's often the most aware and successful people who look for help when they really need it.

Your instructor or favorite computer guru will be able to help you out with these ideas if you find them strange and unusual. Ask them for help. They should be able to help you with the training classes that are giving you trouble.

OTHER TIPS FOR STUDYING

Here are a few final tips for your MCSE test preparation.

Study a Subject Every Day

Even if you don't have any reading or assignments for a class, review the subject every day and once on weekends. Even 15 minutes to a half-hour can help reinforce your understanding of the subject.

Take Book and Lecture Notes on the Same Page

Divide your notebook paper into two columns. In one column, take book notes. Take lecture notes about a topic right next to the same topic book notes. Then you can compare the two. One may help you learn the other.

Learn to Type

Take a typing class or keyboarding class in a local community college. You will find that fast typing skills make your job much easier as a computer specialist.

Test Yourself

Before you take an actual certification exam, take a practice exam. This way you can anticipate the types of questions on the test and feel a lot more relaxed when taking the exam. You will also be able to reliably test out how much you really know about a subject prior to the actual exam.

Salary Negotiation Tips

UNDERSTAND THE BASICS

The first and most important point about salary negotiation is understanding that you have no ability to negotiate without first having a job offer! You would be amazed how many individuals jump the gun by bringing up the issue of salary *before* a job offer is made to them. Never under any circumstances quote, bring up, write down, or say what you made at your last job before an offer is made to you.

The second most important aspect of salary negotiation is making sure you that you have all of the bases covered with respect to salary and benefits *before* accepting the job. It is important to identify the minimum salary requirements you would be willing to accept in addition to any benefits or perks that are important to you during the negotiation period. Don't overlook important perks such as bonuses, cell phones, car expenses—anything important to your job, self-esteem and general well-being.

This crucial time period, from the time the offer is made to your acceptance of the offer, should take place over a period of 2-3 days and no more than a week. During this period, stay cool and try not to be the first to come back with an answer if at all possible. Let the employer sweat it out while you raise the ante! You have something they want—not the other way around.

THE PROCESS OF NEGOTIATION

Negotiation is a give-and-take process of communication that allows the parties with an interest in the outcome to reach a mutually satisfying agreement, or win-win situation. The main purpose of negotiation is to allow both parties a fair and reasonable outcome. One of the key factors in *fair* negotiations is reason. Responding to a job offer that pays a maximum of $85K in the industry with a counter-offer of $100K is not reasonable, no matter how good you think you are in your field. On the other hand, don't bow to low-ballers just because your last job was in another field or you were caught up in corporate downsizing. Currently, the computer industry is experiencing a "sellers" market and the industry is willing to compensate individuals who are inexperienced or new to the industry.

Some important points to keep in mind while preparing to negotiate:

- **Know the going rates for your field.** Know the salary ranges for your area of expertise by referring to trade magazines, salary surveys, and the library.

- **Understand your bargaining power.** Know what you're worth! Properly assess your skills, abilities, whatever you bring to the table that can help your prospects of negotiation. Remember, too that a "bird in hand" or a job offer is the best bargaining ship you have!

- **Know what to say and when during negotiation.** Memorize what you want to say during the negotiation. Develop convincing rebuttals to possible objections. Remember, the employer expects to bargain.

FINALIZE THE OFFER

A job offer is not complete until you finalize the negotiations. Once you reach a verbal agreement concerning compensation and benefits, you still need to do several things before signing off on the deal. How you handle these final steps may affect how well you get along on the job.

Take your time when considering the final offer. Ask for several days to think it over. A common professional courtesy is to give you at least 48 hours to consider an offer. During this time you may want to carefully examine the offer one last time and consider other important questions at this stage of the negotiation process.

- Is it really worth what I am being offered?
- Can I still do better?
- What are the other employers willing to offer me?

If one or two other employers are considering you for a job, let this employer know his job offer is not the only one under consideration. This should give you a better bargaining position. Contact the other employers and let them know you have a job offer and that you would like to have your application status with them clarified before you make any final decisions with the other employer. Depending on how much leeway an employer may have to accelerate a hiring decision, you may be able to go back to the first employer with another job offer. With a second job offer in hand, you may greatly enhance your bargaining position.

GET IT IN WRITING

Talk is cheap and often it leads to misunderstandings if not put into writing; just ask any attorney at law. Questions of duties and responsibilities, expected performance, evaluations, and compensation lie at the heart of any job. These are important questions that require some form of written agreement or contract, as well as commitment on the part of the employer.

Verbal agreements may be okay between close and trusted friends, but they don't have much weight in employment situations. After all, the employer who made verbal agreements with you may be gone tomorrow, and he most likely will not share the commitments with the next employer. Verbal agreements that are important to you and your job should always be put in writing. You can start doing this by taking notes from day one of the negotiation period. At some point, preferably near the end, when you are expected to either accept or decline the offer, ask the employer to summarize your verbal agreement. As this is being done, write down each point. When he finishes summarizing the agreement, read back the agreement as you have written it down in your notes. If the employer has not been taking similar notes, make a copy for his reference. Then ask him to put the vital points into the agreement (written job offer) and sign it. Ask for the written agreement to be returned to you in 1-2 days.

At the conclusion of the negotiation period if you accept the position, reassure the employer that he made the correct decision. You can do this by restating your interest in the job, your delight in joining the organization, and your commitment to performance. Finally, you should consummate the entire affair with a signed thank-you letter of appreciation including a reiteration of the same points you made at the conclusion of the salary negotiation period.

Additional Information Resources

Sunbelt Software: Sunbelt Software is a major distributor of Windows NT Utility and applications software. It offers a free newsletter and e-mail alerts on the Windows NT market. Subscription is a must for any bona fide Windows NT expert. Sunbelt's Web site is located at `http://www.ntsoftdist.com/`.

NT Links: An Internet Web site hosted by Rusten & Ilene's. NT Links has just about every major Window NT-related link on the Web. The NT Links Web site is located at `http://www.activexserver.com/bbs1/links.asp`.

Windows NT Resource Center: An Internet Web site run by Beverly Hills Software, Inc., offers a plethora of Windows NT support and links to NT-related Web sites. Its Web site is located at `http://www.bhs.com`.

Microsoft InfoSource CD: A compendium of Microsoft Solution Providers Worldwide and third-party ISVs. The InfoSource CD is an excellent source for information on these organizations.

What's on the CD-ROM?

CD-ROM Contents

The CD-ROM included with this book contains the following materials:

- Adobe Acrobat Reader
- An electronic version of this book, *MCSE Career Microsoft®!* in Adobe Acrobat Format
- Microsoft Internet Explorer version 3.01
- Microsoft Training and Certification Offline CD-ROM, including: Microsoft Certified Professional Program Exam Study Guide
- Selections from *Windows NT® 4.0 MCSE Study Guide* (IDG Books Worldwide, 1997)

Installing and Using the CD-ROM

The following sections describe each product and include detailed instructions for installation and use.

Adobe Acrobat Reader and the Adobe Acrobat Version of *MCSE Career Microsoft*®*!*

The Adobe Acrobat Reader is a helpful program that will enable you to view the electronic version of this book in the same page format as the actual book.

TO INSTALL AND RUN ADOBE ACROBAT READER AND VIEW THE ELECTRONIC VERSION OF THIS BOOK, FOLLOW THESE STEPS:

1. Start Windows Explorer (if you're using Windows 95) or Windows NT Explorer (if you're using Windows NT), and then open the `Acrobat` folder on the CD-ROM.

2. In the `Acrobat` folder, double-click `ar32e30.exe` and follow the instructions presented onscreen for installing Adobe Acrobat Reader.

3. To view the electronic version of this book after you have installed Adobe Acrobat Reader, start Windows Explorer (if you're using Windows 95) or Windows NT Explorer (if you're using Windows NT), and then open the `Books\Career Microsoft` folder on the CD-ROM.

4. In the `Career Microsoft` folder, double-click the chapter or appendix file you want to view. All documents in this folder end with a `.pdf` extension.

Microsoft Internet Explorer Version 3.01

This is a complete copy of Microsoft Internet Explorer. With Internet Explorer you'll be able to browse the Internet if you have an Internet connection, and view the contents of the Microsoft Training and Certification Offline CD-ROM (included on this CD-ROM).

TO INSTALL AND RUN MICROSOFT INTERNET EXPLORER, FOLLOW THESE STEPS:

1. Start Windows Explorer (if you're using Windows 95) or Windows NT Explorer (if you're using Windows NT), and then open the `Mscert\Ie` folder on the CD-ROM.

2. In the `Mscert\Ie folder`, double-click `Msie301r.exe` and follow the instructions presented onscreen for installing Microsoft Internet Explorer.

3. To run Microsoft Internet Explorer, double-click the Internet Explorer icon on the desktop.

Microsoft Training and Certification Offline CD-ROM

This offline CD-ROM includes the entire contents of a key Microsoft Web site where you can obtain MCSE certification requirements and view Microsoft Certified Professional exam objectives and Microsoft course information. In addition, you can view the most current version of this Web site by connecting to www.microsoft.com/train_cert/ on the Internet.

TO INSTALL AND ACCESS THE OFFLINE VERSION OF THE MICROSOFT TRAINING AND CERTIFICATION WEB SITE, FOLLOW THESE STEPS:

1. Start Windows Explorer (if you're using Windows 95) or Windows NT Explorer (if you're using Windows NT), and then open the Mscert folder on the CD-ROM.

2. In the Mscert folder, double-click Setup.exe and follow the instructions presented onscreen for installing the Microsoft Train_Cert Offline Web site.

3. After the installation is complete, you can view the Web site by selecting Start ⇒ Programs ⇒ Microsoft Train_Cert Offline ⇒ Microsoft Train_Cert Offline.

 note **You must have Microsoft Internet Explorer installed *before* you can view this Web site.**

Microsoft Certified Professional Program Exam Study Guide

This study guide presents interesting and valuable information about the Microsoft Certified Professional exams, including how the exams are developed, a description of the types of questions asked on exams, and some exam preparation tips.

TO VIEW THE *MICROSOFT CERTIFIED PROFESSIONAL PROGRAM EXAM STUDY GUIDE,* FOLLOW THESE STEPS:

1. Start Windows Explorer (if you're using Windows 95) or Windows NT Explorer (if you're using Windows NT). Open the `Mscert\Download\Cert` folder.

2. In the `Cert` folder, double-click `Studgde4.doc`.

 note   **You must have Microsoft Word, WordPad, or Word Viewer installed *before* you can view this study guide.**

Windows NT® 4.0 MCSE Study Guide Chapters

This Microsoft Approved Study Guide prepares you for three MCSE exams that test implementing and supporting Windows NT products: No. 70-73 (Workstation 4.0), No.70-67: (Server 4.0), and No. 70-68 (Server 4.0 in the Enterprise). You'll find three chapters in Adobe Acrobat format on the CD.

TO VIEW *WINDOWS NT® 4.0 MCSE STUDY GUIDE* CHAPTERS, FOLLOW THESE STEPS:

1. If you've already installed Acrobat Reader to view the electronic version of this book, skip to Step 3. If you haven't installed Acrobat Reader, start Windows Explorer (if you're using Windows 95) or Windows NT Explorer (if you're using Windows NT); then open the Acrobat folder on the CD.

2. In the Acrobat folder, double-click `ar32e30.exe` and follow the instructions presented on-screen for installing the Acrobat Reader.

3. To view chapters after you've installed Acrobat Reader, start Windows Explorer (if you're using Windows 95) or Windows NT Explorer (if you're using Windows NT); then open the `Books\MCSE WINDOWS NT 4.0` folder on the CD.

4. In the `MCSE WINDOWS NT 4.0` folder, double-click the chapter you want to view. All documents in this folder end with a `.pdf` extension.

Glossary

Authorized Academic Training Partner (AATP): Same as an ATEC, except AATPs are located in colleges or universities. They teach the same MOC courses as private ATECs, but the courses are considerably longer.

Authorized Technical Education Center (ATEC): Microsoft ATECs are a select group of technical training providers that meet the high standards of excellence that Microsoft demands. Their primary goal is to work together with Microsoft to develop a strong education and certification channel that is capable of delivering consistent, high-level, hands-on technical training on the full range of Microsoft products, including the Windows and the Windows NT operating systems, the Microsoft BackOffice family of server software, and Internet/intranet platform development products.

Microsoft Certified Product Specialist (MCPS): An MCPS demonstrates in-depth knowledge of at least one Microsoft operating system. A candidate may pass additional Microsoft certification exams to further qualify his skills with Microsoft BackOffice products, development tools or desktop applications.

Microsoft Certified Professional (MCP): An information technology professional who has passed at least one of the core Microsoft certification exams. The MCP can be any one of the four classifications of certified professionals under the MCP program, that is, systems engineer, products specialist, trainer and/or software developer.

Microsoft Certified Solution Developer (MCSD): An MSCD is qualified to design and develop custom business solutions with Microsoft development tools, Internet technologies and platforms, including Microsoft Office and the Microsoft BackOffice family of server products.

Microsoft Certified Systems Engineer (MCSE): An MCSE is qualified to effectively plan, implement, maintain and support information systems in a wide range of computing environments with the Microsoft Windows NT Server network operating system and the Microsoft BackOffice family of server products.

Microsoft Certified Trainer (MCT): An MCT is instructionally and technically qualified by Microsoft to deliver MOC through Microsoft-authorized education sites, including Microsoft ATECs.

Microsoft Official Curriculum (MOC): Courses developed by Microsoft product groups to educate computer professionals who develop, support and implement solutions using Microsoft technology. MOC courses prepare computer professionals to become certified as Microsoft Certified Professionals.

Microsoft Solution Provider (MSP): MSPs are independent companies or organizations that team with Microsoft to solve business challenges for organizations of all sizes in many industries. MSPs use Microsoft products as the building blocks for various value-added services, such as systems integration, computer consulting, software customization, application development, technical training, and technical support.

Index

IDG BOOKS WORLDWIDE, INC.
END-USER LICENSE AGREEMENT

<u>Read This</u>. You should carefully read these terms and conditions before opening the software packet(s) included with this book ("Book"). This is a license agreement ("Agreement") between you and IDG Books Worldwide, Inc. ("IDGB"). By opening the accompanying software packet(s), you acknowledge that you have read and accept the following terms and conditions. If you do not agree and do not want to be bound by such terms and conditions, promptly return the Book and the unopened software packet(s) to the place you obtained them for a full refund.

1. <u>License Grant</u>. IDGB grants to you (either an individual or entity) a nonexclusive license to use one copy of the enclosed software program(s) (collectively, the "Software") solely for your own personal or business purposes on a single computer (whether a standard computer or a workstation component of a multiuser network). The Software is in use on a computer when it is loaded into temporary memory (i.e., RAM) or installed into permanent memory (e.g., hard disk, CD-ROM, or other storage device). IDGB reserves all rights not expressly granted herein.

2. <u>Ownership</u>. IDGB is the owner of all right, title, and interest, including copyright, in and to the compilation of the Software recorded on the disk(s)/CD-ROM. Copyright to the individual programs on the disk(s)/CD-ROM is owned by the author or other authorized copyright owner of each program. Ownership of the Software and all proprietary rights relating thereto remain with IDGB and its licensors.

3. <u>Restrictions on Use and Transfer</u>.

  (a) You may only (i) make one copy of the Software for backup or archival purposes, or (ii) transfer the Software to a single hard disk, provided that you keep the original for backup or archival purposes. You may not (i) rent or lease the Software, (ii) copy or reproduce the Software through a LAN or other network system or through any computer subscriber system or bulletin-board system, or (iii) modify, adapt, or create derivative works based on the Software.

(b) You may not reverse engineer, decompile, or disassemble the Software. You may transfer the Software and user documentation on a permanent basis, provided that the transferee agrees to accept the terms and conditions of this Agreement and you retain no copies. If the Software is an update or has been updated, any transfer must include the most recent update and all prior versions.

4. <u>Restrictions on Use of Individual Programs</u>. You must follow the individual requirements and restrictions detailed for each individual program in Appendix D, "What's on the CD-ROM" of this Book. These limitations are contained in the individual license agreements recorded on the disk(s)/CD-ROM. These restrictions may include a requirement that after using the program for the period of time specified in its text, the user must pay a registration fee or discontinue use. By opening the Software packet(s), you will be agreeing to abide by the licenses and restrictions for these individual programs. None of the material on this disk(s) or listed in this Book may ever be distributed, in original or modified form, for commercial purposes.

5. <u>Limited Warranty</u>.

(a) IDGB warrants that the Software and disk(s)/CD-ROM are free from defects in materials and workmanship under normal use for a period of sixty (60) days from the date of purchase of this Book. If IDGB receives notification within the warranty period of defects in materials or workmanship, IDGB will replace the defective disk(s)/CD-ROM.

(b) IDGB AND THE AUTHOR OF THE BOOK DISCLAIM ALL OTHER WARRANTIES, EXPRESS OR IMPLIED, INCLUDING WITHOUT LIMITATION IMPLIED WARRANTIES OF MERCHANTABILITY AND FITNESS FOR A PARTICULAR PURPOSE, WITH RESPECT TO THE SOFTWARE, THE PROGRAMS, THE SOURCE CODE CONTAINED THEREIN, AND/OR THE TECHNIQUES DESCRIBED IN THIS BOOK. IDGB DOES NOT WARRANT THAT THE FUNCTIONS CONTAINED IN THE SOFTWARE WILL MEET YOUR REQUIREMENTS OR THAT THE OPERATION OF THE SOFTWARE WILL BE ERROR FREE.

(c) This limited warranty gives you specific legal rights, and you may have other rights which vary from jurisdiction to jurisdiction.

6. <u>Remedies</u>.

   (a) IDGB's entire liability and your exclusive remedy for defects in materials and workmanship shall be limited to replacement of the Software, which may be returned to IDGB with a copy of your receipt at the following address: Disk Fulfillment Department, Attn: MCSE Career Microsoft®!, IDG Books Worldwide, Inc., 7260 Shadeland Station, Ste. 100, Indianapolis, IN 46256, or call 1-800-762-2974. Please allow 3-4 weeks for delivery. This Limited Warranty is void if failure of the Software has resulted from accident, abuse, or misapplication. Any replacement Software will be warranted for the remainder of the original warranty period or thirty (30) days, whichever is longer.

   (b) In no event shall IDGB or the author be liable for any damages whatsoever (including without limitation damages for loss of business profits, business interruption, loss of business information, or any other pecuniary loss) arising from the use of or inability to use the Book or the Software, even if IDGB has been advised of the possibility of such damages.

   (c) Because some jurisdictions do not allow the exclusion or limitation of liability for consequential or incidental damages, the above limitation or exclusion may not apply to you.

7. <u>U.S. Government Restricted Rights</u>. Use, duplication, or disclosure of the Software by the U.S. Government is subject to restrictions stated in paragraph (c) (1) (ii) of the Rights in Technical Data and Computer Software clause of DFARS 252.227-7013, and in subparagraphs (a) through (d) of the Commercial Computer—Restricted Rights clause at FAR 52.227-19, and in similar clauses in the NASA FAR supplement, when applicable.

8. <u>General</u>. This Agreement constitutes the entire understanding of the parties and revokes and supersedes all prior agreements, oral or written, between them and may not be modified or amended except in a writing signed by both parties hereto which specifically refers to this Agreement. This Agreement shall take precedence over any other documents that may be in conflict herewith. If any one or more provisions contained in this Agreement are held by any court or tribunal to be invalid, illegal, or otherwise unenforceable, each and every other provision shall remain in full force and effect.

CD-ROM Installation Instructions

Each software item on the *MCSE Career Microsoft®!* CD-ROM is located in its own folder. To install a particular piece of software, open its folder with My Computer or Internet Explorer. What you do next depends on what you find in the software's folder:

- Look first for a ReadMe.txt file or a .doc or .htm document. If this is present, it should contain installation instructions and other useful information.

- If the folder contains an executable (.exe) file, this is usually an installation program. Often it will be called Setup.exe or Install.exe, but in some cases the filename reflects an abbreviated version of the software's name and version number. Run the .exe file to start the installation process.

- In the case of some simple software, the .exe file probably is the software — no real installation step is required. You can run the software from the CD-ROM to try it. If you like it, copy it to your hard disk and create a Start menu shortcut for it.

The ReadMe.txt file in the CD-ROM's root directory may contain additional installation information, so be sure to check it.

For a listing of the software on the CD-ROM, see Appendix D.